GARROD'S GLOUCESTER:

Archaeological Observations 1974–81

by A. P. Garrod and C. M. Heighway

with contributions by T. Darvill, S. Fern, C. Goudge, J. Graham-Campbell,
C. Ireland, C. Morris, A. Peacey, J. Price, A Saville, and F. Wild.

'Had a person of judgement been present
when these things were discovered, many
curious particulars might have been preserved'.

Samuel Rudder, *New History of Gloucestershire*, 1779.

Frontispiece   Roman and medieval streets under Northgate Street. See Fig. 31 & site 33/76, VIII.

WESTERN ARCHAEOLOGICAL TRUST
(formerly Committee for Rescue Archaeology in Avon, Gloucestershire and Somerset)

SURVEYS

1. *Small Medieval Towns in Avon: Archaeology and Planning*
   Roger Leech (1975)

2. *Historic Towns in Somerset*
   Michael Aston and Roger Leech (1977)

3. *Historic Towns in Gloucestershire*
   Roger Leech, et al. (1981)

4. *The Upper Thames Valley in Gloucestershire and Wiltshire: An Archaeological Survey of the River Gravels.*
   Roger Leech (1977)

5. *Archaeological Sites in the Avon and Gloucestershire Cotswolds.*
   Alan Saville (1980)

6. *Medieval Villages in South-East Somerset*
   Ann Ellison (1983)

EXCAVATION REPORTS

1. *Excavations in Bath, 1950–75*
   Barry Cunliffe, ed. (1979)

2. *Excavations at Catsgore 1970–73; A Romano-British Village*
   Roger Leech (1982)

3. *Ilchester Volume I. Excavations 1974–75*
   Peter Leach (1982)

4. *The East and North Gates of Gloucester and associated sites – Excavations 1974–81*
   Carolyn Heighway (1983)

5. *Uley Bury and Norbury Hillforts. Rescue Excavations at Two Gloucestershire Iron Age Sites*
   Alan Saville (1983)

7. *Catsgore, 1979 – Further Excavations of the Romano-British Village.*
   Peter Ellis (1984)

8. *The Archaeology of Taunton – Excavations and Fieldwork to 1980*
   Peter Leach (ed.) (1984)

OCCASIONAL PAPERS

3. *Excavations at West Hill, Uley: 1977: The Romano-British Temple — Interim Report*
   Ann Ellison (1978)

4. *Clay Tobacco Pipes in Gloucestershire*
   Allan Peacey (1979)

5. *A Romano-British settlement at Cattybrook, Almondsbury, Avon.*
   Julian Bennett (1980)

6. *Recent work at Cow Common Bronze Age Cemetery, Glos. 1974.*
   Alan Saville (1979)

7. *Excavations at Guiting Power Iron Age Site, Glos. 1974.*
   Alan Saville (1980)

8. *The Wincanton By-pass – a study in the archaeological recording of road works*
   Ann Ellison and Terry Pearson (1981)

9. *Excavations at West Hill, Uley: 1977–9 – 2nd Interim Report; a Native, Roman and Christian Ritual Complex of the 1st Millennium A.D.*
   Ann Ellison (1980)

10. *Excavations at West Hill, Uley: 1979. The Sieving and Sampling Programme*
    Bruce Levitan (1982)

© Western Archaeological Trust   ISBN 904918 22 X

Obtainable from Alan Sutton Publishing, 17a Brunswick Road, Gloucester

Designed by Richard Bryant
Cover Designed by Shelagh Davies
Produced for the Trust by Alan Sutton Publishing, Gloucester
Printed in Great Britain

CONTENTS		Page no.	Microfiche
PART 1	Introduction and summary	1–9	
PART 2	The Sites: Gloucester City and District	11–58	
PART 3	The Sites: Kingsholm	59–68	
PART 4	The Sites: Beyond the District boundary	69–71	
PART 5	The Pottery:		
	Prehistoric pottery by T. Darvill	72–3	
	Roman, medieval and Post-medieval pottery by C. Ireland	74–84	
	Samian pottery by F. Wild	84–6	
	List of Gloucester fabric types	87–8	
PART 6	The pottery from Lower Quay Street (28/79) by C. Ireland	89	
PART 7	Small finds	93–8	
PART 8	Small finds from Lower Quay Street (28/79)	99–104	
APPENDIX	A full list of Gloucester archaeological sites, 1900–1982	105–9	
INDEX	An alphabetical index by Street name	110–11	
BIBLIOGRAPHY		112–114	

MICROFICHE

I	Identifications of pottery, by site (excluding Lower Quay Street)	A2–D6
	Section A: Sites in Gloucester District (excluding Kingsholm) by C. Ireland	A2–C5
	Section B: Kingsholm by C. Ireland	C6–C10
	Section C: District area by C. Ireland	C11
	Section D: Samian pottery by F. Wild	C12–D6
II	Catalogue of published pottery; by C. Ireland	D7–D14
III	Coins by Susan M. Fern	E1–E3
IV	Clay pipes by Allan Peacey	E4–E7
V	Inventory of small finds; edited by C. Heighway:	E8–F4
	Bone	E8
	Copper Alloy	E9–E11
	Flint by Alan Saville and Tim Darvill	E12–E13
	Glass by J. Price	E14
	Gold	F1
	Iron	F1
	Jet	F2
	Lead	F2
	Leather by C. E. Goudge	F3
	Pewter	F3
	Stone	F4
	Wood by Carole Morris	F4
VI	Identifications of pottery from Lower Quay Street (28/79); by C. Ireland	F5–G2
VII	Catalogue of published pottery from Lower Quay Street; by C. Ireland	G3–G8
VIII	Inventory of small finds from Lower Quay Street; by C. Heighway	G9–G13
IX	Table 2.	G14

LIST OF TABLES

TABLE 1	– Stratified groups: Kingsholm	75	
TABLE 2	– Sites The *vicus* area; proportion of different pottery types.		G14
TABLE 3	– King Edwards Gate (12/77) and Berkeley Street (1979); distribution of pottery types in the street-sequence.	83	
TABLE 4	– Clare Street (59/74); the medieval pottery sequence from Period 3.	83	
TABLE 5	– King Edwards Gate (12/77) the medieval pottery sequence.	83	

LIST OF FIGURES

1. Gloucester: excavations and watching brief sites 1974–81. vi
2. Roman Gloucester, c. 250 AD. 2
3. Central Gloucester: 10th century sites and finds. 4
4. Central Gloucester: 11th century sites and finds. 6
5. Central Gloucester: 12th century sites and finds. 7

                                                                                              Page no.

6.   Central Gloucester: 13th century sites and finds.   9
7.   Site 9/74, Brunswick Road. Section of Roman coffins.   11
8.   Site 26/74. Lime kiln, Mitcheldean. Section.   12
9.   Sites 37/74, 77/74, 33/76 XIII, XI. Location of Roman and medieval
       discoveries.   13
10. Site 37/74: 10–11 Market Parade: sections.   14
11. Site 38/74: Kings Walk, sections.   15
12. Site 59/74: Clare Street, section.   17
13. Site 65/74: Robinswood Hill Barracks, section.   18
14. Site 77/74: Norris' Garage, Market Parade. Section accross line of medieval
       boundary of N. suburb.   18
15. Site 66/75. Ladybellgate House, plans.   21
16. Site 98/75 and others: Saintbridge Roman and prehistoric sites. Location
       plan. Scale 6″ = 1 mile.   23
17. Saintbridge site. Prehistoric features.   24
18. Saintbridge site. Roman features.   25
19. Saintbridge site. Burials 1, 2, 4, 5.   26
20. Saintbridge site. Plans and sections of individual features.   27
21. Sites 25/76, 12/77, 19/79, the western wall of the Roman town. Location
       plan.   29
22. Site 25/76, Berkeley Street. Section.   30
23. Site 28/76, Quedgeley, Roman site. Plan and section.   31
24. Site 29/76, Foreign Bridge and Swan Lane. Section.   32
25. Site 33/76. I. London Rd, nr Wotton Pitch. Section.   34
26. Site 33/76. II. London Rd, nr. Heathfield Rd. Section.   34
27. Site 33/76. III. London Rd/Horton Rd. Section.   34
28. Site 33/76. IV. Barnwood Rd/Wotton Brook. Section.   34
29. Site 33/76. V. Oxbode/Northgate St. Section.   35
30. Site 33/76. VI. Barnwood Rd/railway bridge. Section.   35
31. Site 33/76. VIII. Northgate St/Worcester St. Section.   35
32. Site 33/76. X. Section.   36
33. Site 33/76. XII. Section.   37
34. Site 63/76. Cathedral Treasury. Location Plan.   38
35. Site 63/76. Section.   38
36. Site 12/77. King Edward's Gate. Development Plan.   40
37. Site 12/77. King Edward's Gate. Section.   41
38. Site 38/78. Prince Albert site: Plan.   45
39. Site 38/78. Prince Albert site: Section.   46
40. Site 19/79. Berkeley Street. Sections.   47
41. Sites 28/79 and 59/74. The riverside area.   49
42. Site 28/79, 10 Lower Quay Street. Section.   50
43. Site 30/79. St Catherine Street. Section.   52
44. Site 11/80. Church House, Gloucester Cathedral. Plans and section.   53
45. Site 4/81. South Gate. Plan and section.   54
46. Site 14/81. Westgate Street, outside St. Nicholas Church. Section.   56
47. Site 26/81. Saintbridge. Location plan of 1981 trenches.   56
48. Site 26/81. Prehistoric and Roman features, plan.   57
49. Kingsholm, 1st century finds.   59
50. Kingsholm, late Roman finds.   61
51. Site 57/74. 9–11 St Oswalds Rd. Section.   61
52. Kingsholm. Central area of 1st century fort or fortress.   62
53. Site 4/78. 76 Kingsholm Rd. Plans.   64
54. Site 5/81. 17 Sandhurst Rd. Plans and section.   67
55. Minor sites. Prehistoric pottery and 1st-century pottery from Kingsholm.   74
56. Minor sites. Roman pottery.   76
57. Minor sites. Roman pottery.   78
58. Minor sites. Medieval pottery.   80
59. Minor sites. Post-medieval pottery.   82
59A. Samian pottery.   85
60. Site 28/79, Lower Quay Street. Roman, medieval, and post-medieval pottery.   90
61. Site 28/79, Lower Quay Street. Post-medieval pottery.   91
62. Site 28/79, Lower Quay Street. Post-medieval pottery.   92
63. Minor sites. Small finds of bone and copper.   94
64. Minor sites. Small finds of copper, glass, gold and iron.   95

		Page no.
65.	Minor sites. Small finds of iron, jet and lead.	96
66.	Minor sites. Leather.	97
67.	Minor sites. Leather and wood.	98
68.	Site 28/79, 10 Lower Quay Street. Small finds of bone, copper and iron.	100
69.	Site 28/79, 10 Lower Quay Street. Leather footwear.	101
70.	Site 28/79, 10 Lower Quay Street. Small finds of metal, silver, stone and wood.	102

LIST OF PLATES

PLATE I	King Edwards Gate: site 12/77.	42
PLATE II	Roman road in Mitcheldean; site 27/74. View south from the north end of Silver Street.	69
Frontispiece	Street sections in Northgate Street – see site 33/76, VIII and Fig. 31.	

ABBREVIATIONS

B	– Building
F	– Feature
TF	– Type Fabric
GADARG	– Gloucester and District Archaeological Research Group
Pd.	– Period
D	– Diameter
L	– Length
TBGAS	– Transaction of the Bristol and Gloucestershire Archaeological Society
PNFC	– Proceeding of the Cotteswold Naturalists Field Club

ACKNOWLEDGEMENTS

The cost of watching briefs in 1974–81 was met both by Gloucester City Council, who provided the salary and administrative costs of the Field Archaeologist and Unit Head, and by the Department of the Environment who provided the necessary grants for field work. Post-excavation work was also funded by the Department of the Environment and the City.

We are grateful to all those who contributed to this report in many ways, especially John Rhodes, Museum Curator, for his comments and support. The excellent work of Caroline Ireland, Pottery Researcher, was incomplete when she resigned to follow her husband to Cambridge; we are grateful to her for allowing us to use her work, unfinished as it was, in this report. We also wish to thank her predecessor, Cherry Goudge, for her considerable contribution.

Many volunteers and assistants helped on all the sites reported on: we would like to mention John Smith, John McKiernan, Paul Kent, Dave Kear, Lynne and Chris Marley, Alan and Joanna Vince, and the Gloucester and District Archaeological Research Group.

Nearly all tracings of plans and sections reproduced here were done by Lynne Marley from the original site drawings of A. P. Garrod. We are grateful to Richard Bryant for his considerable help both in compilation and production of this report. Some of the microfiche sections were typed at the Western Archaeological Trust, who also administered project funds in 1983–4.

Carolyn Heighway
Patrick Garrod
20th January 1984

DEDICATION

TO THE GLOUCESTER AND DISTRICT ARCHAEOLOGICAL RESEARCH GROUP and all those citizens who value Gloucester's past.

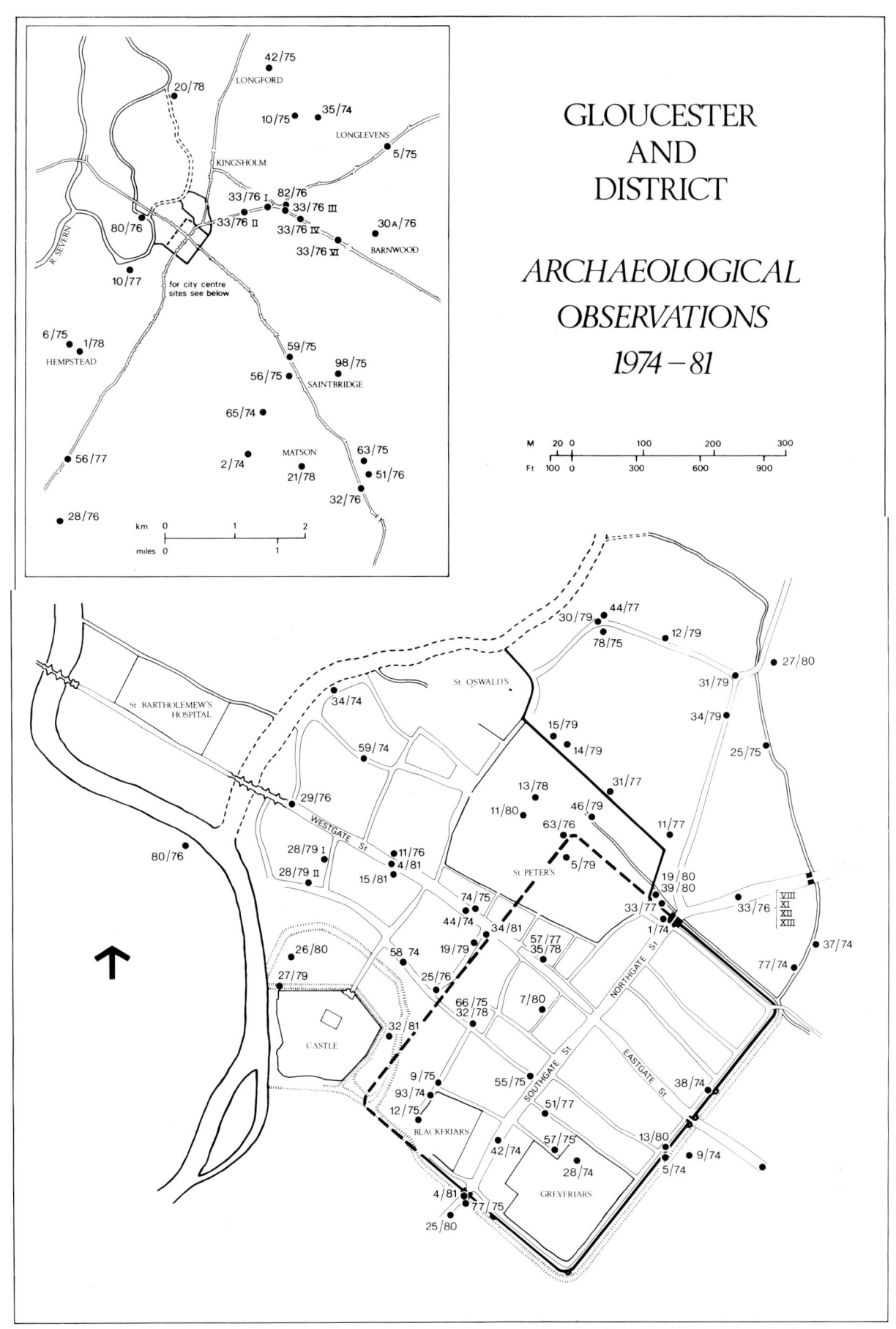

Figure 1. Gloucester: location of 'watching brief' sites 1974–81. Inset shows sites outside the central City area. Drawn by Jean Williamson.

INTRODUCTION: GLOUCESTER AS AN ARCHAEOLOGICAL SITE by C. M. Heighway

The historic core of Gloucester is set on a small hillock overlooking the River Severn. Founded as a Roman fortress in the 60's AD, it became a *colonia c.* AD 100. More or less abandoned in the post-Roman period, the town was restored in the 10th century, was a shire-town in the 11th, and became one of the prosperous small towns of medieval England.

The town had a nearby Roman and medieval quay on a navigable arm of the Severn which had silted up by post-medieval times. The quay and docks are now further south.

Suburbs, both Roman and medieval, extended down the slope across the lower alluvial clays and gravel terraces to the north and west. The site of an earlier Roman fort *c.* AD 50 and a Royal Saxon Palace lies in the northern suburb close to the river at Kingsholm.

Ever since the 19th century, archaeological excavation has been carried out in Gloucester. In the earlier years, invaluable records were made on building sites by interested individuals such as the architect Henry Medland, who worked in Gloucester in the 1880's and 1890's. In the 1930's the Gloucester Roman Research Committee was set up by W.H. Knowles in his capacity as President of the Bristol and Gloucestershire Archaeological Society. This committee carried out and published several important excavations. From 1951, the Museum had an archaeological assistant who organised excavations as important sites were built on. In the mid 1960's the building boom began, and thousands of cubic metres of archaeological deposits were threatened with destruction. In 1967 a successor to the Gloucester Roman Research Commmittee, the Gloucester and District Archaeological Research Group (GADARG) was formed, its aims being to widen the scope of the previous committee to include the area around the town and other periods of history. The Museum did its part by appointing, in 1968, a Field Archaeologist (H. Hurst) to deal with the archaeological problem. During the next five years excavations were carried out almost without pause. In 1973 an Excavation Unit was set up, with a Unit Head, a Field Officer, (A.P. Garrod), and Administrative Assistant, and a Finds Research Assistant. Since the Unit was set up, the pace of development has slowed, but still at least one major excavation has taken place every year until 1979; in 1981 the unit was re-absorbed into the Museum.

Since 1973 the Field Archaeologist has undertaken a number of excavations in both the City and its District. However the greater part of his time has been dedicated to the observation and recording of all ground disturbances, whether during building constructions or the laying of service trenches.

Long familiarity with excavations, prior to and throughout the city redevelopment, has enabled Garrod to relate even the smallest stratigraphic section to the known archaeological sequence. The process of archaeological retrieval under these circumstances has been highly cost-effective.

Sequences of dated occupation deposits have been recorded from nearly all areas of the town; these sequences are vital to the production of period maps (Figs 3–6). The groups of pottery obtained are small, but still useful, if use is made of the knowledge of pottery dating gained from other controlled excavations. The many records of street sections have proved invaluable. They provide a dating method for the earliest streets and can often determine a street alignment, so that a series of plans showing the development of the towns street pattern can ultimately be compiled. Street sections are also important for the economic information they contribute; the leather, pottery, bones etc. lying on a street surface are not usually residual, for streets were seldom disturbed by pitting, or building activities, even in the medieval period.

The Field Archaeologist also keeps a record, usually photographic, of buildings which are being demolished (detailed drawn building records are done by GADARG, which currently maintains a record of Gloucester buildings which is kept at the Folk Museum). The Field Archaeologist also keeps a record of medieval and post-medieval cellars. A full survey of cellars was begun in 1974, when it was discovered that the tower of the medieval East Gate still existed as a cellar. There may be other discoveries of this type to be made. The systematic cellar survey was shelved, due to lack of time, but a few obvious sites (sites of the Roman west and south gates) have been checked with negative results.

ROMAN GLOUCESTER

The plans of the fortress and colonia have been published by Hurst (1974, 18–22). Watching briefs of 1974 to 1981 have added the following information.

There is a large structure on the road north from Gloucester 90m. outside the North Gate. The structure may be a monumental arch (33/76 VIII). Also at this point is a massive wall (33/76 XI). This is large enough to be defensive but its line (alongside the main road) is puzzling.

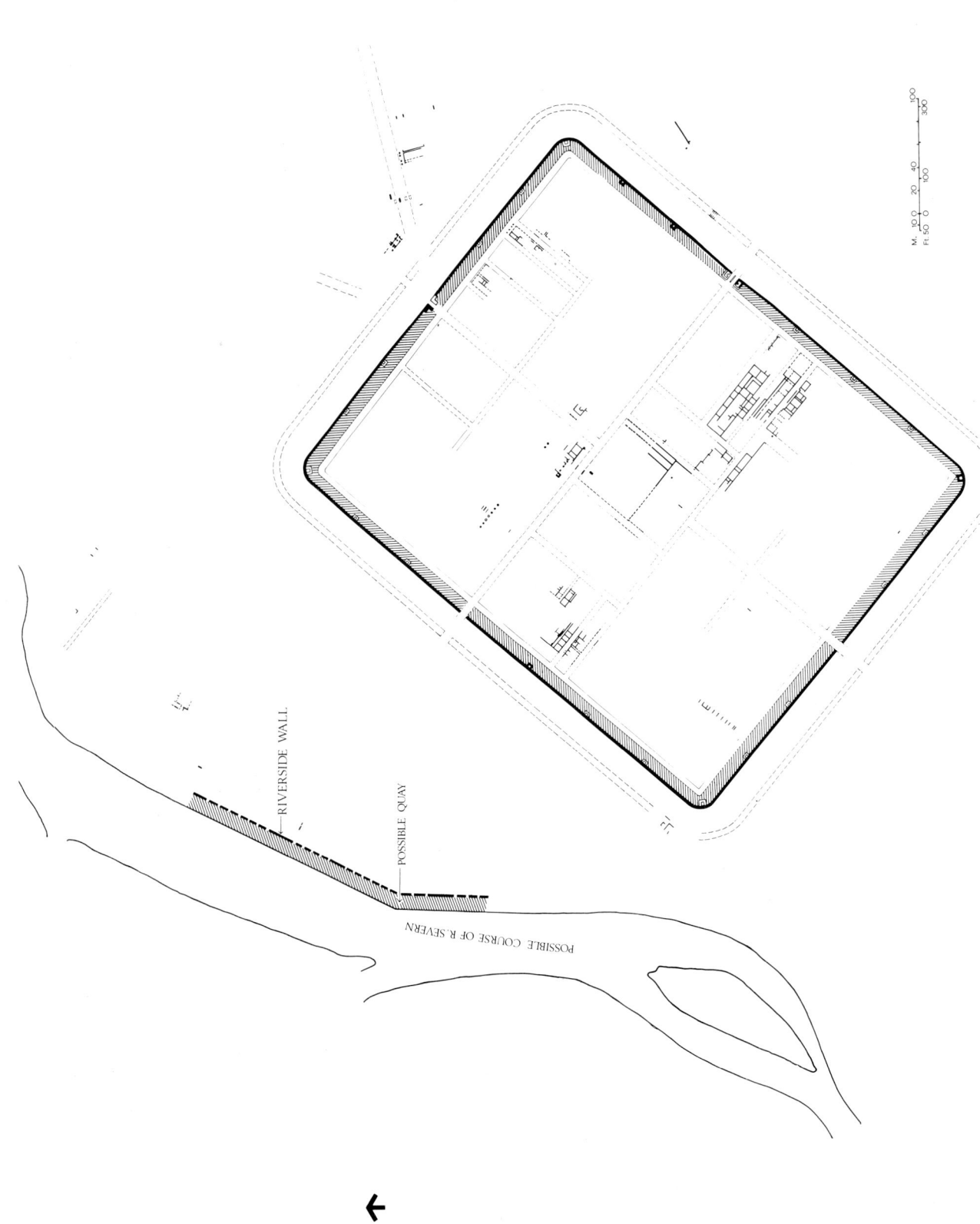

Figure 2. Roman Gloucester, c. 250 AD. Buildings recorded to 1979 are included. Drawn by Richard Bryant, after Hurst 1974, Fig. 7.

Under St. Johns Lane a new road line has been established (69/76, 14/76).

Another Roman road is now known to occupy the line of Worcester Street (33/76 XII, XIII).

Several burials have been added to the plots of the Brunswick Road cemetery (sites 9/74, 7/76, 43/79).

The area of the Wotton cemetery (Heighway 1980) has also been clarified; two sites provided negative evidence (82/76, 26/78); others extended the known information (27/76, 33/81).

The source of Gloucester's water in the Romano British period has always been assumed to have been the springs on the hillside above the town. This is confirmed by the discovery of what is almost certainly the base of an aquaduct entering the town from the east (38/78).

Glevum had extensive suburbs. Watching briefs have added to the known area of these (44/77, 7/76, 38/78, 34/79, 12/79, 30/79, 17/81). A large late Roman ditch to the north of the town (12/79) could have defended Gloucester's large northern suburb.

Almost all the information that exists on the Roman waterfront has been compiled from watching briefs.

In the 19th century several observations suggested the line of the Roman quay (Heighway and Garrod 1981, 124). The discovery of the quayside wall and quay was recorded by Garrod in a building excavation in 1973 (Hurst 1974, 46). The wall, 1.4m thick, was constructed of coursed rubble and founded on a masonry platform at 6.75m. AOD. A quay at this level would 'provide scope for mooring and working vessels over a useful range of tides' (Rowbotham 1978, 7). Roman occupation was at *c*. 8.9m AOD or higher. The quayside wall would revet higher ground to the east and prevent erosion during the flooding that would certainly have occurred.

Since 1973, this wall line has been confirmed (59/74), and a trial excavation carried out (28/79). The results of this are given below, but it is sufficient to mention here that the quayside wall was probably defensive, and that since it survived until the 12th century, the implications for the later topography of the waterfront are considerable.

This wall, if defensive, can be assumed to be later than the late 2nd century external wall-towers on the west side of the original walled circuit. Pottery indicates a late 3rd to 4th century date.

A major post-Roman topographical alteration at Gloucester was the elimination of the original *via principalis* and the re-routing of the main street to the north. Victorian records, a small excavation (57/77), and a subsequent watching brief (35/78) have established that the new route passed through a monumental building, probably the baths *palaestra* (Heighway and Garrod 1980).

The sequence of Gloucester's Roman defences is fairly well established, but watching briefs continue to amplify the available information (38/74, 77/75, 33/77, 12/79). There is evidence for deliberate levelling of buildings outside the defences in the 2nd century (77/74).

POST-ROMAN GLOUCESTER

No occupation sites are known from the 5th to the 8th centuries. 9th century levels are almost a-ceramic (Heighway, Garrod and Vince 1979) and it is reasonable to suppose that the earlier centuries were also. The problem is worsened by the fact that on most sites, levels of 5th–10th century date have been eroded by later activity (Hurst 1972, 43). This means, once again, that the most complete stratigraphic record is under streets, particularly under the cardinal streets which probably date back to the immediate post Roman period. Here the post-Roman centuries are represented by a disturbed loam containing Roman pottery and building debris. There is a visual difference, according to A.P. Garrod, between this and the "dark earth" which survives elsewhere and which is probably due to cultivation (Hurst 1974, 23). The dark earth in the principal street could result, not from cultivation, but from the constant churning of traffic on unmetalled tracks. A sampling programme carried out in conjunction with the watching brief could establish the nature of all these "dark earth" deposits.

9TH CENTURY

The physical framework of the settlement at Gloucester in the 9th century was still that of the Roman walls. The material culture of the settlement was nearly all of wood or other organic material: there was virtually no pottery (Heighway Garrod and Vince 1979: Heighway forthcoming a; Heighway 1984). The decay of the

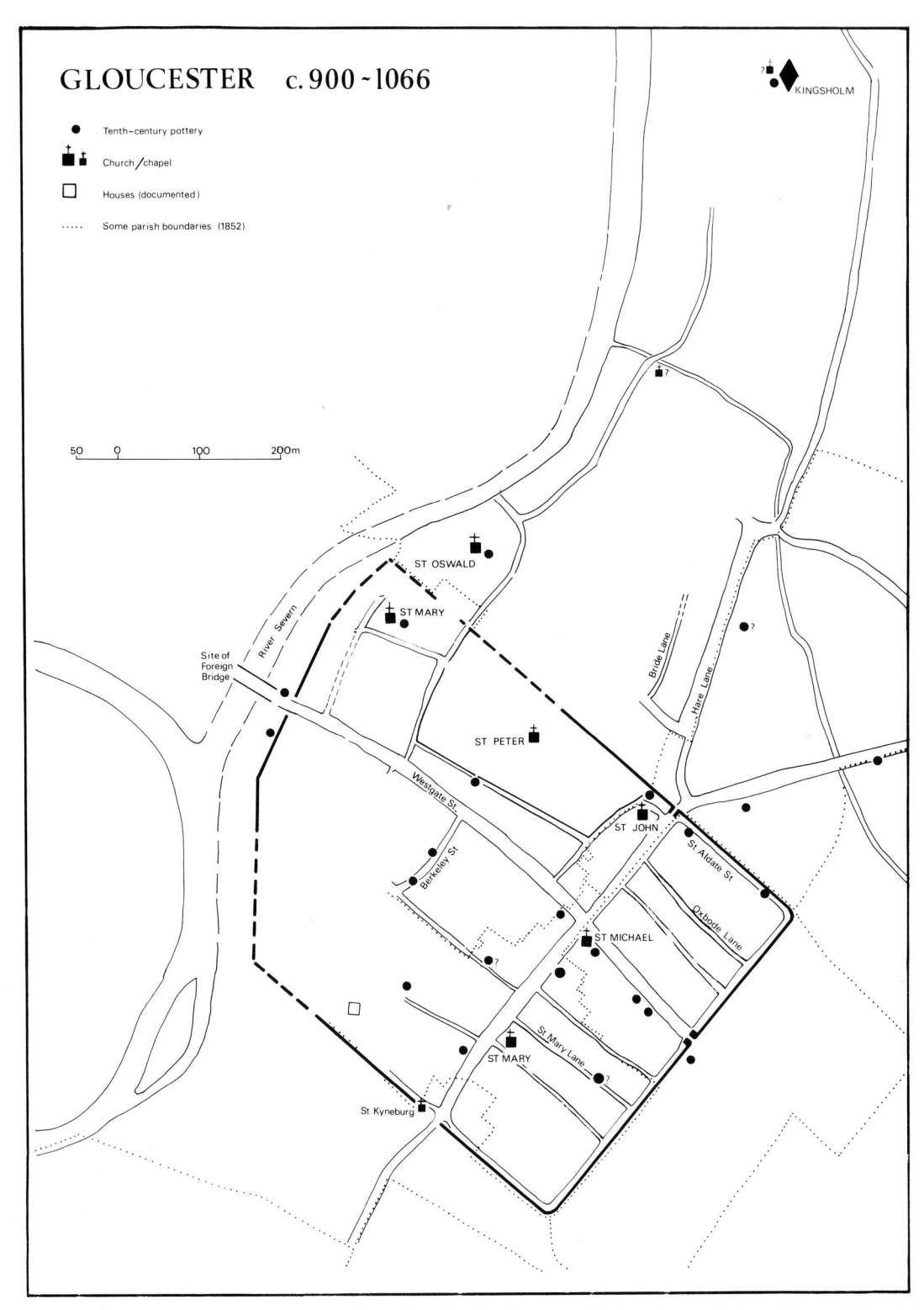

Figure 3. Gloucester in the 10th century, based on finds of pottery Fabric Type 41A, without 41B. All finds spots and excavations to 1979 are shown. The key applies also to Figures 4–6. Drawn by Western Archaeological Trust.

organic remains may partly explain why remains of this period are few, but it is probable that occupation at this stage of the city's development was confined to the central area, perhaps occupying the open space where the old Roman forum had been. It is likely, though not yet proved, that there was also occupation in the waterfront area. 9th century occupation has not so far been discernable from watching briefs, but in the future it may be possible, especially with the aid of radio-carbon dates, to distinguish 9th century levels even in a very small excavation.

10TH CENTURY

An important development of the 10th century is held to be a re-laying of the streets by Aethelflaeda of Mercia, before 914, as part of the foundation of a *burh* in the Alfredian tradition (Hurst 1972, 66–8; Radford 1978, 133).

Since watching briefs are particularly productive of evidence about streets (above, p.1) we might expect them to provide confirmation of this hypothesis.

Unfortunately, 10th-century dating evidence is rare and difficult to interpret. Large collections of pottery cannot be expected, and there is always the possibility that odd sherds may be residual. Added to this is the problem of dating the pottery itself. Type TF 41A was in use in the 10th and 11th centuries; somewhere in the mid to late 11th century a change was made to TF 41B (Vince 1979, 175–6). If a sequence of streets indicates such a change, *i.e.* with TF 41A in earlier streets, TF 41B in later ones, then an approximate indication of date may, with reservations, be obtained (see, for instance, Table 3, site 19/79). Ideally, other dating evidence is needed to corroborate pottery evidence.

Evidence for the date of the main area of 'Saxon' street pattern *i.e.* in the E. area of the walled town, has not yet been forthcoming. There is one sherd of 10th-century pottery from under an intra-mural metalling in St. Aldate Street (-/47); St. Mary Street had a second surface dated to the 12th century or later (Hassall and Rhodes, 1974, 30). All the many street sections recently recorded either did not go deep enough (42/74, 44/74, 58/74, 25/80) or had insufficient dating evidence (14/76, 25/76, 35/78).

The best evidence for tenth-century streets comes surprisingly from the area just west of the Roman fortress.

An important topographical event was the demolition of the W. wall of the Roman fortress and town. Hurst (1974, 13) thought this might have occurred as late as the late 11th century. There is now further evidence.

The W. wall and ditch have to be considered separately, since the two elements could have gone out of use at different times.

Berkeley Street, roughly on the berm of the W. ditch, crosses the ditch at its S. end (Fig 44). Sherds of pottery from the upper fills of the ditch (site 25/76, Trench II) provide a *t.p.q.* of the mid 11th century for the final silting of the ditch, and for the construction of tenements on the W. side of Berkeley Street at its S. end.

The parish boundary of St. Nicholas and Holy Trinity, probably 11th century or later (Heighway forthcoming a) respects tenements fronting onto Westgate St., but its straight line S. of this may indicate that there were no tenements fronting the W. side of Berkeley St. when it was formed. By contrast there were 11th-century tenements on the E. side of the street, at its S. end (Hurst 1974, 43). All this seems to suggest that in the 11th century a short stretch of the W. ditch survived W. of Berkeley St., at its S. end. The ditch was shallower, perhaps resulting only from subsidence of earlier ditch fills, but it was apparently not yet worth building on.

The best evidence for the demise of the W. wall comes from the metallings of Berkeley Street. The street was metalled at least fourteen times from when the Roman wall was robbed to sometime in the 13th century. Under Street 3 was an 11th-century scramasax sheath (Fig. 66 and p.98), a 10th century shoe, and late 10th to 11th century pottery (site 19/79). At Winchester, the streets of the *burh* were remetalled every 25 years (Biddle 1970, 285–7). It is unlikely that Gloucester streets would have been resurfaced so often, but at the latest, Berkeley St. must have been first metalled in the early 11th century. The Roman wall was thus demolished before that date.

The lane which surrounds the abbey precinct, excavated at a point W. of the W Roman wall, was also in existence by the 11th century (site 12/77) (p.39).

Burials found under the west range of the Norman Abbey show the abbey already had a burial-ground outside the W. wall by the 11th century (site 11/80).

Thus the accumulated evidence suggests that by the 11th century the W. wall of the Roman city was no longer in existence. Indeed, if the Saxon burh had been contained within the fortress wall, there should have been a 10th century intra-mural street on the W., inside that wall. No evidence survives for such a street (Hurst 1974, 13); although it could have been removed altogether when the wall was demolished.

If the W. wall was gone by the 11th century, it is necessary to suggest a defensive limit further W. This is simple, since the Roman quay wall, excavated in 1979 (site 28/79), has been shown to have been in existence until the early 12th century (see Heighway & Garrod 1981, and below, site 28/79). It survived until the early 12th century, so could have defended the Saxon *burh*.

Eight out of twenty find-spots on the plot of 10th-century finds in Gloucester derive from watching briefs. The plan demonstrates a modest expansion of occupation, concentrated however on the frontage of the two main streets.

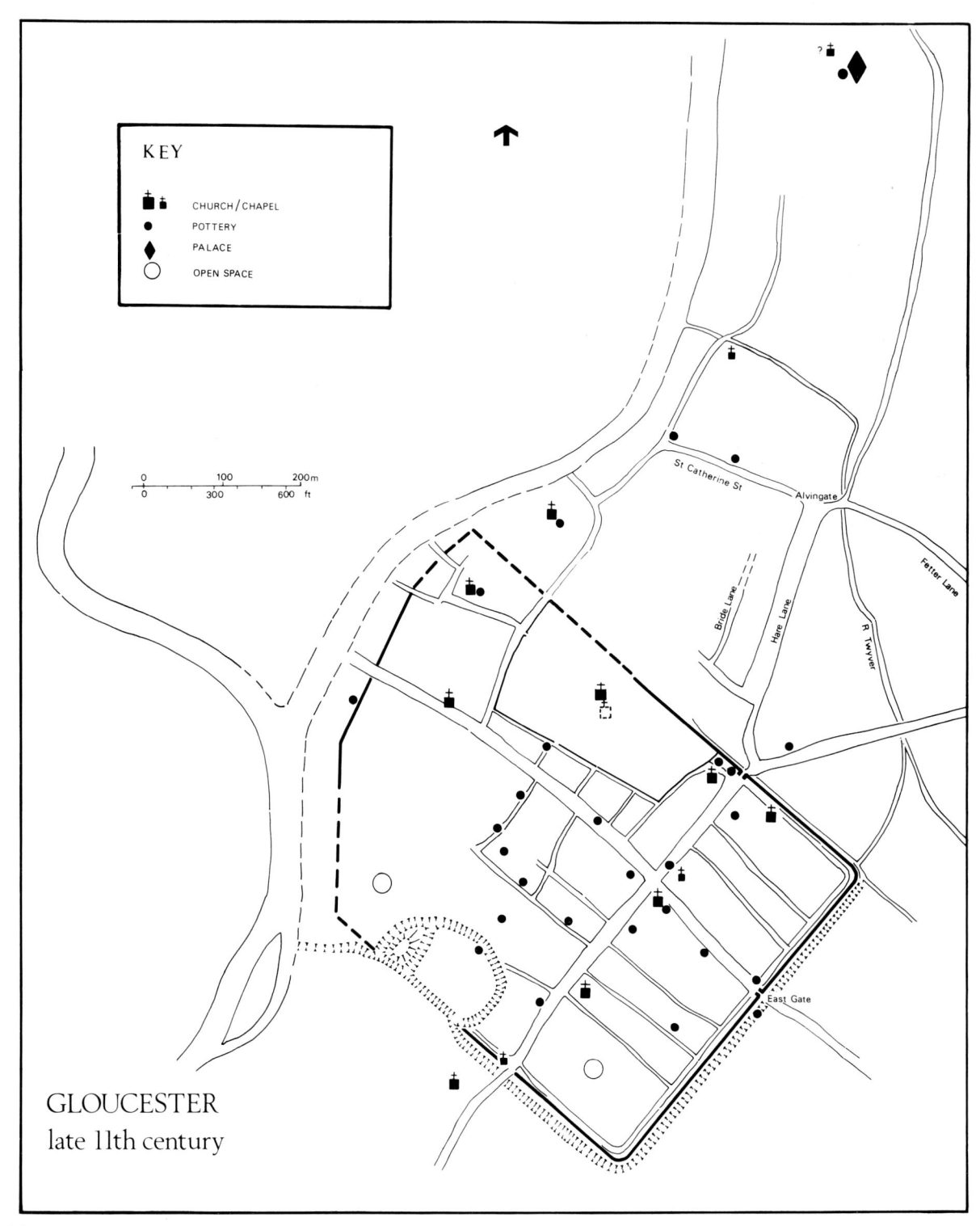

Figure 4. Gloucester in the 11th century, based on finds of pottery Fabric Type 41B without 41A. All finds spots and excavations to 1979 are shown. For key, see Figure 3. Drawn by Western Archaeological Trust.

THE 11TH CENTURY

Nine out of twenty-four sites marked on Fig. 4 show finds derived from watching briefs.

The evidence of general trading patterns in pottery suggests a considerable increase in trade in the 11th century (Vince 1981, 313). The distribution maps do not show much increase in the area occupied, but detailed research on the pottery shows that the quantity and variety of wares is much greater in the 11th century than in the 10th. This change may be a pre-conquest one. On ceramic evidence it could go back to c. 1000 but it is probably closer to c. 1050.

The Conquest imposed important new buildings on the town's landscape: the new abbey, built by Serlo from 1089 onwards, and the royal castle. From information derived from Garrod's watching briefs in 1973, and subsequently (9/75), it is now known that the original motte and bailey castle was in the Blackfriars area, and that the early 12th century stone castle was built further W (Hurst 1974, 12; and forthcoming).

THE 12TH CENTURY

Two important innovations in the early 12th century were the building of the stone castle, and the demolition of the Roman quayside wall, which took place at about the same time (below, site 28/79). The two may even be connected in that the stone taken from the quayside wall could have contributed to the building of the castle.

The demolition of the Roman wall freed a large tract of land for settlement. Almost immediately Lower Quay Street (then Walkers Lane) was formed and houses developed along its frontage. The area around the N side of the castle was soon in use for tanning and dying.

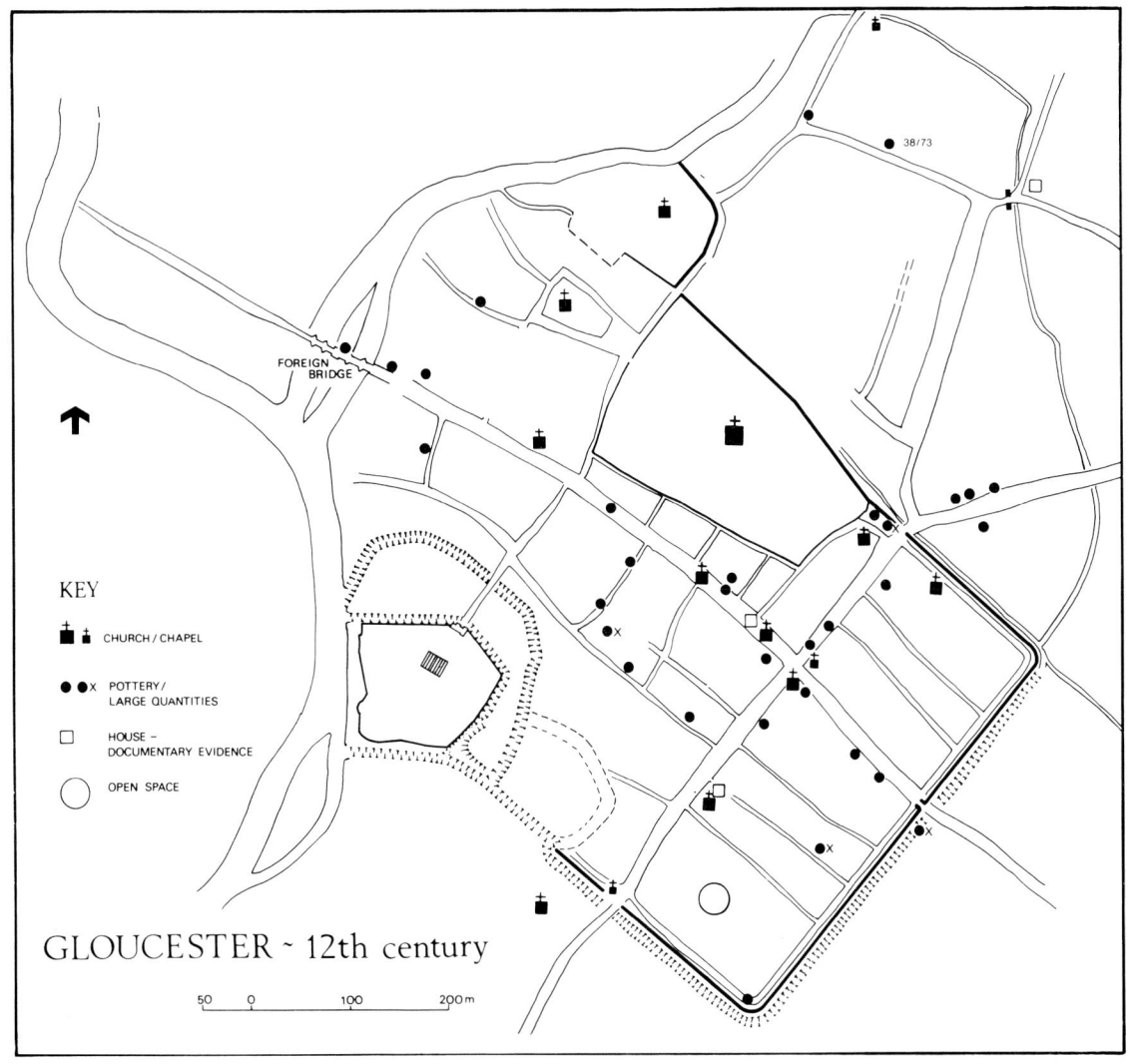

Figure 5. Gloucester in the 12th century, based on finds of pottery Fabric Type 40. All finds spots and excavations to 1979 are shown. Drawn by Western Archaeological Trust.

The 12th century town, as demonstrated by pottery distributions (twelve out of twenty-seven find spots from watching briefs) was still expanding within the Roman walls, but the availability of space for 13th century religious houses shows that there was still plenty of open space. A suburb outside the north gate was already beginning to develop in the 12th century.

The market was by now established in Westgate Street, where the Butchery and Mercery were (Lobel 1969). Two churches had been built in the middle of the street – St. Mary de Grace and Holy Trinity – and the centre of the street was occupied by timber shops (Heighway and Garrod 1980, 83) and even stone houses (Kirby 1967, IV/7).

The 12th century also saw the construction of Foreign Bridge (Hurst 1974, 46). The exact position of the waterfront in the post-Roman period is uncertain, but the known position of Foreign Bridge (ibid, and below site 29/76) gives an indication of where the E. channel flowed in the 12th century. It is very puzzling that Lower Quay Street, the street known in the 13th century as Walkers Lane, should have properties on its W. side backing onto the river Severn; one at least of these properties was 27 yards long. The river cannot have flowed this far east. Either this is an error of lease survey, or the reference is to an otherwise unknown channel.

THE 13TH CENTURY

The most conspicuous additions to the towns topography in the 13th century were the insertions, into various unoccupied areas of the town, of the religious houses.

Most of these have been partly excavated, and there is ample documentary evidence for them. The position of the claustral buildings of Greyfriars (Mynard, unpublished) Blackfriars (Saunders 1963) and St. Oswalds (Heighway 1978, 1980a) is known. The position of the claustral buildings of the Carmelite Friars however, has always been uncertain, although its precinct area is known (Lobel 1969) and can be checked from leases.[1] The house of the Carmelite Friars in Gloucester was founded in the reign of Henry III (Page 1907, p.112). The Friars built 'an oratory' in the area 'near Brook Street' in 1269–70.[2] The evidence below (37/74) is a useful indicator of the position of the White Friars house. A building with a tiled floor and containing burials, and with 13th century mouldings in association with it, is unlikely to be anything other than the Friars church (Fig.9). It stands in the position occupied by the White Friars church on Speed's map of 1610.

It is possible that the church is identical with a building known as the 'White Barn' which is mentioned in 1657 as having been recently demolished because of its ruinous state.[3] The adjective 'White' could refer to the Friars, rather than to the barn's colour. A building called 'the Fryers Barn' was filled with earth and formed part of the defensive system in the Civil War (Washbourne 1825, pp lviii, lix, 215, 219, 222); this may have been identical with the 'White Barn', if not with the church.

The lands and buildings of the Whitefriars were acquired at the Dissolution by Sir Thomas Bell[4] (Fullbrook-Leggatt 1952, 71). The exact site of the church was unknown until discovered in 1974.

By the 13th century there was an extensive suburb outside the N. gate, which was defended with gates and perhaps also a bank (Hurst 1974, 15, 17). Further evidence of this bank was looked for in Market Parade (77/74), with inconclusive results. The defence also depended on the River Twyver (25/75).

The waterfront had by now moved considerably W. from its Roman position. Foreign Bridge had been built in the late 11th to mid 12th century (Hurst 1974, 49), Westgate Bridge in the late 12th (ibid, 41, 50).

A lane known in 1842 as White Swan Lane and in 1455 as 'Dockham Lane' probably represented a river frontage N. of Foreign Bridge.[1] A watching brief at the S. end of Swan Lane (site 29/76) showed the parapet of Foreign Bridge across the end of the line of Swan Lane, and that the earliest metallings of Swan Lane probably ran over the parapet wall and were unlikely to have been laid before the late 13th century. Beneath Swan Lane was black river silt. This site thus helps to position the 13th century waterfront somewhat E. of Swan Lane. Evidence was also obtained to confirm a 12th century date for Foreign Bridge.

The probable position of 13th and 17th century waterfronts was established at Clare Street (59/74).

Various finds of boats have been made in the past, but they were undated so cannot help to fix the position of the waterfront (Heighway and Garrod 1981). A boat found under the Petty Sessions Court (now the police station) (Green 1942, 49) is puzzling: being E. of both Roman and medieval waterfronts. Was this boat in the N. castle ditch?

The position of medieval South Gate, known from 19th century maps, has been confirmed (4/81).

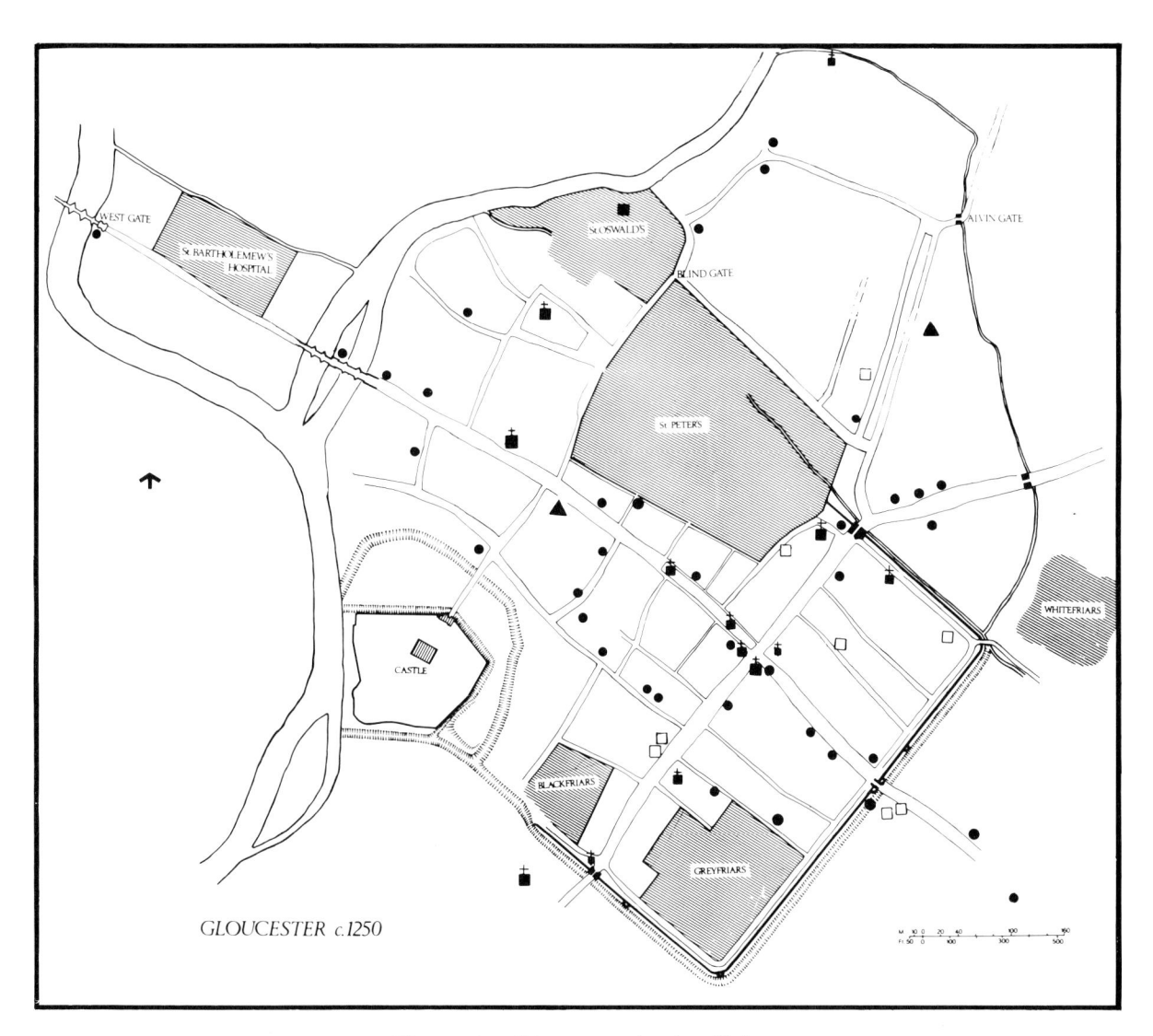

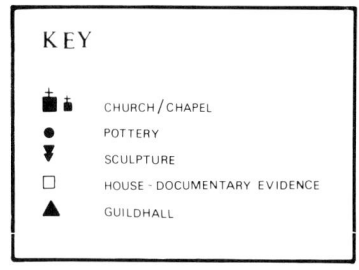

Figure 6. Gloucester in the 13th century.

KEY
- ■✝ ▪︎† CHURCH/CHAPEL
- ● POTTERY
- ▼ SCULPTURE
- □ HOUSE - DOCUMENTARY EVIDENCE
- ▲ GUILDHALL

THE DISTRICT

The work of the Field Archaeologist is not confined to the town centre. The area covered includes Gloucester District, an area of about 39 square kilometres. Wide sheds of oolitic sand, gravel and alluvial clay, cut by small tributaries, extend across the underlying lias clay of the Severn Vale to the quartzite sand and gravel terraces of the River Severn. The area is dominated by Robinswood Hill, an outlier of the Cotswolds.

Watching briefs have shown that the District was occupied by farmers from the Late Neolithic to the late Roman Iron Age period and beyond.

Much more needs to be known, both about the prehistoric periods, and the Romano-British period when the colonia *territorium* was taken from tribal land. B. Rawes has suggested (Rawes 1979) that the territorium is divided by a series of ditches. Although this is likely, all ditches so far excavated are associated with areas of Roman settlements and Garrod has found no evidence for ditched alignments beyond such settlements.

Enormous areas of once-rural land in the last ten years have been swallowed up by housing estates. Recording of sites by the Field Archaeologist and G.A.D.A.R.G. has been continuous ever since. The District is rich with evidence for Roman settlements and villas and it is hoped that continued work in this area will establish a firmer understanding of the relationship of rural occupation to the fortress, the *colonia*, and the medieval manors. Recording of Roman sites in quantity began with work by G.A.D.A.R.G. on the M5 (Fowler 1977) and has continued since (Rawes 1977a, 33).

The combined efforts of G.A.D.A.R.G. and the Field Archaeologist has added to the number of Roman settlement sites (35/74, 65/74, 98/75, 28/76, 20/78, 36/78, 26/81), and prehistoric sites (35/74, 65/74, 98/75, 26/81).

A question posed by Fowler (1977, p.41) was the reason for the absence of early medieval sites on the M5. The problem has still not been solved, but certainly one Roman site (28/76) has produced some 9th to 11th century pottery; but is unoccupied in the later medieval period. There may yet be examples to be found of medieval settlement on Roman sites. The problem is exaggerated by the knowledge that Gloucester, and presumably its area, was virtually a-ceramic in the 5th–9th centuries. (Heighway, Garrod and Vince 1979).

ROMAN ROADS NEAR GLOUCESTER

The line of the Roman road which leads out of Gloucester's E. gate has never been entirely clear. The Roman road is the same as the medieval line and runs straight to a point about 1 km. S.E. of Gloucester. Here there is a fork; the medieval road turns S. and takes a sinuous course up the Cotswold scarp to Painswick. The N. road at the fork is a minor one which eventually becomes a track known as 'the Portway' which passes across the common fields of Upton St. Leonards.

A section across 'the Portway' (site 51/76) showed it to have three superimposed metallings, of which the last two were probably post-medieval. The first contained no dating evidence. The Roman road west from Gloucester was metalled only once (site 50/76).

Further east a Roman line for the 'Portway' is not apparent. If it was a Roman road it presumably gave access mainly to the city's fields. Its course up the scarp face is described by John Milner (1980) who claims that it is a medieval road.

Several sections of Roman roads have been noted, both on 'Ermin Street' (33/76 I, II, III, IV, VI, VII, X; 27/77, 10/81, 16/81) and on the road from the East Gate (59/75).

A marked feature of these is that where medieval roads followed the Roman line, they gouged great hollows in the underlying levels, often nearly removing the Roman street metallings.

1. GRO City Leases 1646–1644, 730, 580–84.
2. By licence of the Archbishops of York: *Reg. Giffard, Surtees Soc.* col 109, 92–3. The jurisdiction of York came about because the area was in the parish of St. Oswalds Priory, then in the hands of York. See Thompson 1921.
3. GRO City Leases 1646–1664, 580–84.
4. See also lease of 1657 cited in fn 3.

PART 2 THE SITES

The following account of the discoveries takes the form of a brief summary of the sites: the researcher is referred to the original records for fuller details. An alphabetical index of streets and a numerical index of sites is provided. Sites in the Kingholm area, and those beyond the District boundaries, have been assigned separate sections (Parts 3 and 4).

Sites are given a Museum accession number (e.g. 1/74): all finds and records are so prefixed.

It must be remembered that the work detailed in this report took place under less than ideal conditions. Often only a few minutes were available for the making of the record. Therefore accuracy is not of the order that might be expected on a formal archaeological excavation. Layers were usually measured in from pavement level: levels given are computed from the nearest OS spot height and may be up to 400mm off the true height. However, the stratigraphic sequence is quite clear. Levels in brackets are approximations, calculated from nearest O.S. street levels.

Only significant or dateable finds are mentioned in the summaries

1/74   45–9, Northgate Street.

Watching brief, during complete mechanical excavation of site following major excavation on the Roman and medieval North Gates. See Heighway et.al. 1983.

2/74   Robinswood Hill, Well House   SO 84001561

Observations made before underpinning of Well-house.

The existing Well-house, probably medieval, of oolitic limestone blocks, was found to be set on a Victorian brick-built sump; a 140mm (outside diameter) glazed earthenware pipe drained the sump and a similar pipe fed it. A short length of unseamed lead pipe had been built into the front of the structure, perhaps to feed a cattle trough.

Records: drawings

5/74   Bell Lane

Service trench

18th and 19th century buildings demolished when Bell Lane was widened earlier this century.

Records: Plan

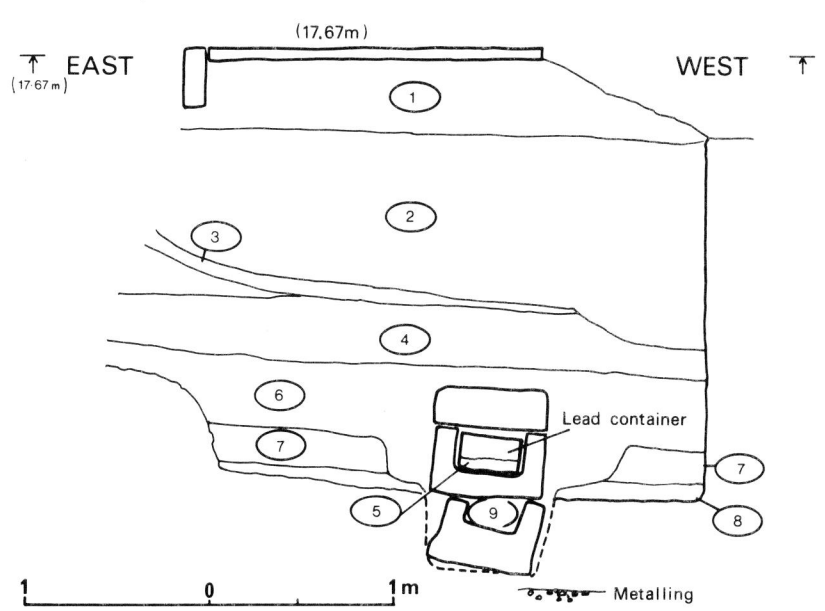

Figure 7. Brunswick Road: section of Roman coffins found under road.

26/74 STENDERSHILL, MITCHELDEAN

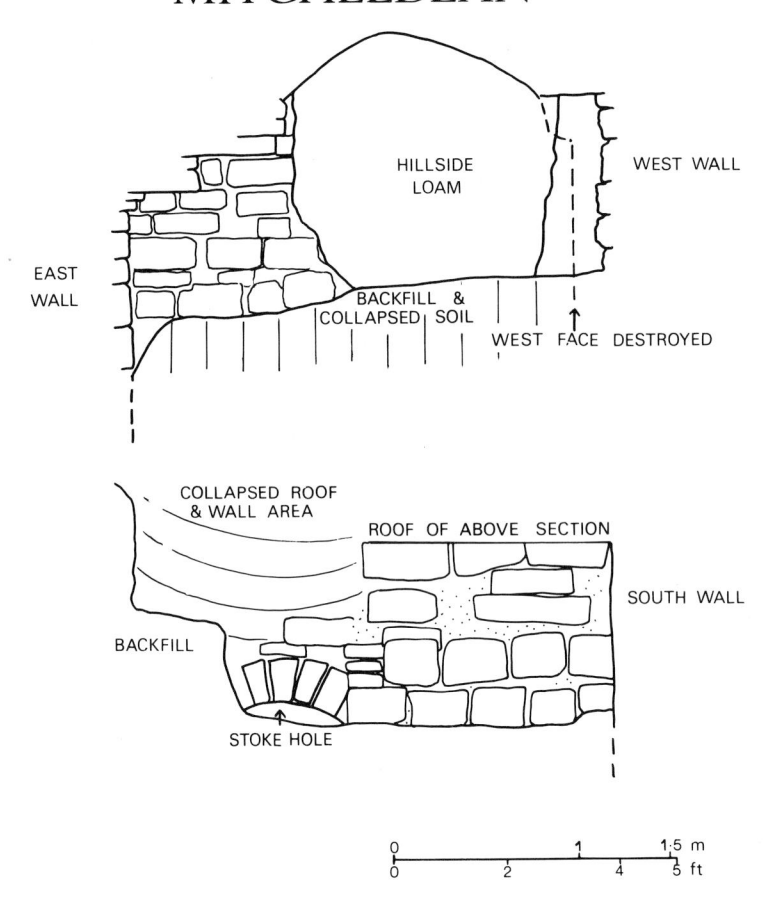

Figure 8. Section of lime kiln at Stenders Hill, Mitcheldean.

9/74 Brunswick Road

Service trench

Two Roman stone coffins were found, one with a lead lining. These are related to the Roman cemetery which exists in this area (Heighway 1980b, 66–7; Heighway et al, 1983, p.39. The coffins cut through a small area of oolite gravel metalling; further west the edge of a ditch was seen (Fig. 7).

Records: SNB 31, pp.4–6; photos.

Finds: pottery, 4 sherds BB1 (TF4), 3rd–4th century. The coffins are on display in Gloucester City Museum (unmarked).

28/74 Greyfriars

This excavation was directed by Howard Davies and John MacKiernon for the D. of E. Guardianship Monuments section. All records are with the D. of E: the pottery is presently stored at Blackfriars, Gloucester.

Records: SNB 42, 43; plans; photos.

34/74 In road outside 26, Priory Road.

Observation of a sewer trench revealed river silts at a depth of 2m. although this is not a certain indication that the old Foreign Bridge river channel ran along this line.

Records: SNB 31, pp.12–13; plans;

35/74 Squires Gate, Longlevens. SO 85042020

Housing Development

A scatter of abraded Roman sherds was found in the spoil heaps. Fragments of tegulae, some unabraded Roman pot sherds and body sherds of a prehistoric vessel, possibly Neolithic, were also found (see p.72). No archaeological features were observed.

Records: SNB 31, p.14

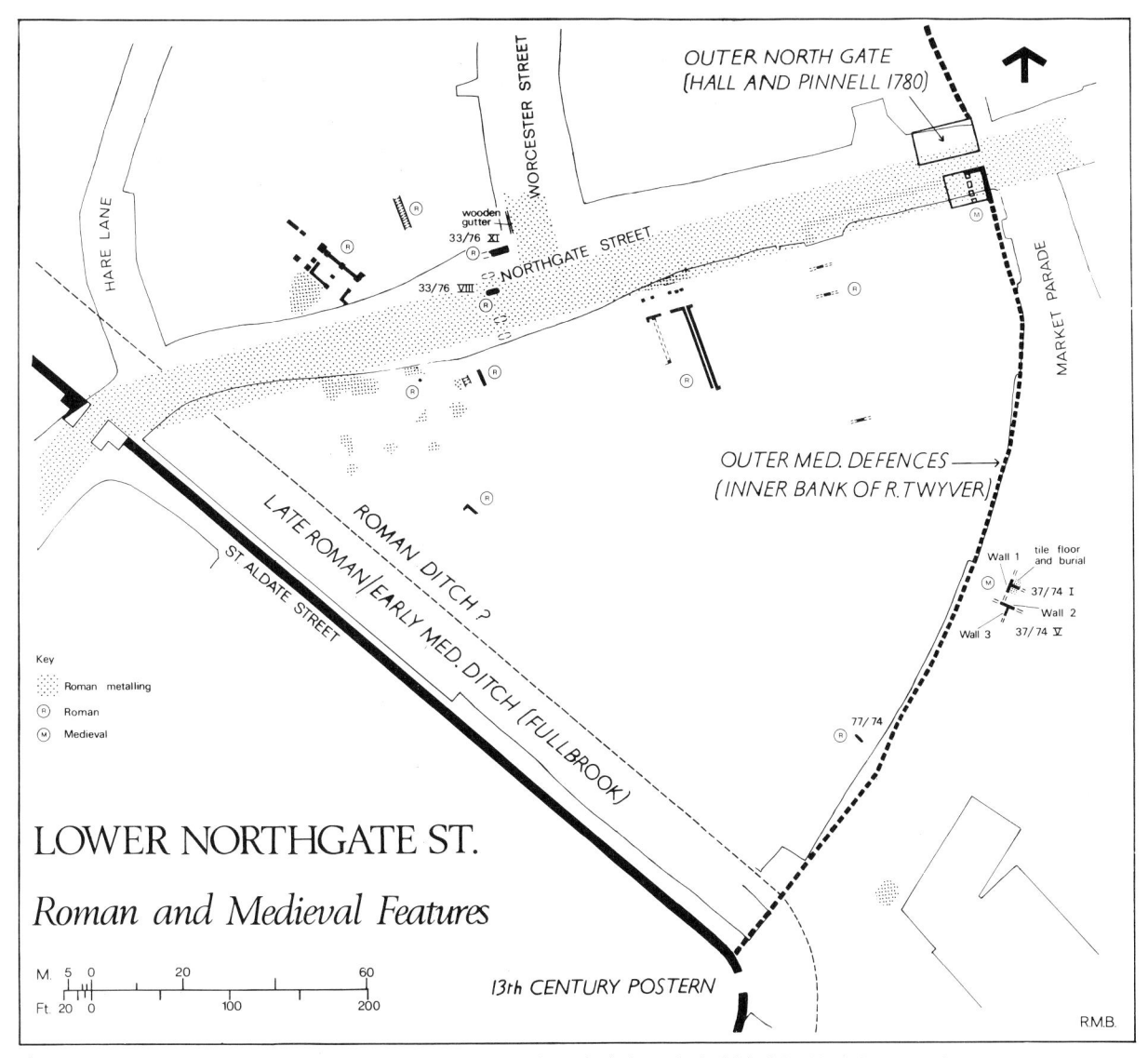

Figure 9. The north-east suburb of Gloucester: sites 37/74, 77/74, 33/76 XIII, XI. Location of Roman and medieval discoveries. Plan based on Hurst 1974, Fig. 10, with additions.

37/74 10–11, Market Parade (Figs. 9 and 10)

Repairs to a gas main: a series of small trenches in the road.

A floor of plain medieval glazed tiles were found, with a burial inserted into it. The floor was limited to the W. by a mortared limestone Wall 1, and to S. by a robbed Wall 2 which had used similar mortar. A third wall 3 at right angles to Wall 2, of lias limestone on oolite footings, was bonded with a different mortar. The building formed by the first two walls was aligned approximately E-W.

This may represent part of the SW corner of the church of the Carmelite Friars which stood in this area (see above, p.8).

Unstratified finds included two pieces of 13th century roll-moulding.

Records: SNB 31, pp.15–25.

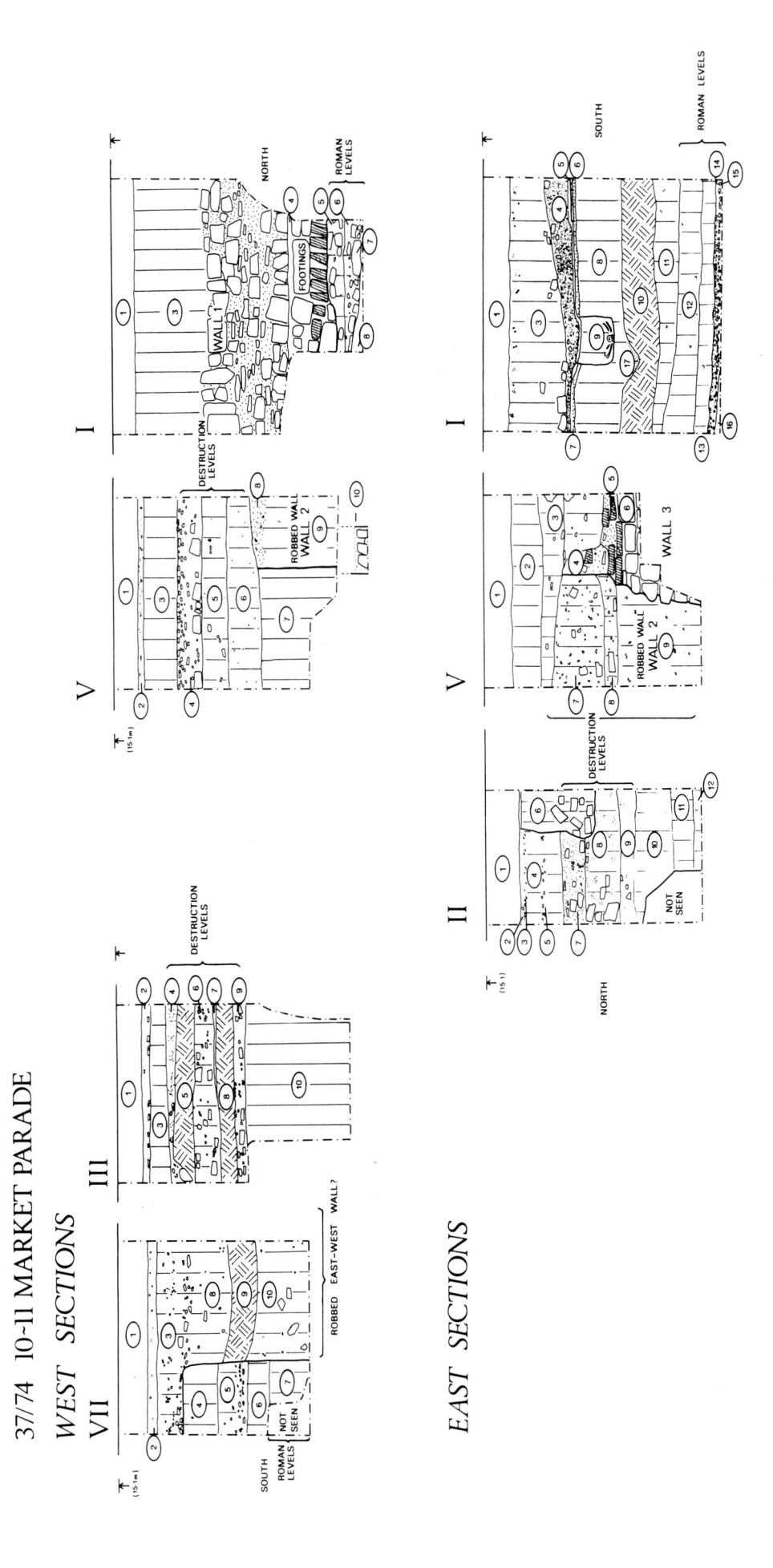

Figure 10. Market Parade, site of Whitefriars' church. Sections.

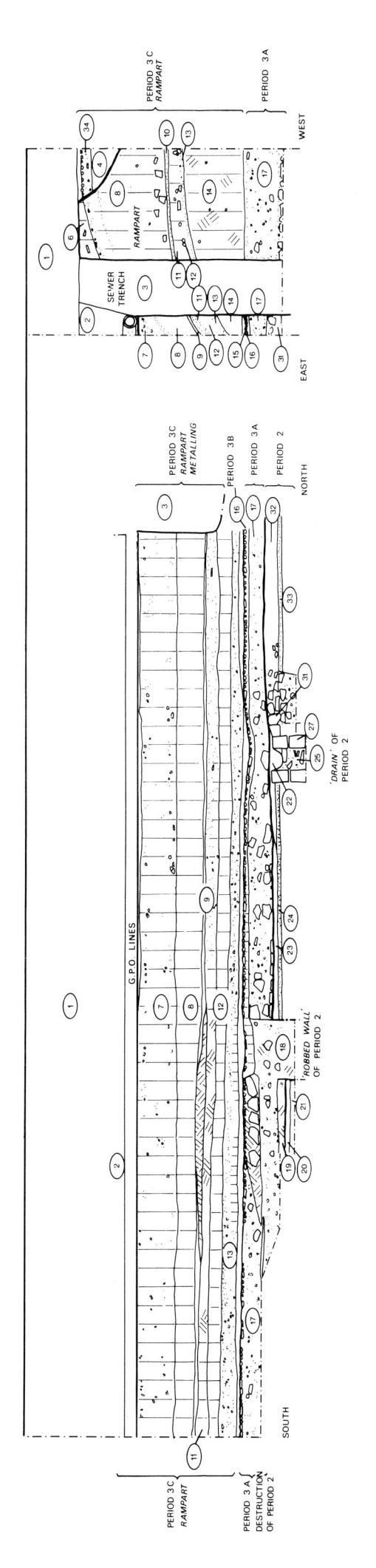

Figure 11. Kings Walk, Sections.

38/74   Entrance to Kings Walk Viewing Chamber (Fig.11).

Construction of a new entrance to the underground chamber where part of the Roman city Wall and a medieval bastion are preserved.

Period numbers (except for suffixes) are those used in Hurst 1972:

Period 2:   A demolished building whose occupation level II (22) contained a Samian stamp of Flavian/Trajanic date. The building had floors of *opus signinum* and puddled clay: a stone-built drain ran W.E. which would have flowed towards the defences.
Pottery: early 2nd century including stamped white-ware base. The pottery compares well with other groups of the early second century.

Period 3a: Destruction of Period 2.

Period 3b: A metalling II (34) overlay the demolished building to the west: this may have been a temporary intervallum street surface for the construction of the period 3 rampart.

Period 3c: A rampart of topsoil as described in Hurst 1972, p.29. The surface of the rampart had apparently been metalled with small pebbles II (16) (cf Heighway et al. 1983 p.30 where a similar metalling was found over the Period 3 rampart near the North Gate).

Records: SNB 31, pp.26–28, 30–32, 40, 41; drawings.

42/74   Outside 40 Southgate Street.

Gas pipe trench

A tree-trunk water conduit 40cm. in diameter was recorded 70cm. below the modern road surface.
An oolite and lias stone cobbled surface was recorded 1.30m. below the street surface.
The wooden water-conduits are often found under Gloucester's main street; one is preserved in Gloucester Folk Museum. Another was found under Westgate Street (see site 44/74 below). They are 17th century in date (inf. Bryan Jerrard).

Records: SNB 31, p.29.

44/74 Outside 68, Westgate Street.

Sewer pipe trench

A metalled surface of oolite gravel and lias was recorded at a depth of 90cm. Beneath it was a layer of sticky organic loam (12) 1.3m. or more in depth, containing 12th century pottery.
A 17th century timber water-conduit D:400mm. cut all these surfaces. A similar conduit was found under Southgate St. (site 42/74).

Records: SNB 31, p.33.

45/74 East Gloucester Development

Three burials recorded during building operations are now known to be associated with a Roman settlement nearby (site 98/75).

46/74   38–44, Eastgate Street.

Excavations in 1974, 1978 and 1979 of the Roman, Norman and Medieval East Gates, a length of City wall and ditch. Excavation 1974: the 1978 work was a six month watching-brief on the building works carried out by A. P. Garrod. See Heighway et al. 1983.

58/74   Longsmith Street and Quay Street (medieval 'Bareland').

Construction of water-main along the length of the two streets.

At a depth of about 0.5m, a 10m. length of metalling (3) lay beneath the Quay St. S. carriageway, W. of Upper Quay Street. 17th century pottery came from loam (2) above this metalling. Under (3) was a stony black gritty organic loam (5) containing 13th century pottery. This was cut to the S. by organic material (14) (13) filling a large feature, perhaps a ditch. This could have been either a street drainage channel or the outer (N.) edge of Gloucester Castle ditch.
All these layers were cut to the E. along the S. side of Quay Street by brick cellars of the demolished 19th century Central Police Station and former Petty Session Court.
Along Longsmith Street S. carriageway, E. of Ladybellgate Street, medieval stone footings, with associated estuarine-clay floors, were observed, indicating the extensive widening of the S. side of Longsmith Street in the 20th century. At the junction of Longsmith Street and Southgate Street, there was an 18th to 19th century barrel-vaulted cellar 2.75m wide beneath the S. carriageway.

Records: SNB 31, p.75; SNB 33, p.19.

59/74 CLARE ST

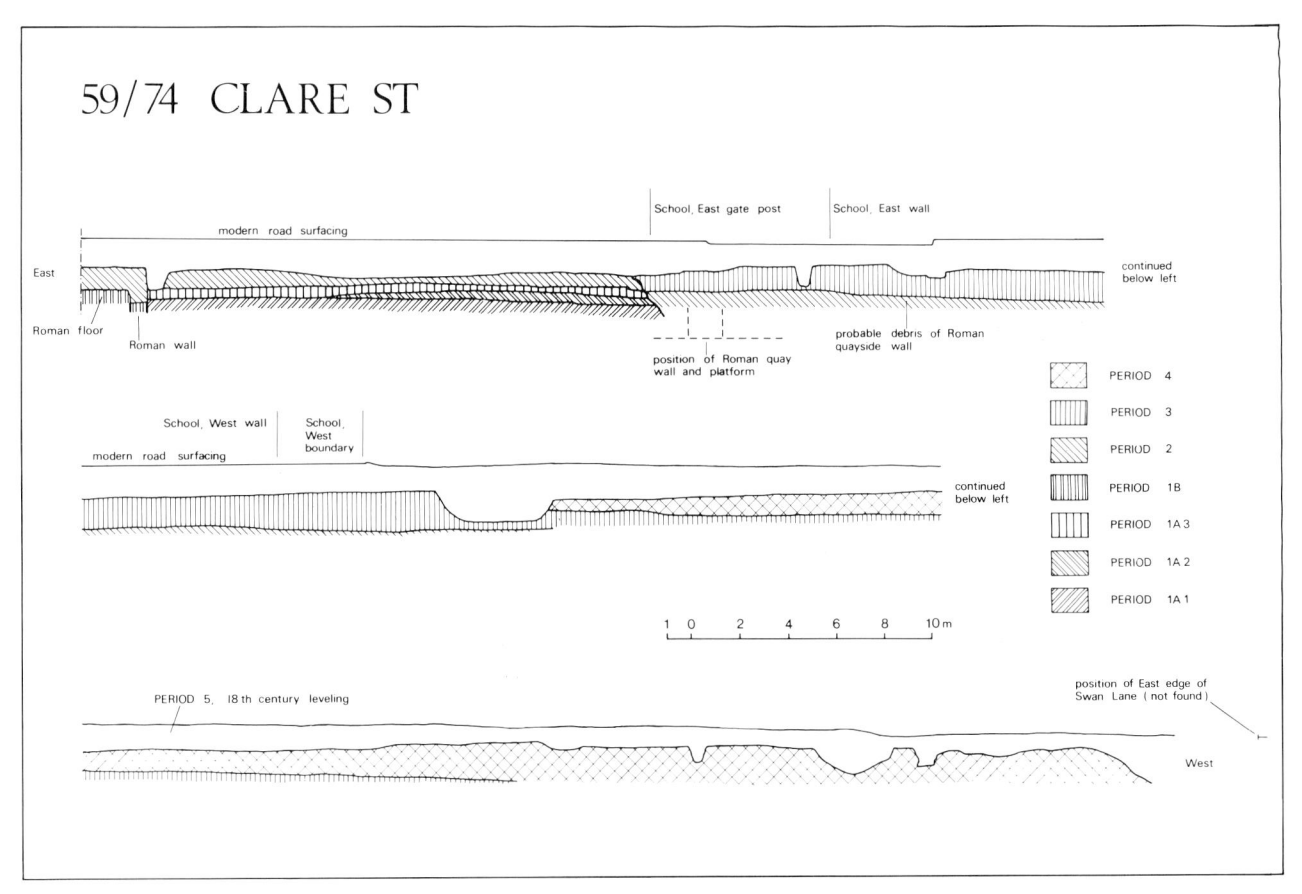

Figure 12. Clare Street, section across the Roman waterfront. Drawn by J. Williamson. The positions of late medieval metalling of Swan Lane (from site 29/76) have been plotted.

59/74 Clare Street (Fig.12, Fig.41)

Sewer trench dug the length of Clare Street, about 2.7m. deep.

Period 1B1: A Roman building represented by a robbed wall, with an *opus signinum* floor to E. of it.

Period 1B2: Occupation levels within the building.

Period 1B3: Fallen wall plaster and destruction debris from the building.

Period 1A1: Metalling W. of the Roman building extended for 20.7m. to what appears to be a robbed wall. Other evidence (see 28/79) suggests that this robbing represents the 'Roman Quay wall', a revetting-wall for the Roman river bank.

Period 1A2: Loam in the waterfront area, over the metalling, was covered by a possible second metalling.

Period 1A3: The waterfront area was covered in silty loam.

Period 2: The abandoned Roman building was robbed: the area W. of the quay wall silted up; the quay wall was also robbed.

Period 3: The floors of buildings dated by pottery to the 12th and 13th century were laid over the robbed quay wall. Early metallings of Clare Street dating from the 13th century were found, as wll as the road-side ditch.
The Period 3 levels sloped down to the W. towards the river; clearly the 12th and 13th century river front was not far west of this point, and if the trench had been deeper the waterfront might have been seen.

Finds included smithing slag and a weaving (?) pin.

Periods 4 & 5: The Period 3 'river slope' was filled with pinkish estuarine silt. A cut still further W. was filled with early and mid-18th century material and may represent the 17th century river bank. If it does, medieval Swan Lane cannot exist here, except at a lower level than recorded elsewhere (see 29/76). The area was levelled up in the 18th century by the dumping of rubbish.

Records: SNB 31, p.65; SNB 38, pp. 16-31; drawings; photos.

65/74
ROBINSWOOD BARRACKS

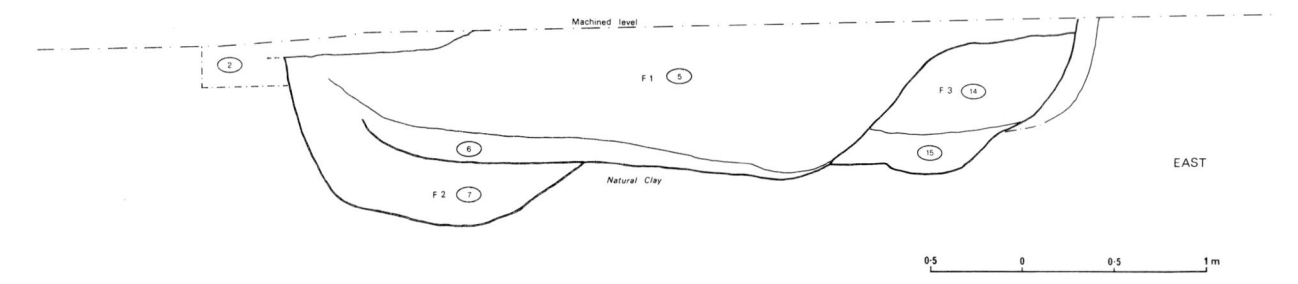

Figure 13. Robinswood Hill, barracks site. Section of ditches indicating Romano-British settlement.

65/74 Robinswood Hill Barracks (Fig.13)   SO 842162

Housing development; Water pipe trench. Some further excavations also took place.

Two ditches F2 and F3 were recorded, cut by a wider, shallower ditch F1. F3 contained a brooch, and 1st century Roman and late Iron Age pottery (see p.72). F2 contained 3rd century pottery. F1 contained 1st to 2nd century and 3rd century material; also Roman glass vessels, flints, and bronze objects including a seal-box (p.94 no.10).
   Another ditch, F4, further W., contained 3rd century pottery.
Pottery from contractors' spoil tips included samian ranging in date from Flavian to Late Antonine.
   The ditches and the large quantities of domestic refuse, suggest the existence of a Roman settlement which appears to have co-existed with the Kingsholm fort and with the early years of the Gloucester fortress (see p.77), and to have continued into the late 3rd century.

Records: SNB 38, pp.35–44; photos, drawings.

77/74 NORRIS' GARAGE, MARKET PARADE
SOUTH SECTION

Figure 14.

77/74   Norris' Garage, Market Parade (Figs. 9 and 14)

This site is close to the course of the R. Twyver as it curves around the outer medieval defences (Hurst 1974, 30). Hall and Pinnell's map of 1789 shows land within (SW of) the stream as open ground; the medieval defence may never have been very substantial, since in 1643 there was only a 'small work newly raised' (Washbourne 1825 p.42). By 1852 however the stream was culverted and buildings occupied some of the line of the stream, fronting onto what is now Market Parade. The property in question was a 'coach manufactory' in 1852 (Board of Health) and this building, with its stables and mangers, was still intact in 1974, although it had in 1937 been converted to a garage (inf. Mr. Norris, the owner, in whose family the property had been for three generations). The smithing equipment and horse trappings were acquired for the Lloyd Baker collection (now at Northleach).

Period 1:   The outside wall of a Roman building was recorded: the building had an *opus signinum* floor at a depth of c. 12.8m AOD. The building had been deliberately demolished; the wall had been flattened, leaving no debris. A loam layer (53) accumulated above the building.

The building was unexcavated so its exact date is uncertain. The Roman pottery from the site ranges in date from the late 1st to 4th centuries, with the majority dated to the late 1st or early 2nd century. The demolition of the building was possibly related to the clearance of an area around the defences in the early 2nd century (Hurst 1974, p.14).

The building continued E. under Market Parade, which is thus not a Roman boundary: this implies that the Twyver, too, is here not running on a Roman line (for the Roman course of the Twyver, see Heighway et al 1983 p.6).

Mr. Norris says that, when digging trenches for petrol tanks in the 1950's, he saw the corner of a massive building at a depth of about 12 feet in the NW corner of the courtyard. This would be at a similar depth to the Period 1 building described here.

Period 2A   Horizontal deposits about 1m thick of redeposited green natural clay may be the levelled remains of a medieval boundary bank, or else result from dumping to raise the ground level. Pottery indicates a 12th century date or later.

Period 2B   Loam deposits and possible field drains (F21/F23 and F22) show the areas was used for agriculture. The possible edge (F17) of the Twyver stream was located. Pottery: medieval and late 18th century.

Period 3   Further loam levels with 18th and 19th century pottery show the ground remained open. Field drains flowing E. into the Twyver were replaced in brick at the end of the period. The date-range of clay pipe from these levels is *c.* 1630 to the 19th century.

Period 4   The excavation area was in the courtyard of the coach manufactory of 1852, so there was no evidence of the 19th century building, although there were 19th century clay pipes from Period 4, which represents the garage showroom built in 1937.

Period 5   The garage was modernised in about 1950.

Records: SNB 39, pp.1–51, photos, drawings.

93/74   Ladybellgate Street.

Waterpipe trench. See 9/75.

Medieval walls and floors were recorded, probably part of Blackfriars precinct before widening of the street. Under the building was made-up ground of heavy clay-saturated loam.

Records: SNB 41, pp.3–11; drawings.

5/75   Horsebere Bridge, Cheltenham Road   SO 859198

Partial demolition of a brick culvert which carried the Horsebere Brook across the Cheltenham Road at Longlevens.

Under the brick culvert was a lias limestone single-arched bridge. The E. side of this bridge rested on oak beams (morticed and re-used) pinned with vertical stakes; these are either supports for the stone bridge, or remains of an earlier timber bridge. Fragments of fractured brick in a road surface beside and perhaps contemporary with the stone bridge suggest the latter was 16th century or later (for dating of brick, see Vince in Heighway et al 1983). Earlier road surfaces at a very low level indicate a pre-existing plank bridge or ford.

Records: SNB 41, pp.12–14, 21–27; drawings; photos.

Finds: mortar and timber samples from bridges.

6/75 Hempstead School

Digging of foundations.

No archaeological features: medieval and post-medieval pottery found in topsoil, the latest being of late 18th century date.

Records: SNB 41, p.15.

9/75 Ladybellgate Street

Complete re-surfacing of road.

The earlier levels uncovered provide evidence for the earlier Gloucester Castle and they will be fully published, with a description of the pottery found, in H. Hurst, 'Gloucester Castle', forthcoming.

A medieval wall 8 shows there were once buildings outside (W of) the present Blackfriars area. Medieval walls were also found under the E. side of Ladybellgate Street in 1974: see site 93/74.

A post-medieval wall 4, probably represented the W. wall of Bell's Place, as Blackfriars became after Dissolution. This wall appears on Hall and Pinnell 1780. Metalled surfaces, III (5) (6) (7), one containing blast furnace slag, were associated with this wall. East of wall 4 were back-filled cellars.

Brick wall footings, of Victorian date were recorded on the W. side of Ladybellgate Street, under the road to the E. of wall 4, showing that the street was originally only 6m wide.

Records: SNB 41, pp.17–20, pp.42–3; drawings; photos. see also 93/74.

10/75 Longford School, Longford Lane   SO 847 202

Service trenches.

No archaeological features. Pottery from spoil tips was 18th and 19th century, with one 13th century jug handle.

Records: SNB 41, p.16.

12/75 17 Ladybellgate Street

A record made by Howard Davies for Department of the Environment of a service trench through the front door of the houses. No. 17 is one of a row converted in the 16th century from the W. range of Blackfriars. The section shows the medieval foundations.

Records: 1 drawing.

13/75 Greyfriars

Records of works N. of the church: records with D. of E. see site 28/74.

25/75 Railway viaduct, Worcester Street.

Trench I dug for inserting concrete reinforcement between piers of second viaduct arch.

A metalling (19) was recorded at a depth of 2m. containing Roman and late 11th to 12th century pottery.

Trench II, dug against E. pier of first viaduct arch.

Under post-medieval made-up ground was a clay/silt layer (6) with twigs and snail shells which may represent the bed of the Twyver before it was culverted. Late medieval pottery.

Records: SNB 41, pp.38-41, 72.

42/75 Longford Lane   SO 843208

An aerial photograph of ridge and furrow N. of Longford Lane, taken by H. Wingham.

55/75 1–3 Longsmith Street

Service trench beneath S. carriageway.

A series of brick-filled 18th and 19th century cellars represented the old building frontage.

Records: SNB 41, p.61.

56/75 Lamprey Estate, Painswick Road   SO 846167

Housing development

No archaeological features: area S. of Sudbrook infilled with rubbish in 19th–20th centuries. A 12m wide linear feature below this might be a backfilled post-medieval sandpit.

The junction of the Sudbrook and Painswick Road was observed, but no medieval bridge found, although the name Saintbridge (c. 1200) might suggest that one existed (Smith 1964, 141).

Records: SNB 41, p.62; photos.

57/75 Greyfriars Lane

Road surfacing in the courtyard W. of Greyfriars church.

Record made of walls as marked here in the 1852 map, representing medieval properties.

Records: SNB 41, pp.67–8; photos.

Finds: Mortar samples.

59/75 Painswick Road/Eastern Avenue, roundabout

Machining of roundabout.

Three successive roadmetallings were recorded resting on natural subsoil. No dating evidence.
There may be a Roman road on this line, but this is not certain negative evidence, since medieval roads have commonly worn well down into the Roman surfaces, eroding the Roman layers (e.g. 33/76, I, VII, X).

Records: SNB 41, p.65.

63/75 The Wheatridge, Upton St. Leonards.

Survey of merestones prior to housing development.

The common fields of Upton St. Leonards, enclosed only in 1897 (Scobell 1899), are now developed for housing.

Merestones were recorded on the OS map of 1885, but none of these could be found in 1975. Those found seemed to be in positions other than those of 1885, and to be wrongly placed in relation to the headlands.
Mr. and Mrs. B. Rawes, who also watched this site, believe that all the stones have been moved since 1897 (Rawes 1977b, 32).
For records of the 'Portway' track and Roman and prehistoric sites, see sites 98/75, 29/77 and 36/77.

Records: SNB 55, pp.30–34; photos.

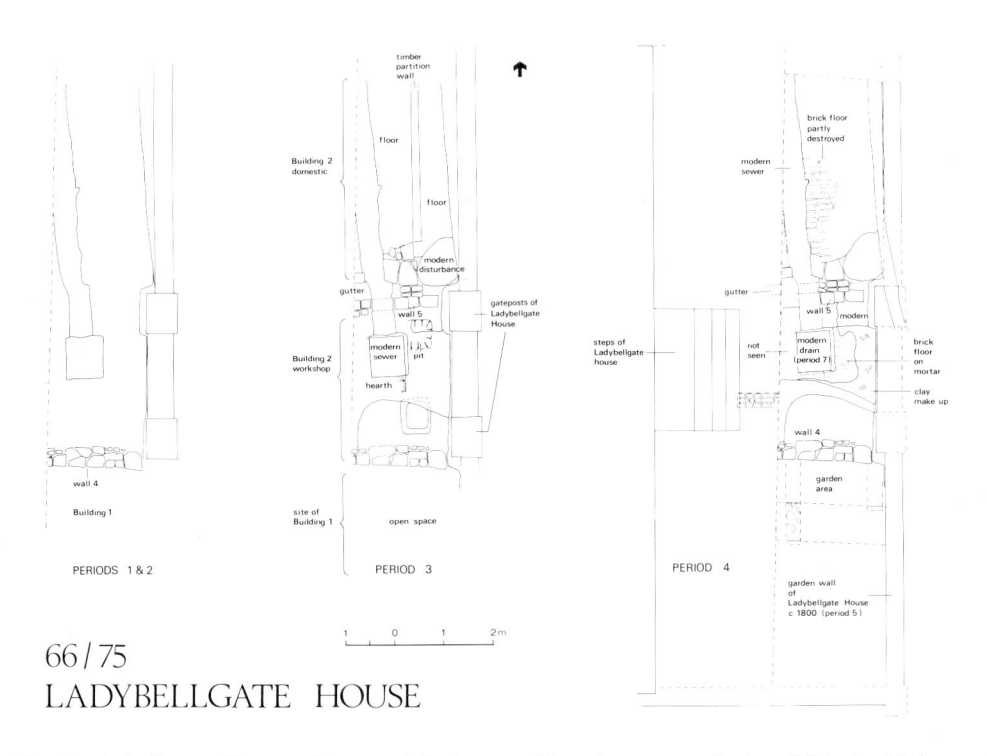

Figure 15. Ladybellgate House, Longsmith Street. Development of site, 15th to 17th centuries.

66/75 Ladybellgate House, Longsmith Street (Fig. 15).

Forecourt of Ladybellgate House cut back about 2.7m for road widening.

A record was made of two buildings 1 and 2 beneath the forecourt which date at least from the fifteenth century.

Period 1 Building 1 with clay floor, hearth or furnace, and spreads of charcoal and iron slag.

Period 2 Building 2 had occupation saturated with smithing hammer-scale and charcoal. Building 1 seems to have become an open space. 15th to 16th century pottery.

Period 3 Building 2 was divided down the centre by Wall 5. The E. half of building 2 was divided by a timber partition. Two pits were cut into the floor; they were filled with loam and hammer-scale. Building 1 still seems to have been open space. 17th century pottery.

Period 4 Building 2 acquired floors of brick over clay make-ups. Wall 5 was cut down and used as a support for a stone and brick drain. 17th century pottery. Clay pipe (19th century, intrusive?).

Period 5 Front Garden walls contemporary with the construction of Ladybellgate House c. 1700. Early 18th century clay pipe bowl. 18th century pottery.

Period 6 Flagstones in the courtyard of Ladybellgate House.

Period 7 Modern service trenches.

The medieval plot boundaries in the block of tenements between Bell Lane and Berkeley Street have already been researched by Henry Hurst (Hurst 1972, 46–60; 1974, 24–27). Buildings 1 and 2 correspond to Hurst's plots XA and XB which can be dated back to 1230. This investigation could not examine the earlier levels, but provided information about the use of these plots from the 15th century onwards, when Longsmith Street, as its name implies, was a smithing and industrial area.

Ladybellgate House, and the tenements which it occupied are well documented. Before the house was built the site contained a messuage occupied by John Wagstaff, brewer (Rogers 1975, p.7).

See also site 32/78

Records: SNB 41, p.74–79; SNB 52, pp.3–16; drawings.

74/75 66 Westgate Street

Alterations to rear of building.

A builders trench cut through a brick built cesspit containing a fine group of Victorian pottery, clay pipes of 1830–70 including one dated *c.* 1870, and glass medicine bottles.

Records: SNB 52, pp.18–20.

77/75 71–3 Southgate Street

A hole was dug by the occupier against the Roman city wall.

Most of the material removed was post-medieval fill which covers the plinth to a height of c.900m. Against the plinth was a large oolite block about 500m. high, resting on rubble in orange sand. This could be an external tower. It does not resemble the Roman external towers, which have lias footings, not oolite as here. It could be part of a medieval bastion of which others are known (Hurst 1972, 33), although it seems rather close to the South Gate for this; it could also be any medieval or post-medieval building or shed constructed on the berm of the ditch.

Records: SNB 52, pp.22–23.

78/75 Hopkins yard, St. Catherine Street.

Excavation for crane base.

Dark brown loam, obviously made-up ground, was noted to a depth of 1.5m. It contained 18th century pottery.

98/75, also 29/77, 36/77, 45/74 East Gloucester Development: Heron Estate (Figs. 16–20) centred on SO 852 167

45/74 Housing Development

Roman burials

Three burials were recorded on the 100ft. contour line just above the stream which takes water from the

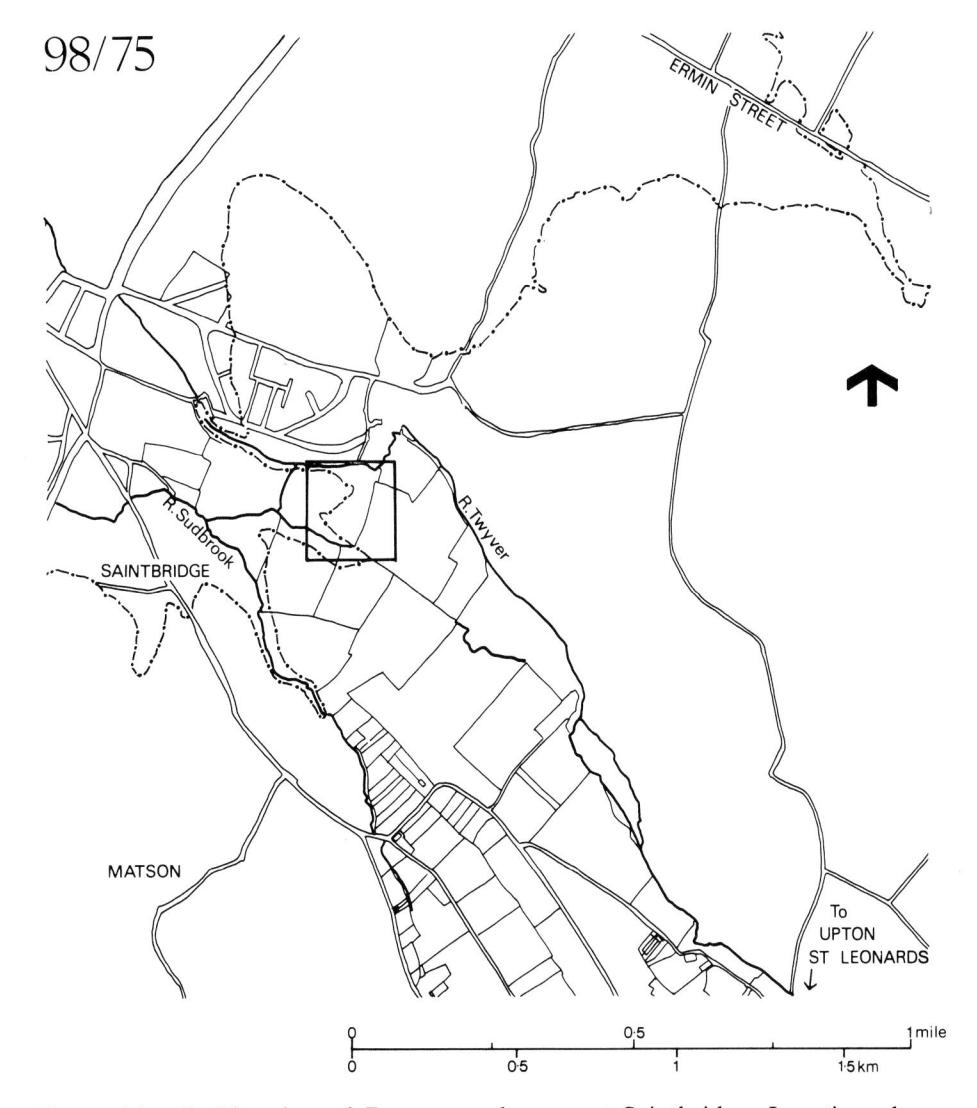

Figure 16. Prehistoric and Roman settlement at Saintbridge. Location plan.

Twyver to the Sudbrook. This stream, to judge by the position of the contours in the area (Fig.16), represents the original bed or feeder of the Sudbrook tributory before it was diverted to flow round the N. of Gloucester (Fullbrook-Leggatt 1964), and re-named the Twyver.

The burials were badly damaged by machining. The physiological notes were provided by Dr. C. Oyler.

Burial A NW/SE. Lower half destroyed. Head to W(?). A person of small build, perhaps 5ft. tall. Age over 50. Sex uncertain.

Burial B NW/SE. Two iron nails indicate a coffin. The long bone of the upper arm suggests a small, slight person. Muscle development on the bone nil. Sex female.

Burial C NE/SW. Crushed remains of vertebrae and pelvis. Bones too fragmentary to provide physiological information.

All three burials were particularly shallow, probably 50cm. below the original plough surface. In the grave fill were a few sherds of Roman pottery. A small ditch was found just west of Burials A and B; the ditch contained 10th century pottery.

Records: SNB 31, pp.37–9; photos.

98/75 Prehistoric and Roman settlement.

Key to trenches (See Fig. 17).
98/75 Trench I: Field and building trenches west of Hawthorne Rd.
Trench II surface finds collected by Rawes.
Trench III surface finds from 855167 and 855165
37/77 Trench I: building trenches south of 98/75.
29/77 Trench I: area E. of 98/75; surface finds.
II: – IV: building trenches as indicated on fig.17.

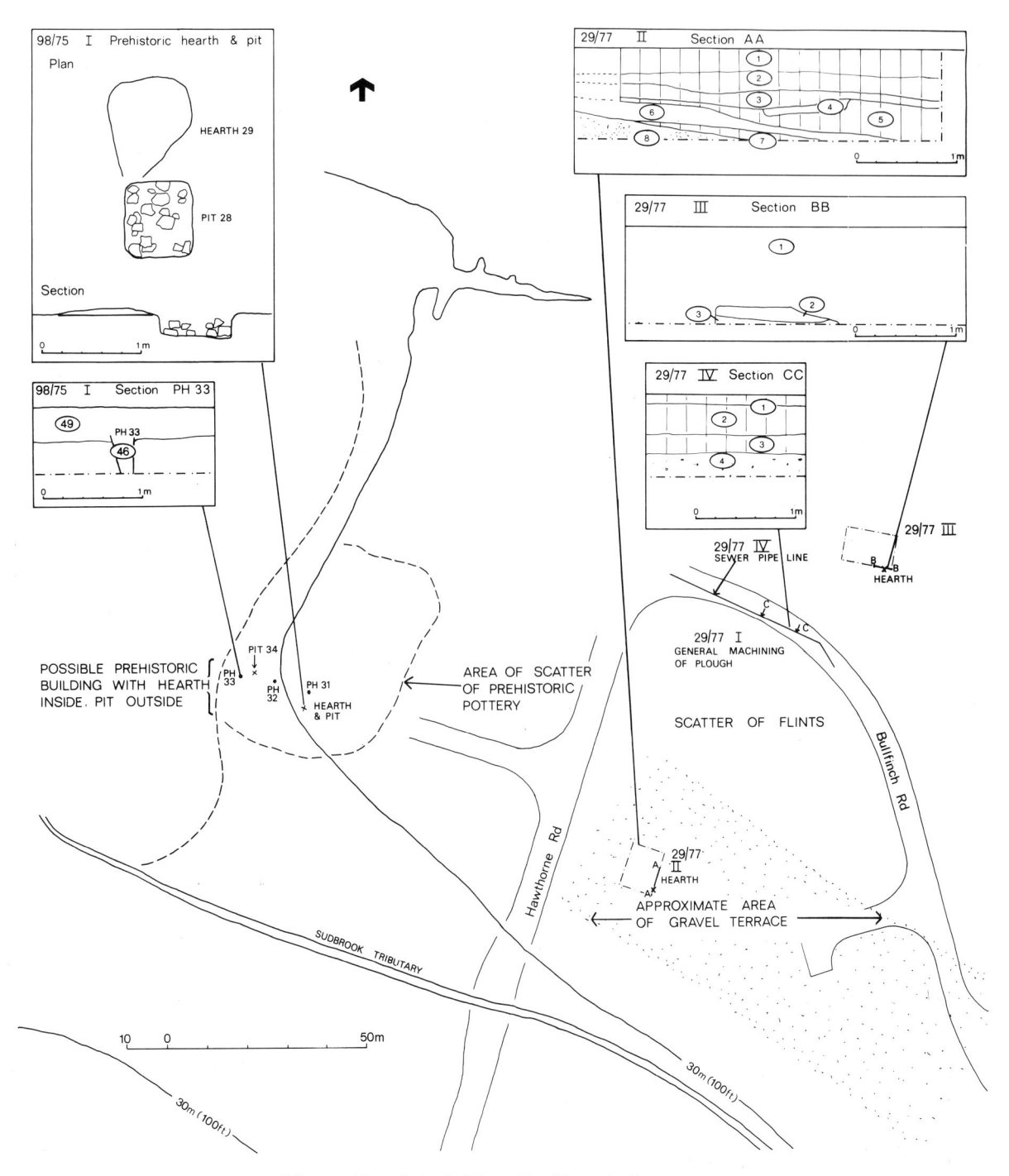

Figure 17. Saintbridge: Prehistoric features.

The site was originally located in 1974 by Mr. and Mrs. B. Rawes during field walking.

The topsoil and plough soil were machined away prior to building, leaving only the deeper ruts of ridge and furrow.

A further area W. of this site has since been excavated by T. Darvill for Gloucester City Museum (site 26/81).

Prehistoric

P1,P2 Three hearths (P1) of burnt clay 18, 19, 29, were resting on the original ground surface. Hearth 29 was associated with a shallow pit 28 (P2), which was packed with local limestone and sandstone, reddened from burning. The pit was partly covered by loam layer which is a Roman level (see R7 below). Pit 28 contained a flint flake (SF 28). Hearth 29 contained a flint, SF 30.

P3 Three post-pits (P3) 31, 32, 33 under the Roman level R7 contained fired daub and pottery, including sherds of Beaker ware (see p.72–3). Hearth 29 and its associated pit are on the opposite

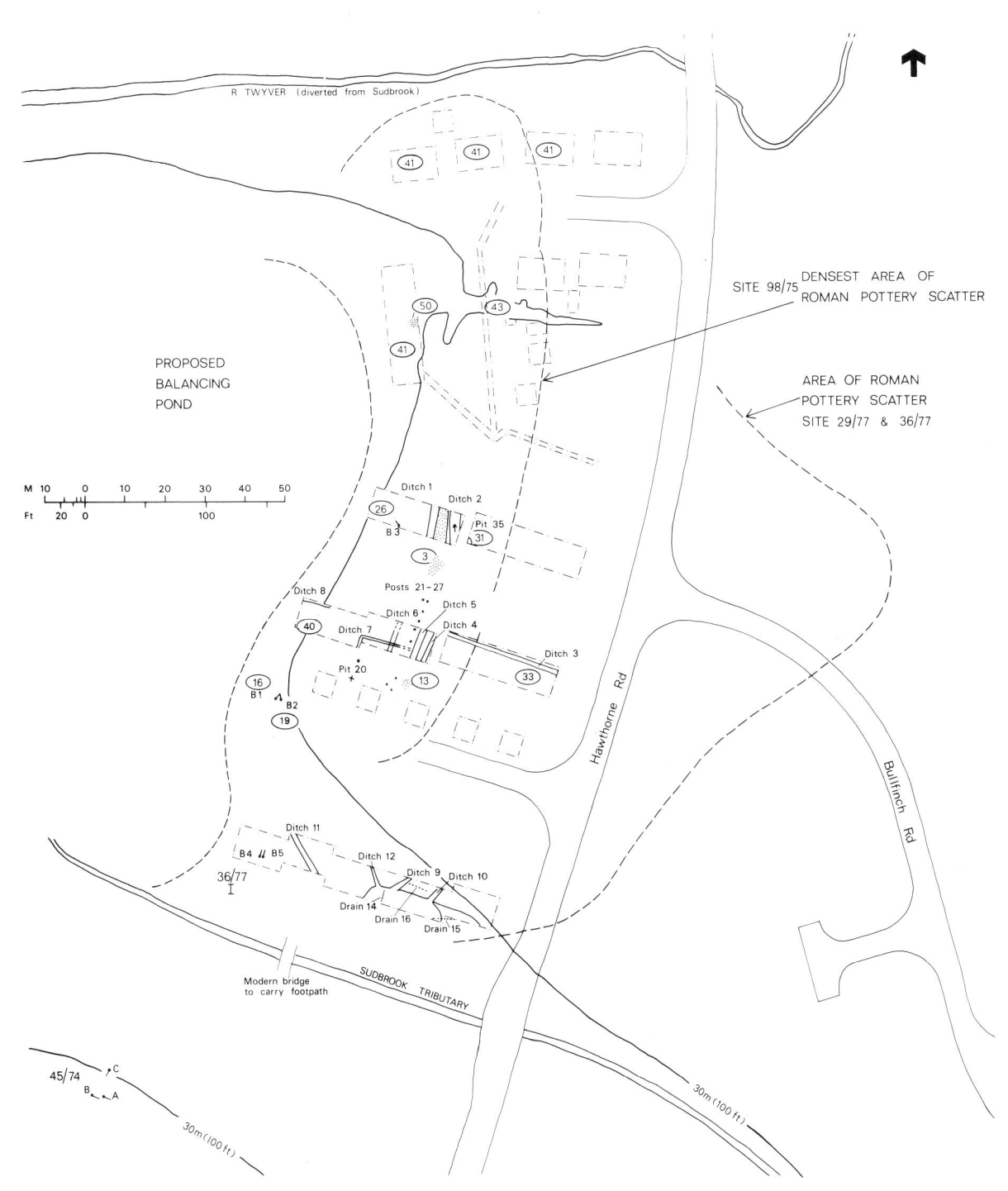

Figure 18. Saintbridge: Roman features.

side of the line of posts to Pit 34: the latter contained daub and pottery.
  A spread of Iron age sherds was noted in the area of (40).

Roman (Figs. 18 and 19)
  An extensive scatter of Roman pottery was recorded, some being collected by Mr. and Mrs. Rawes (Glevensis 10, p.13).

  In addition to the three burials recorded in 1974 (see site 45/74) five burials were recorded near the nucleus of the site.
Burial 1 had the remains of iron hobnails at its feet and had once had a coffin. Head machined away.
Burial 2 also had boots and a coffin. At its head were the articulated bones of a shoulder and leg of baby lamb (22), presumably a burial offering. A sheep bone (23) was just to the left of the head.
Burial 3 The head and most of the body were machined away. Two round-headed iron nails either side of the legs suggested a coffin. The body had been laid on its back with hands over the pelvis.

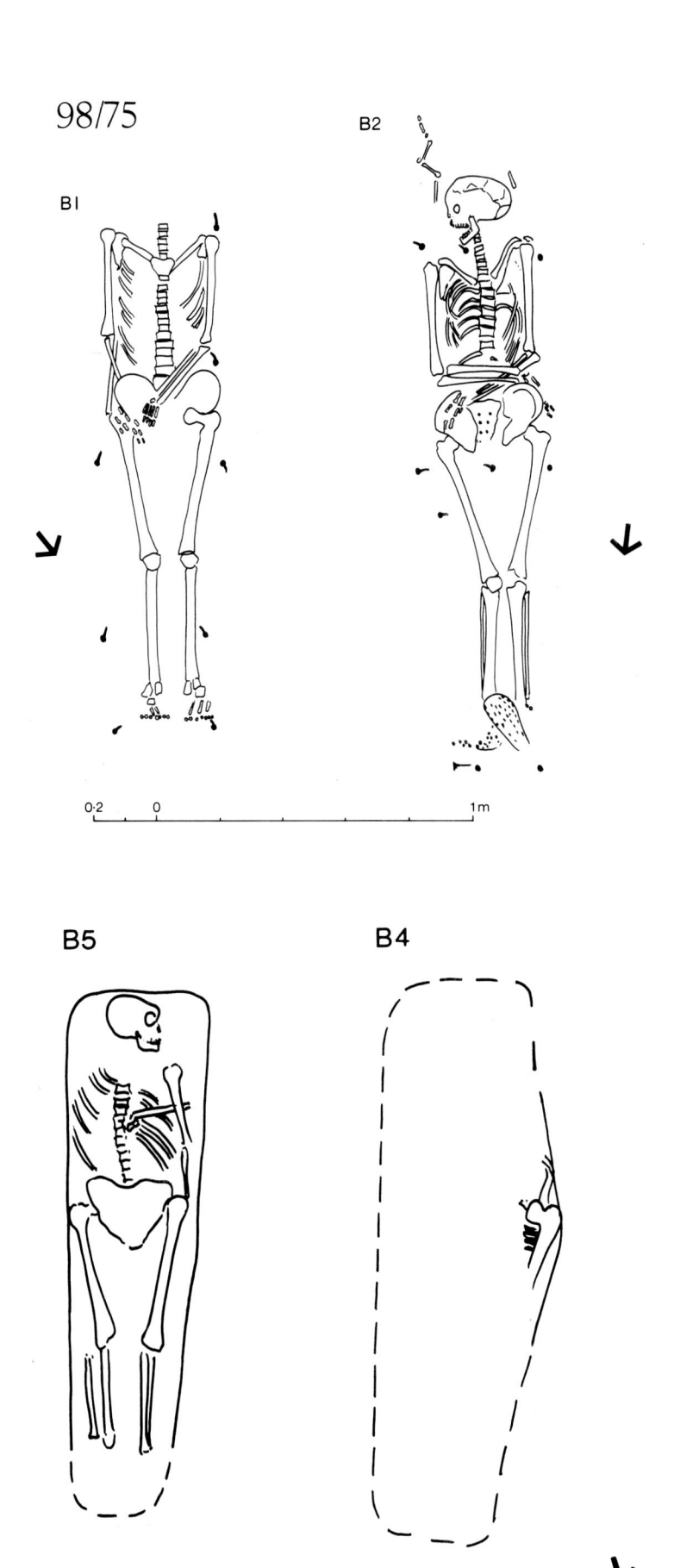

Figure 19. Roman burials, Saintbridge.

Figure 20.

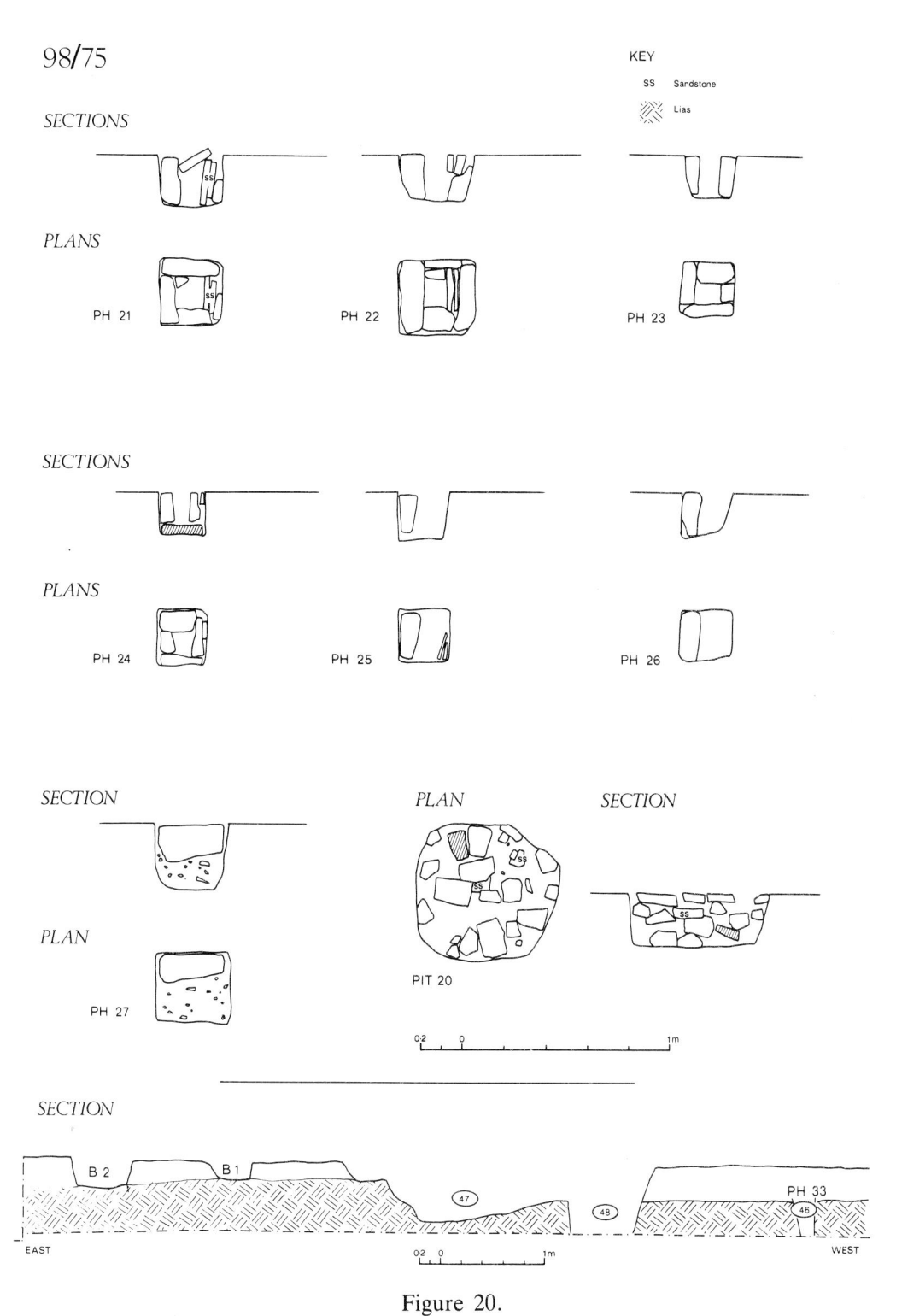

Burial 4 hip bone and pelvis only remaining; the body had apparently been face-down, with the fingers beneath the pelvis.
Burial 5 the body had been turned on its side facing W., with the left arm extended across and beneath the chest, and the right arm full length down the side of the body.

Finds from the burials included hobnails, coffin nails; and prehistoric pottery.

R5 Patches of metalling, 98/75 (3) (13) and (50) were badly damaged by ploughing. The metalling contained a coin of Valentinian 364–78, and one of Antoninianus (307–37).
R6 Ditches 1 to 12 were covered by or cut through a Roman level R3. Ditches 9, 10, and 12 (site 36/77) drained south into a basin filled with silt and thence presumably into the Sudbrook tributory.
Ditches 1 (=6), 2 (=5) drained north down the slope
The ditches contained early 4th century pottery.

R4   A row of posts 21–27 followed the line of ditch 5, so they may have been a boundary fence (sections of posts, Fig.20). The post packings used limestone and sandstone tile and a quernstone fragment.

R7   A loam level 98/75 I (5) cut by the posts contained 4th century Roman pottery, three 4th century coins, fragments of a red sandstone quern, worked flints, prehistoric pottery (see p.72) and some post-medieval finds indicating that the layer had been disturbed by ploughing.

R1   Pit 20 contained two coins of Valentinian, a zoomorphic buckle, mid to late 4th century pottery and a sandstone quern fragment.

R3   Under the machined-off plough soil which sealed the burials was a layer of dark loam 98/75 I (25) which also covered the ditches.

R2   Under R3 in one area was a layer 10cm. thick (26) (see Fig.20) of charcoal-flecked loam containing animal bones, a human jawbone, and much late 1st or early 2nd century pottery, including nearly-whole pots smashed in situ; this layer provides a terminus post quem for the burials. The pottery is possibly contemporary with the Gloucester legionary fortress (see p.77).

Medieval (M = plough soil; M2 = lower plough soil)
Apart from the scatter of medieval pottery in the ploughsoil, the only medieval feature was a pit or ditch, 17, found near the burials of site 45/74 (q.v.). Finds included flints (p.93); a bronze finger ring (Fig. 63, No. 7.), and pottery of Iron Age, Roman, and later date.

Post Medieval (PM)
The ridge and furrow contained domestic rubbish from night manuring of 18th, 19th and 20th century date.

Records: 29/77 SNB 80, pp.20–23
36/77 SNB 80, pp.27–37; drawings
98/75 SNB 52, pp.29–48; drawings.

6/76   Severn Street ('Lime Kiln Lane' in 1843)

Contractors trench 1.7m. deep, 28m long.

The latest archaeological layer was a line of railway sleepers from the 19th century dockland railway track. Metallings beneath this overlay natural clay. Brick fragments were found beneath the metallings which therefore probably also date to the Docks phase.
No evidence was found of any medieval streets.

Records: SNB 52, pp.37–8

25/76   Berkeley Street (Figs. 21 and 22)

Sewer trench and manhole. Trench I: W. half of road; Trench II, W. of I, along kerb. See also site 19/79.

Period 1   Backfill (F.7) of (?) western city ditch (trench II).

Period 2   Street metallings over the backfilled ditch; observed in trench I at a higher level AOD than Period 1, though not certainly covering Period 1.

Period 3   trench (F5) of a robbed medieval building.

Period 4   19th century cellars. These represent the post-medieval and medieval frontage of the west side of Berkeley Street.

Period 5   robbing of 19th century buildings.

Period 6   modern service trenches.

There are about 15 street surfaces of medieval and later Berkeley Street, but there is no adequate dating evidence. A sherd of Ham Green ware indicates that street layer (13), more than halfway through the sequence, was laid after the 13th century. The earliest street was not reached and could not be dated, but it seemed that the street metallings filled a slight hollow in the backfilled western city ditch.

The date at which the western wall and ditch went out of use has important implications for the topography of the late Saxon town (discussed above, p.5). The evidence for the ditch on this site derives only from a sherd of pottery (TF 41B; mid 11th to 13th century) from layer (5), an upper fill of the ditch, and a sherd of the earlier TF 41A from layer (6) below it. These suggest that the ditch was visible, if only as a shallow depression, in the mid 11th century.

Records: SNB 52, pp.76–84 (section opposite p.74); photos.

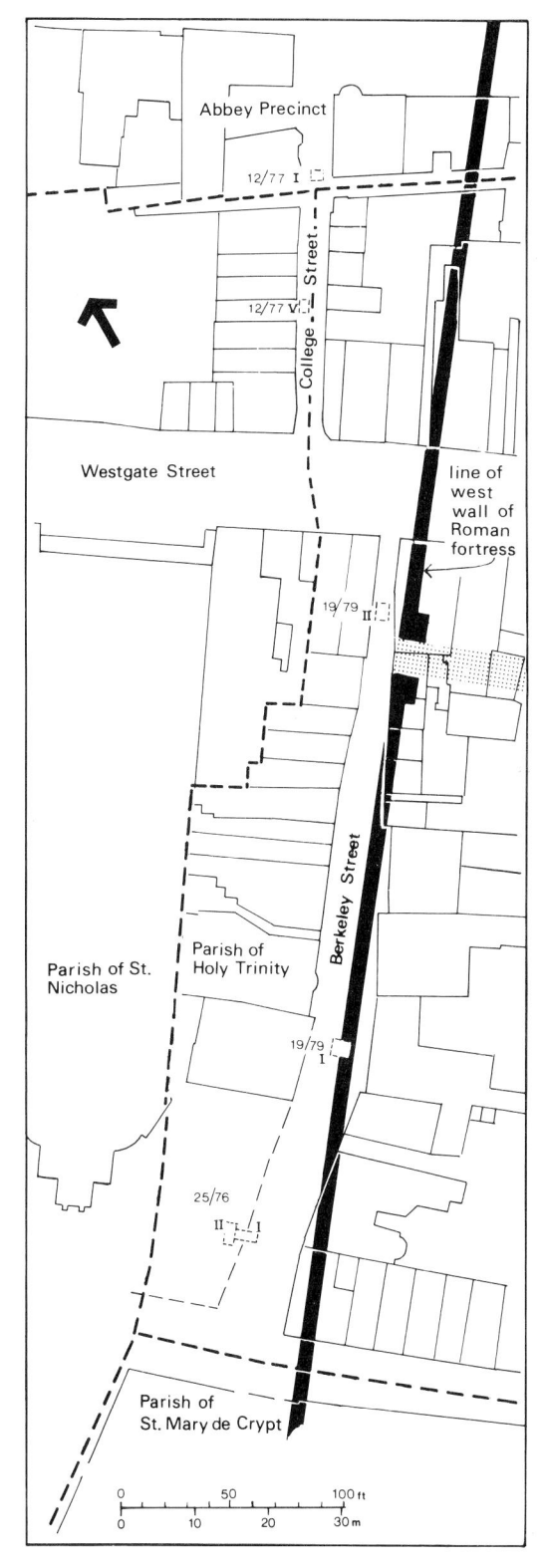

Figure 21. The western wall of the Roman fortress and town; location plan for sites 25/76, 12/77 and 19/79. The line of the Roman wall has been plotted from excavations at 17 Berkeley Street; the property boundaries are those of 1852. The Roman West Gate, though unexcavated, is shown as a mirror image of the East Gate.

25/76 BERKELEY STREET

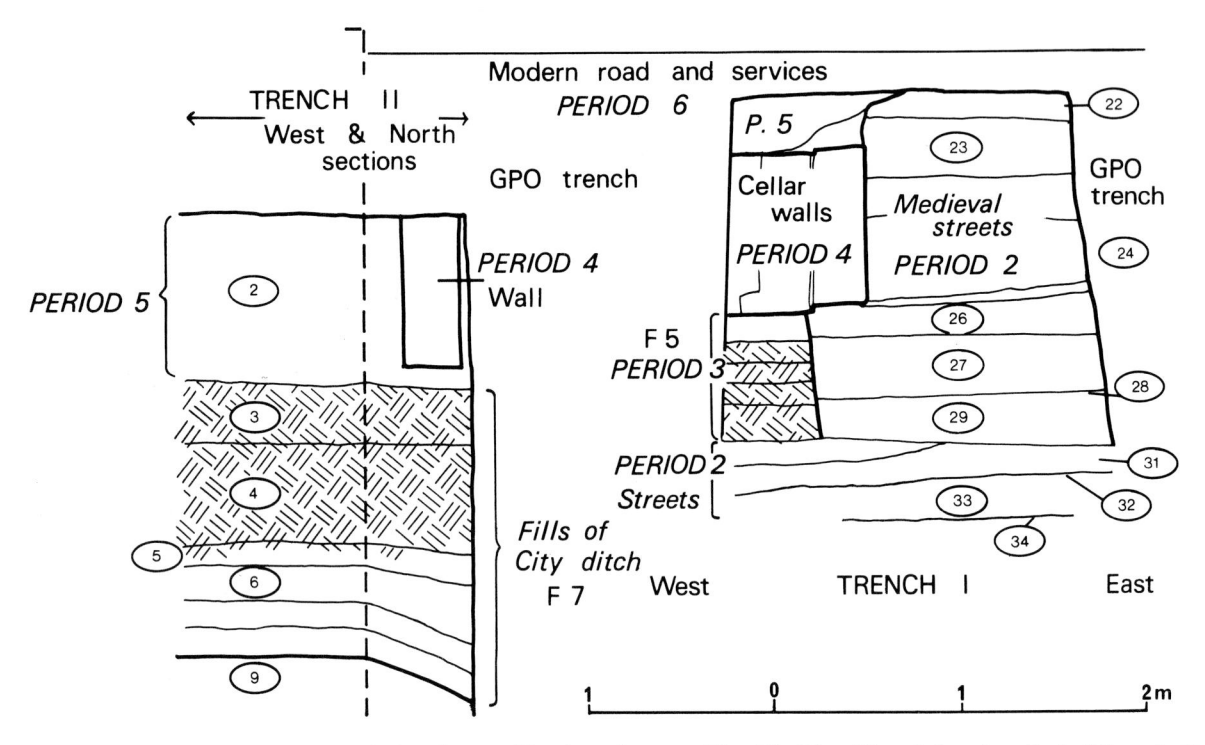

Figure 22. Sewer trench in Berkeley Street. For location see Fig. 21. The fills of the city ditch (Trench II, left) are 11th century or later; the metalled streets of Period 2, Trench I, cannot be related to the ditch fills.

26/76 148 Barnwood Road, Wotton, Gloucester

Construction of new flats

A watching brief failed to find evidence of the Roman cemetery known to exist at Wotton Pitch (Heighway, 1980b; see 27/76).

Records: SNB 58, pp.55–7

27/76 St. Margarets Almshouses, Wotton, Gloucester.

Construction of new almshouses.

Cremation and inhumations of the late 1st century onwards were recorded.
See A. P. Garrod in Heighway, 1980b.

28/76 Gloucester to Hardwick S. M5 Link Road (Fig.23)   SO 813 147

Road Construction

    Trench I new culvert dug for Shorn Brook   SO 80451243
    Trench II earth scraping in Quedgeley farm area   SO 813 147

Fields I – XVII – see plan 28/76/2. Field Walking.

Trench I. A burial (2) was found lying EW parallel with the Shorn Brook. The date of the burial is unknown; the decayed condition of the bones suggest it is ancient.

Trench II. Roman settlement, badly damaged by ploughing. The features on Fig.23 are as follows:-

Medieval
    Ditch 5 was a medieval and post-medieval field boundary; also ditches 6, 7, and 8 (not illustrated).

Roman: first phase
    Building 1 had two phases. In the first, post sockets (10) and (11) were covered by a deposit (4) of stiff charcoal-saturated black loam containing some small gravel, occasional red sandstone and tegulae

28/76 QUEDGELEY

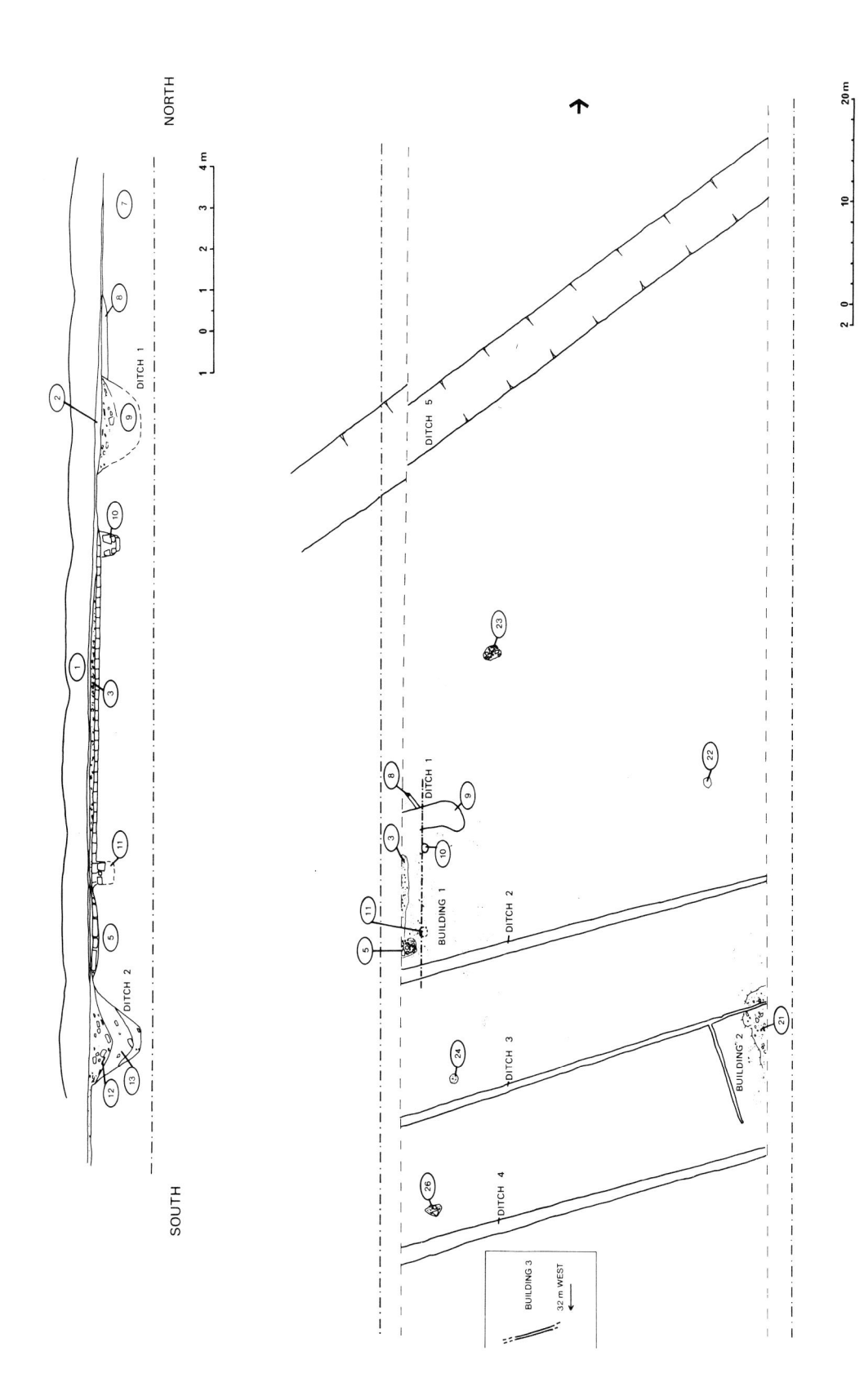

Figure 23. Roman-British settlement at Quedgeley, S. of Gloucester.

fragments, late 3rd to 4th century Roman pottery, smithing slag including hearth lining, and fragments of querns.

To the E. was an area of industrial occupation with a clay floor (7) and a slot (8). Over these was a deposit (6) of charcoal and iron slag.

Ditch 2, apparently contemporary with this layer, contained dark charcoal flecked loam, building materials, scraps of lead (e.g. SF 9).

Ditch 3, also contemporary, had a very similar fill; however in addition to 3rd and 4th century pottery it contained four sherds of late Saxon pottery. It also contained window glass fragments.

Building 2 also had a first phase characterized by an industrial working layer 30. This contained a third century coin and bracelet (SF4)

Roman; second phase

The industrial level (4) was covered with a metalling (3) which incorporated re-used building materials including Roman tegulae, box flue tiles, sandstone tiles. A sunken stone surface (5) included re-used oolite stones and two pieces of a sandstone quern (SFs 6,7).

Building 2 also had a superimposed metalling (21) of a similar nature.

A later Building 3 was represented by patches of metalling and a beam slot (27). 70g. of smithing slag was probably residual from B2.

The very reduced remains of this site may represent a larger complex which still lies to either side of the now completed road.

The extensive re-use of Roman building materials suggests that somewhere in the vicinity was a Romanized farm of stone which was robbed as building material for this small settlement. The settlement itself, or this part of it, was certainly a workshop complex in its first phase.

The conspicuous lack of coins from the site, only one (late 3rd century), may well indicate that it was in use in the fifth century (Reece 1983); this may be borne out by the re-use of Roman building materials. On the other hand, the site was recorded in very adverse circumstances not conducive to the finding of coins.

Field walking: a scatter of medieval post-medieval pottery came from fields on the line of the new roads.

Records: SNB 58, p.97, pp.135–157; photos; drawings.

29/76 SWAN LANE, South end

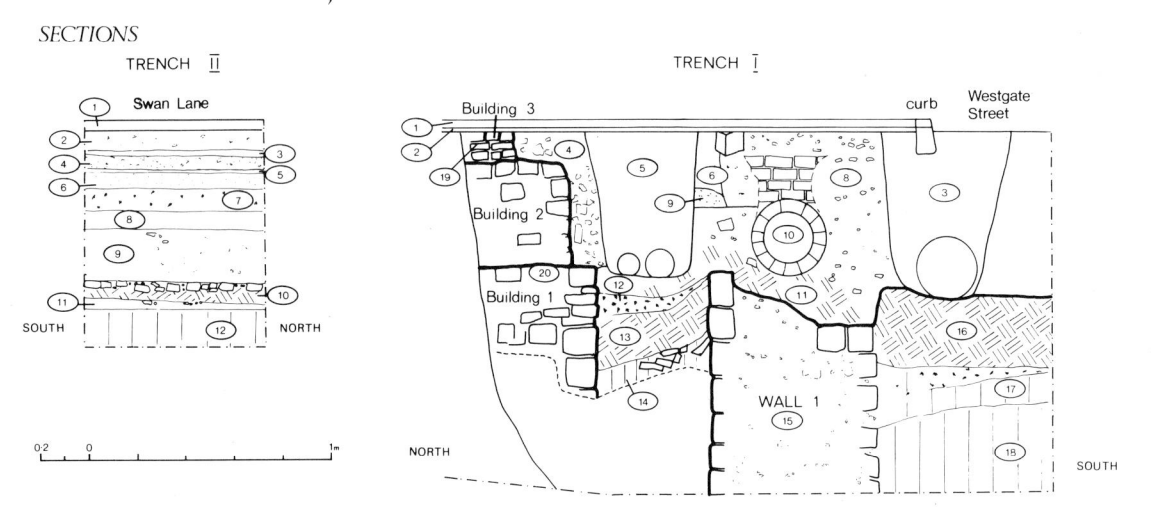

Figure 24. Foreign Bridge: the N. parapet (Wall 1) extended across the S. end of Swan Lane.

29/76 Westgate re-development, Gloucester: near Swan Lane (Fig.24)

Sewer connection trench 16m. long; 3m. deep.

Trench II cut the S. end of medieval Swan Lane (which no longer exists) where it joined Westgate Street; trench I projected into Westgate Street.

Trench II cut a series metallings of Swan Lane; the earliest, (10), was of lias stone cobbles, set above grey-black silt (11) above the estuarine silt of the old river channel (12). The second earliest, (9), contained 14th/16th century pottery.

Trench I sectioned a massive wall 1, 1.3m thick; to the S. it cut thick grey river deposits. N. of it was a series of walls of successive dates (Buildings 1, 2, & 3).

Layer (17) contained 4 sherds of 12th century pottery and presumably represents the ground level of that date.

Wall 1 must be the parapet wall of Foreign Bridge, within which layer (16) was the clay make-up for a medieval street metalling. Thus the bridge parapet is now known to extend further E. than before (site 67/73; Hurst 1974 p.46). It is also dated here by 12th century pottery from layer (17) (pre-dates Foreign Bridge) and 1 sherd of early to mid 13th century pottery from layer (14) (post-dates the Bridge). Hurst's 12th century date for the Bridge (Hurst 1974, 49) is thus confirmed.

The first metalling of Swan Lane was laid on a river silt surface II (12) which is undated but was at a higher level than I (17), of 12th century date. The first suface II(10) of Swan Lane was covered with a thick layer (9) of green gritty silt containing fourteenth to sixteenth century pottery. This suggests that Swan Lane is unlikely to pre-date the 13th century. The street could have crossed the parapet (Wall 1) of Foreign Bridge (see fig. 25). Alternatively, the parapet could have been breached at the point where the street crossed it.

Buildings 1, 2, and 3 represent properties fronting onto Westgate Street. Building 1 cut into layer (14) (early 13th century), and was of lias stone, probably forming a sill for a timber building. Building 2 was constructed on Building 1. Building 3 had a brick foundation, and was probably the 'White Swan Inn' which stood here in 1852 and was demolished in the twentieth century.

Records: SNB 58, pp.76–95.

30A/76   Barnwood, Barclays Bank accounting centre   SO 858 185

Site machined off to natural sand and gravel.

No archaeological features.

32/76   Painswick Road, Glevum Estate   SO 855 152

Sewer Trench.

The first street metalling of the Painswick Road was 3.5m wide and laid in a slight hollow 6m wide; successive metallings were also recorded. These may all be 18th to 20th century, the first metalling being medieval.

Records: SNB 52, pp.25–28.

33/76   Sewerage scheme, Northgate Street to London Road.

A series of circular sewer shafts c. 5m in diameter were dug at intervals from Northgate St. Gloucester to the Barnwood Road. Each shaft was given a trench number. Trenches were, of course, circular in plan, but half of each has been drawn and appears as if in a straight-sided trench.

Trench I: London Road, outside   St. Margarets almshouses, near Wotton Pitch (Fig.25)
A series of undated street metallings were set in a hollow way cut 1m. into natural ground level.

Records: SNB 65, pp.30–33; photos.

Trench II: London Road and Heathville Road Junction (Fig.26).
   The metalled south edge and south ditch of the successive metallings of a road just entered the section: it was judged by its profile to be the Roman road to Cirencester ('Ermin Street'). Later medieval street metallings had apparently been machined off in modern road schemes: traces of medieval or post-medieval metallings were observed in the backfill of a gas pipe trench (9).

Records: SNB 65, pp.34–38; photos.

Trench III: London Road and Horton Road Junction at Wotton Pitch (Fig. 27).
   A series of undated street metallings were recorded. Layer (5) was constructed of slag and was probably post-medieval. Layers (7) (8) (9) (10) were sunk into a hollow way (cf Trench I). The hollow (probably medieval, since this is a typical features of medieval roads, which were seldom metalled and tended to wear down rather than building up) cut still earlier ditches and metallings, the earliest of which are likely to have been Roman ('Ermin Street') surfaces.

Records: SNB 65, pp.49–53; photos;

Trench IV: Barnwood Road at crossing of Wotton Brook (Fig. 28)
   The eastern edge of a series of street metallings, one (layer 11) incorporating Roman tile. These were overlain by silty loam accumulation of considerable depth, probably representing the medieval and post-medieval unmetalled road churned into mud, as well as flood deposits of the adjacent Wotton Brook.

Records: SNB 65, p.54; photos.

Trench V: Oxbode and Northgate Street Junction (Fig.29).
   Wall 1 was the cellar of a demolished 19th century building. Two sections were drawn; one is published

33/76 I

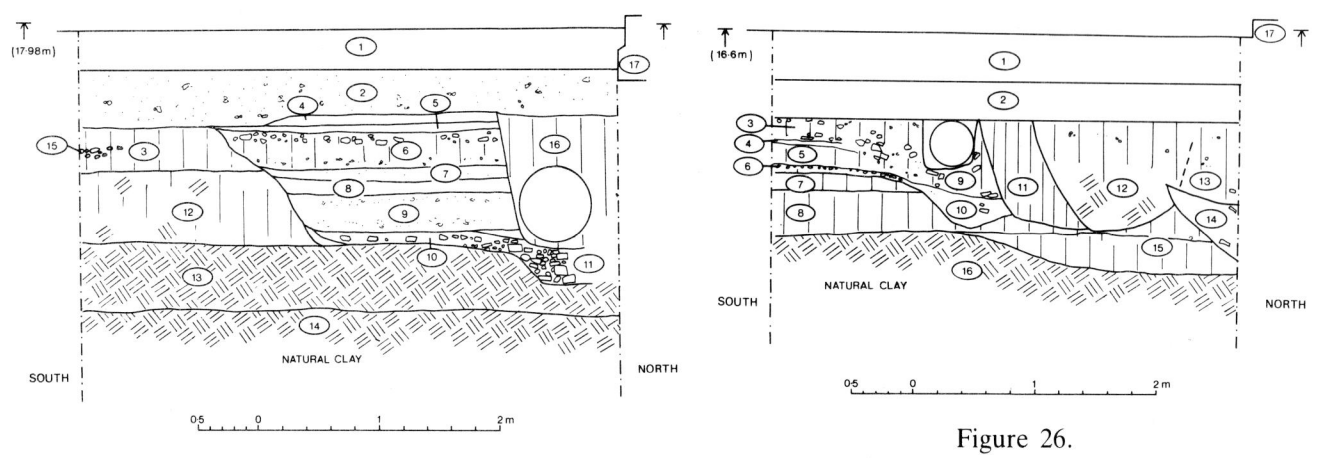

33/76 II

Figure 25.

Figure 26.

33/76 III

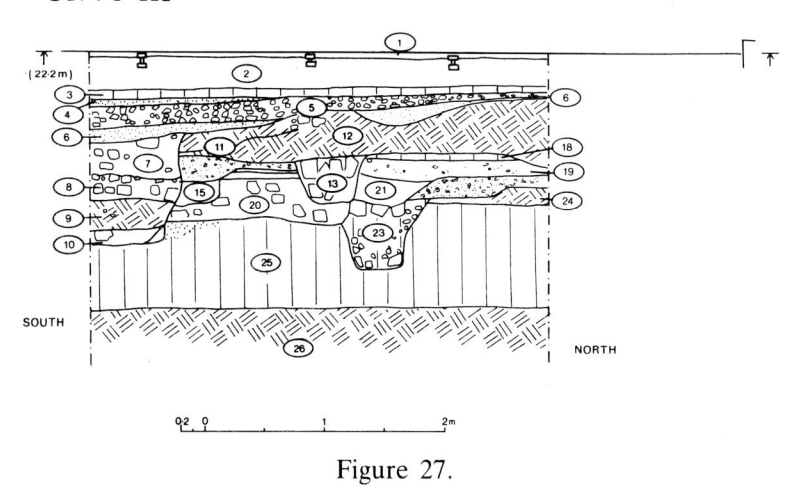

Figure 27.

33/76 IV

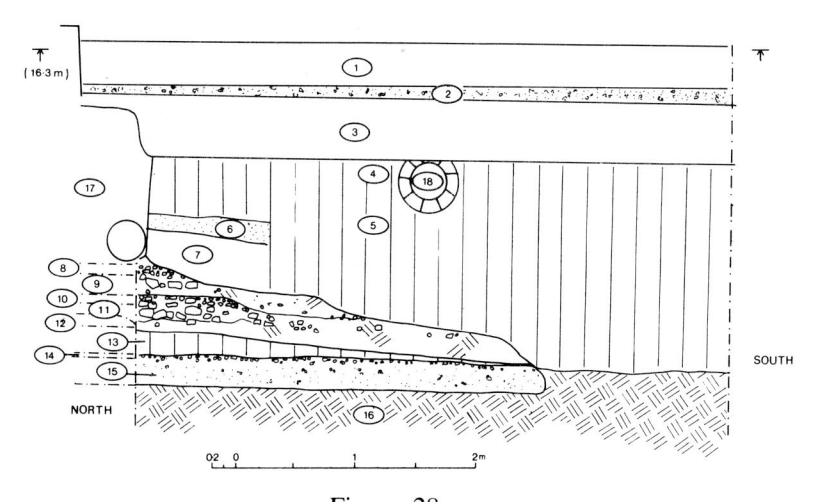

Figure 28.

33/76 V

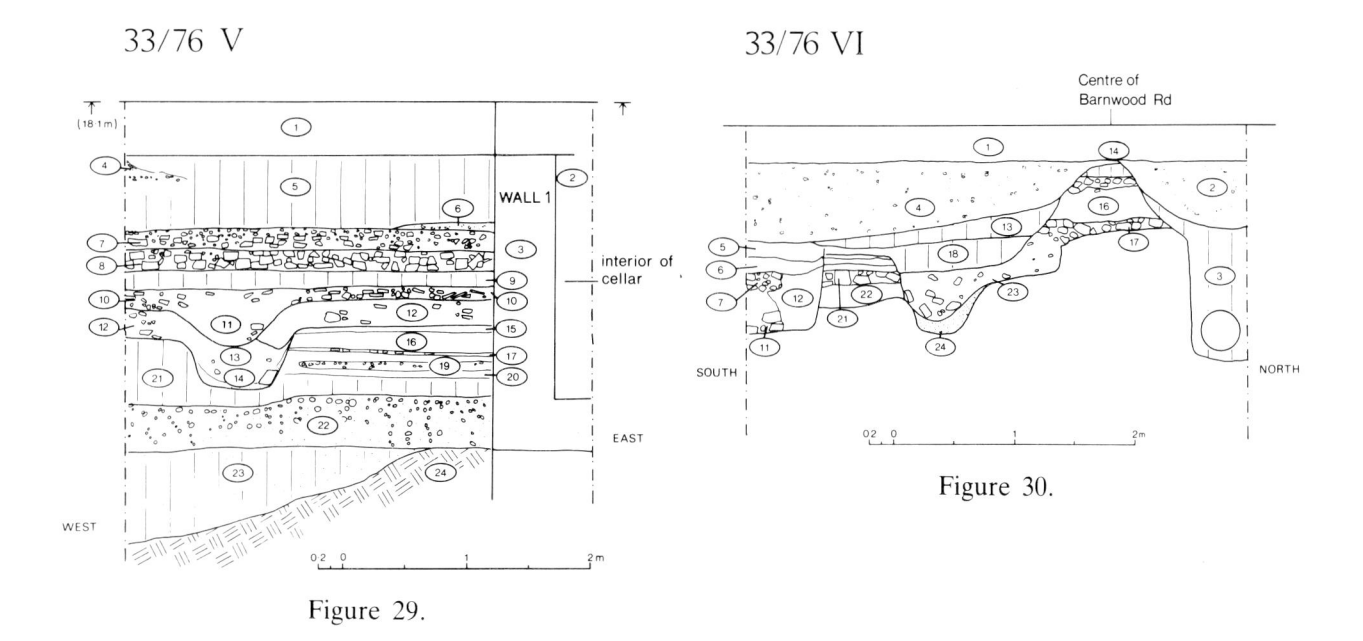

33/76 VI

Figure 29.

Figure 30.

(Fig.29) showing the S. road ditches of the Roman street (under Northgate Street) and stratigraphy to the E. of them. The only dating evidence was late 1st to early 2nd century pottery from layer (36) (on S. section above (19)).

Records: SNB 65, pp.63–71

Trench VI, Barnwood Road near railway bridge (Fig.30)
  Traces of early road metallings ('Ermin Street') with a W. side ditch were cut by later sunken streets of post-medieval date.

Records: SNB 81, 127–37.

33/76 VIII

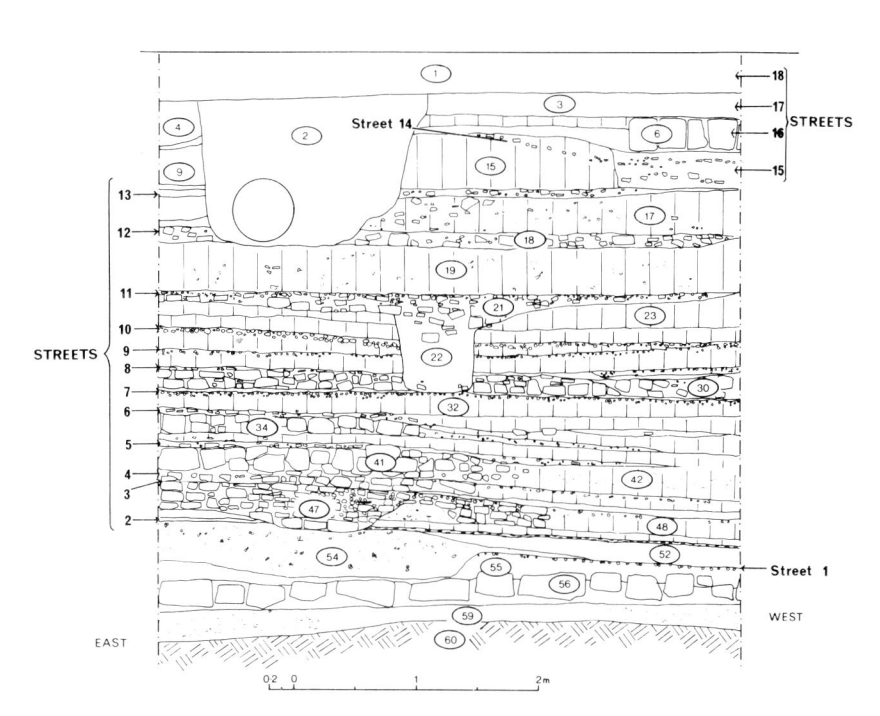

Figure 31. Section of early surfaces of Northgate Street near its junction with Worcester Street. Streets 1–10 are Roman, 11–18 medieval. The 'monumental arch' foundation is not visible in section.

35

Trench VII: Oxford Street and London Road Junction
   Two metallings (no dating evidence) covered a black silty loam (7) with Roman finds: all surfaces sunken and cut into natural soil to W.

Records: SNB 80, pp.18–19.

Trench VIII: Northgate Street and Worcester Street junction (Figs. 9 and 31).
   18 street surfaces were recorded: Roman (streets 1–10) and medieval to modern (Streets 11–18).
   The highest Roman Street 10 had above it layers (24) and (23) of dark loam. The first medieval metalled street 11 was 300mm above the latest Roman street. 12th and early 13th century pottery and a leather shoe came from below street 12.
   In the base of the shaft, cutting Roman street 3, and probably some later streets also, was a rectangular foundation trench 1.8m wide and 3m long, and at least 1m deep. The alignment and massiveness of this structure suggest it may have been one side of a monumental arch.

Records: SNB 80, pp.45–60; photos.

33/76 X

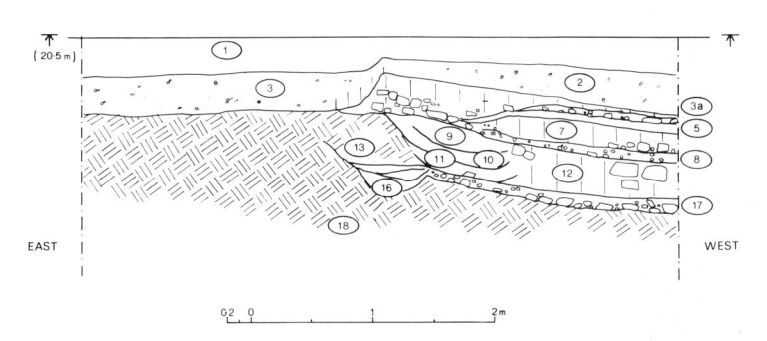

Figure 32. Section of 'Ermin Street', Barnwood Road near Wolseley Road. Roman and medieval street metallings worn into a hollow way.

Trench X: Barnwood Road, near Wolseley Road Junction (Fig.32)
   The E. side of street metallings and ditches were recorded cut into a hollow 0.8m into natural clay.

Records: SNB 81, pp.115–23.

Trench XI (see Trench VIII)
A tunnel dug W. from the shaft Trench VIII.
   Street metallings (10), (8), (7) were observed in the side of the tunnel. The lowest metallings were cut by a wall foundation of oolite stones set on timber piles at a depth of 4.5m from the street surface. The position of this in relation to the metallings suggests it was late Roman. A collection of late 1st century pottery (13) from the spoil heap probably came from the metallings. Pottery from trenches XI, XII, and XIII suggests this was within the *vicus* area of the Gloucester fortress (p.79).

Records: SNB 89, pp.22–5.

Trench XII (see trench VIII) (Fig.33).
   A sewer shaft dug at the end of the tunnel, trench XI. A foundation of oolite stones was recorded as in XI. This is a wall 1.6m wide running approximately E.W. along the N. pavement of upper Northgate Street. The wall cut levels containing 1st–2nd century pottery. N.E. of this wall were Roman street surfaces edged by wooden gutters (35) and (32) and a stone block (30), perhaps the base for a verandah post. All indicate a Roman street roughly on the line of Worcester Street. The wooden gutter contained a coin of Trajan (98–117).
   Medieval street metallings above this belonged to Lower Northgate Street.

Records: SNB 89, pp.33–43.

Trench XIII (see trench XII)
Sewer connection hole at Worcester St. and Northgate St. junction, north of trench XII.
   Record of a street sequence and 'verandah base' as in trench XII. At the bottom of the sequence were Roman streets with 1st to 2nd century pottery, preserved organic material, iron objects, fuel ash slag and a smithing hearth.

Records: SNB 89, pp.51–55.

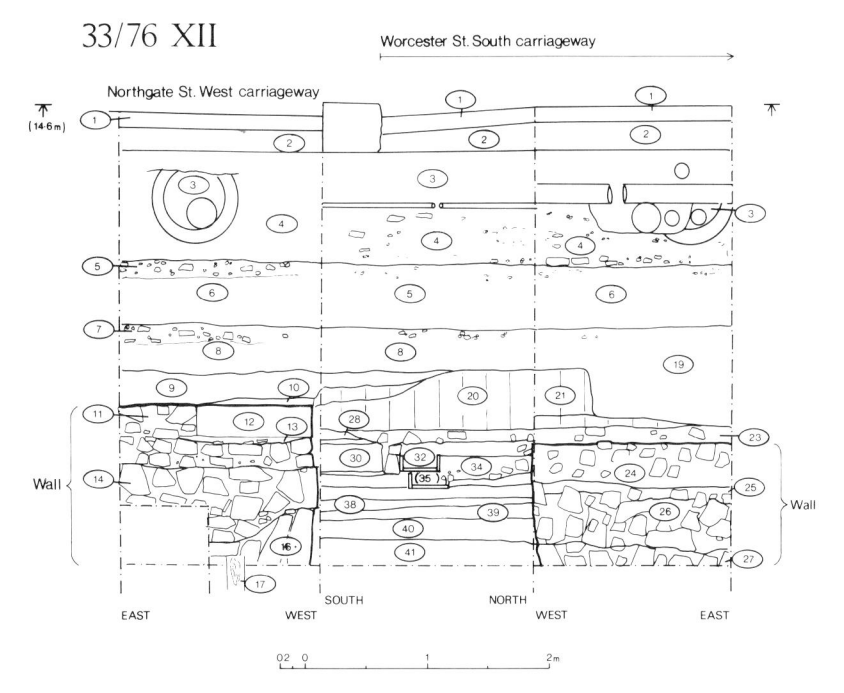

Figure 33. Section of Roman features and metallings at S. end of Worcester Street. The wooden gutters (32) (35) and associated street surfaces indicate a hitherto unknown Roman road on the line of Worcester Street. The wall recorded in either side of the trench is plotted on Fig. 9.

50/76   Churcham, Queen's Farm   SO 765187

Excavation for fence posts.

The site occupier, T. Adamson, carried out an excavation of the Roman road; the Unit made the archaeological record.

Two successive street surfaces were recorded. Below the first street was a Claudian-copy coin.
Loam 0.9m thick over the Roman street contained medieval finds.

Records: SNB 81, pp.5–33 (summary pp.32–3); drawings; photos.

Finds: Unstratified:- SF 1 Iron nail, SF 2 Brooch, SF 3 belt-buckle, SF 4 coin, William II, clay pipes 1830-70. From below first metalling:- SF 5 coin: Claudian copy. Finds with T. Adamson.

51/76   East Gloucester Development: The Portway Track   SO 857154

A section across the 'Portway' (see above, p.10) revealed three oolite metalled surfaces. The first metalling was laid in a shallow depression c. 3m wide. Post-medieval pottery was found under the second metalling (but perhaps intrusive from a nearby gate post pit). The third metalling contained a bronze riveted loop (p.94 no.9).

Records: SNB 58, pp. 101–105; photos; drawings.

63/76   Gloucester Cathedral Treasury by C. M. Heighway and A. G. Vince (Figs. 34, 35)

Works for the conversion of the E. slype into a Treasury involved the cutting of a new door through the N. transept wall (Wall 1). The new door is entered from inside a 13th century screen known as the 'Reliquary'.

The E. slype has on each side a blind arcade of Norman arches with cushion capitals; the new entrance converted two of the arcade arches into a door.
  The E. slype floor was partly removed to build showcases. The floor was of 15th century plain Malvernian tiles (a detailed report on these is included in a PhD thesis on the Malvernian ceramic industries, by Alan Vince).
  There were earlier mortar floors under the 15th century one.
  Detailed elevations were drawn of the part of Wall 1 which was removed (these are not published here), and a cross-section drawn (Fig. 35).
  The opportunity was taken to excavate a small trial trench inside the 'Reliquary'. The excavation recovered a Donyatt-ware pot from under the reliquary floor, showing that the floor was re-laid in the 17th

63/76 CATHEDRAL TREASURY

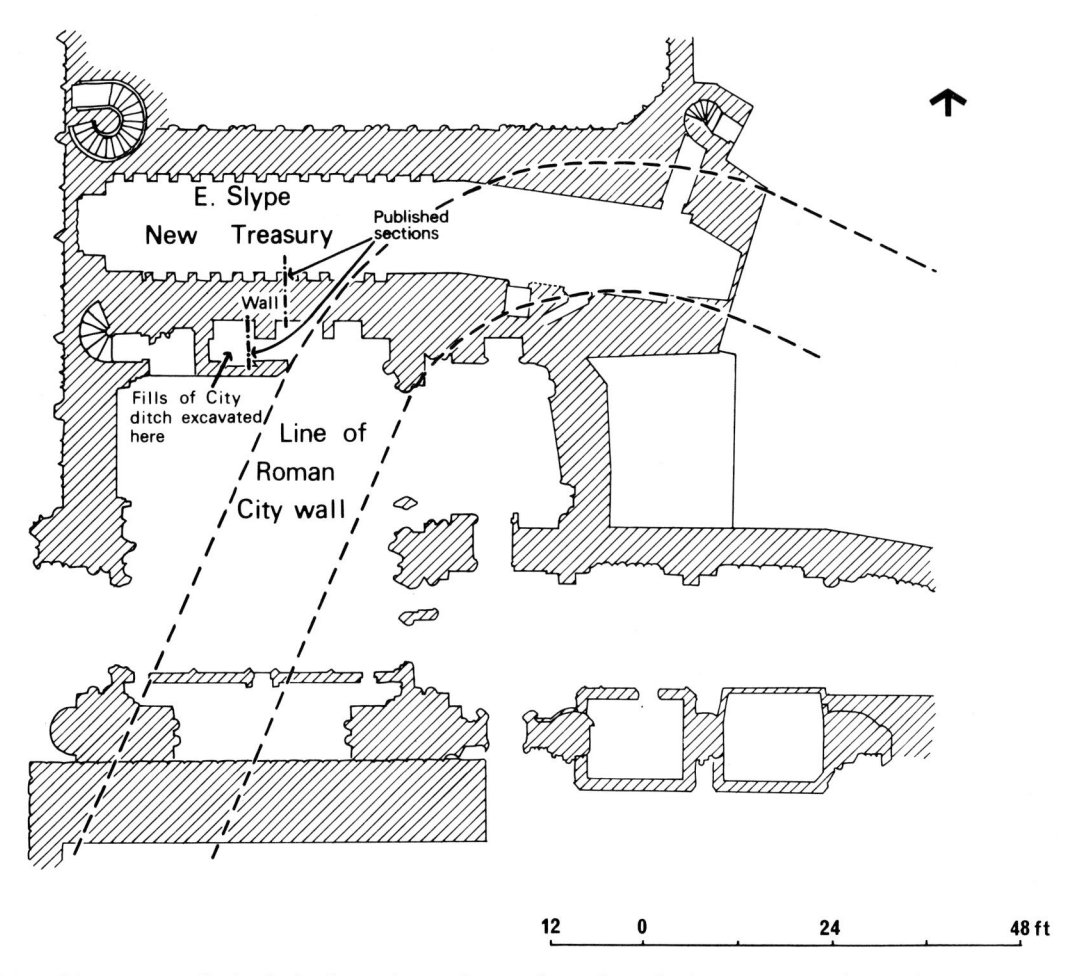

Figure 34. Gloucester Cathedral: Location of trenches dug during construction of new Treasury. Cross-hatching indicates the present standing walls of the Norman N. transept and Slype.

63/76 CATHEDRAL TREASURY

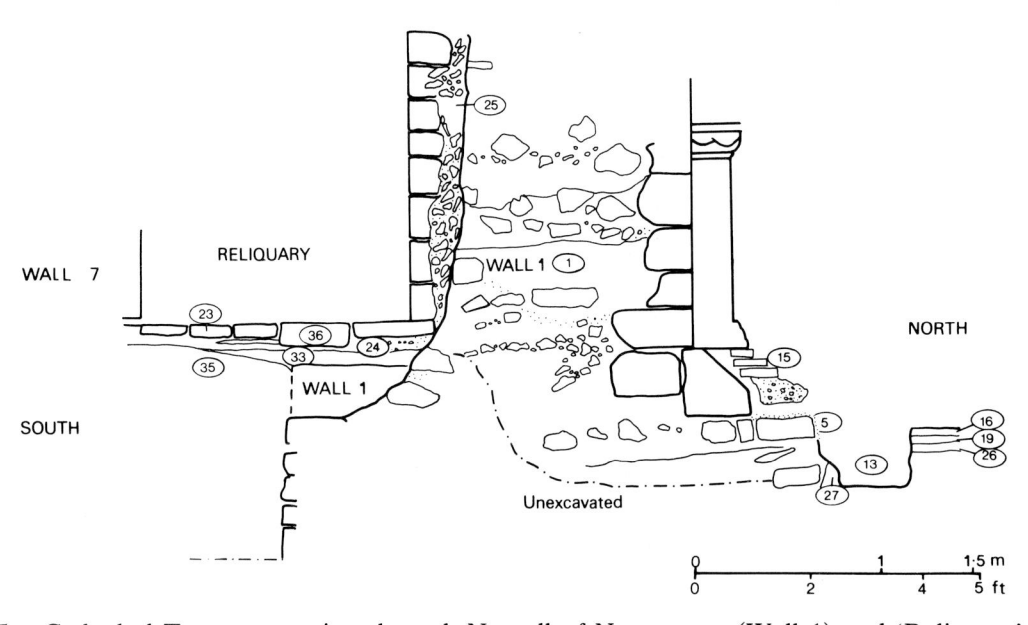

Figure 35. Cathedral Treasury: section through N. wall of N. transept (Wall 1) and 'Reliquary' floor.

century. There were two 17th century clay pipe stems from the same context.

Under the floor of the Reliquary the trench encountered deep loam deposits in the area occupied by the Roman fortress ditch. These fills reached a depth of 1.2m below the N. transept floor and were probed to 0.35m deeper. The finds in the loam fill included some Roman building material, painted window glass (?late medieval), and two small sherds of 10th–11th century limestone-tempered ware. Since the Cathedral is set on the slope of the small hill on which Gloucester is built, these loam fills are possibly from a general levelling of the area before the building of the Norman Abbey, although the finds of painted glass (Fig.64, No.18) suggest late-medieval disturbance.

The N. wall at the E. end of the slype, when washed, showed many graffiti, mostly names, presumably executed by boys attending the Cathedral School. Mrs. Richards (County Record Office) assessed the date of the handwriting as 17th or 18th century. A drawing has been made.

Records: SNB 39, pp.53–89; drawings; photos.

70/76 23 Brunswick Road.

A Roman or medieval ditch aligned E–W was recorded in the back garden.

Records: SNB 65, p.3.

80/76 Castlemeads   SO826 188.

Trench for Severn Water Board.

At 10m from the W. bank of the present channel, a layer of silt at 2.5m depth contained Roman tile (1 imbrex and 12 tegulae) and charcoal probably washed down from the Roman tilery (Heighway and Garrod 1980) and including late 1st-century samian (below, p.86).

Records: SNB 65, p 41–57; photos, drawings.

82/76 Wotton Pitch, site of Wotton Fleece Hotel.

New blocks of flats.

No evidence of Roman cemetery (see Heighway 1980b, p.60, where this site is marked as negative symbol).

Records: SNB 80, p 76.

Finds: Roman pottery, unstratified.

91/76 St. Nicholas Church.

Plaster stripping.

Photographic record of S. wall of S. aisle. The wall had been rebuilt from about halfway up.

Records: photos.

Finds: worked stone.

10/77 13, 17, 21, 23 Llanthony Road, near Llanthony Priory.

Demolition of 19th century terraced housing.

No earlier archaeological structures noted.
A stone carved head, found by contractors at the rear of the houses, is thought to be modern, and has been taken to the garden of Mr. Rigby, 50 Hailes Road, Coney Hill, Gloucester.

Records: SNB 65, p. 55a; photos.

11/77 1–3 Park Street (Back Hare Lane).

New building for Kings School.
Successive medieval domestic and/or industrial floors were recorded on the Park Street frontage. The lowest level seen, (8) at 1.3m deep, contained pottery dated from the late 11th to the 13th century.

Records: SNB 65, p.61–2.

12/77 King Edward's Gate, College Street (Figs. 21, 36, 37; Plate I.)

Trenching for services (trenches I and II) cut through the gate: the excavation was subsequently extended under the road (trenches III and IV). In College Street, 12m to the south, a record was made of street sections (Trench V).

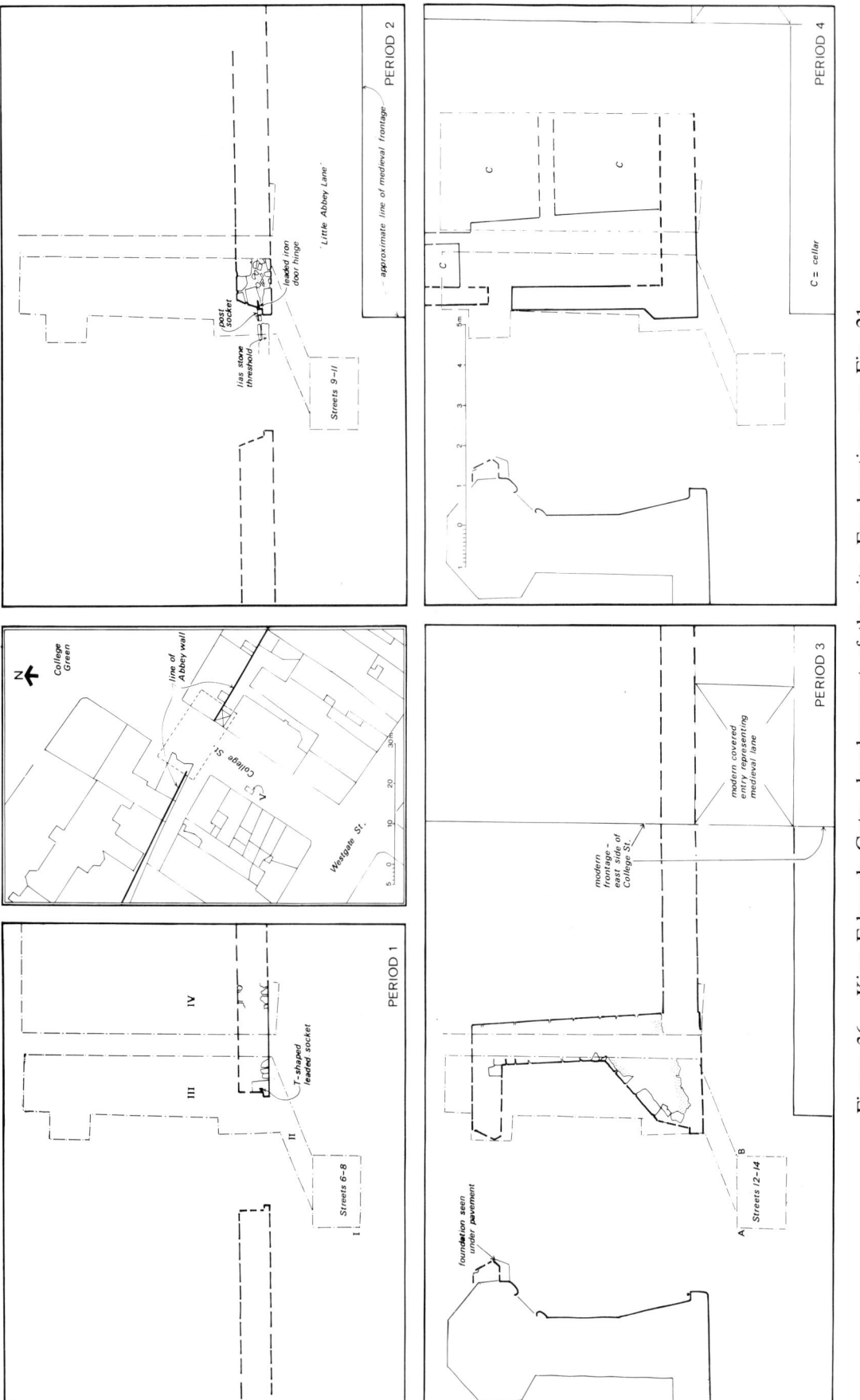

Figure 36. King Edwards Gate: development of the site. For location, see Fig. 21.

12/77 KING EDWARDS GATE

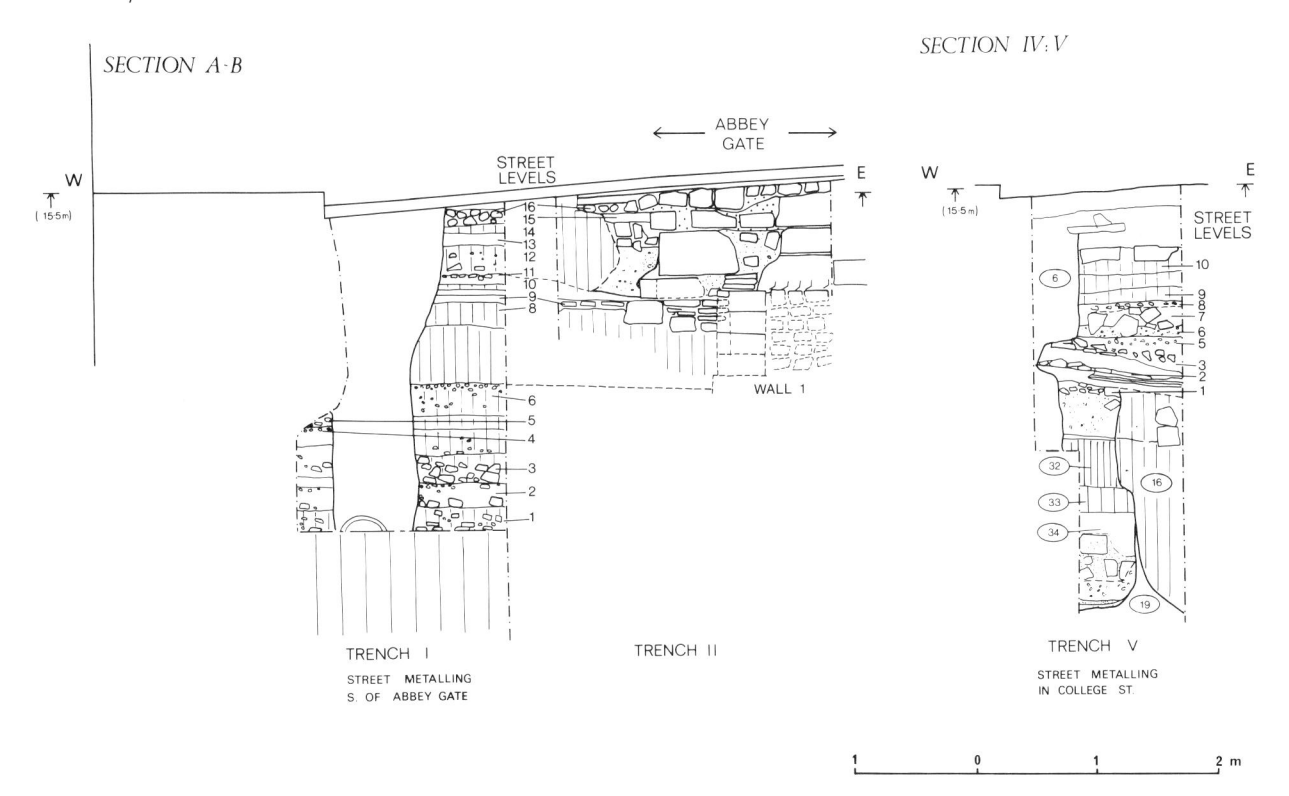

Figure 37. Street sections outside King Edward's Gate. For location see Figures 36 and 21. Streets 1–5 pre-date the first Abbey Gate of (?) 1104–13. The street numberings do not equate from one section to the other. Street 1 of Trench V appears to be contemporary with Street 6 or 7 in Trench I.

A medieval street once skirted the Abbey wall and linked St. Johns Lane to St. Mary's Street. This street was called 'King Edwards Lane' in 1843, but since this is a name also given to College Street, we have referred to this Abbey Wall circuit street as 'Little Abbey Lane'.

College Street used to be known as 'Lych Lane' (Stevenson 1890, p. 40b) and it is first mentioned in c.1291–2 (Stevenson 1893 no. 729). It was widened to the E. in the late 19th century to provide a vista to the Cathedral: thus the E. sides of the successive Abbey gates were under the road. The south tower still stands.

Period 0 The first Abbey Wall of Period 1 cut loam levels inside the Abbey Precinct which contained late 11th century pottery and one sherd (TF 49), which may date to the 12th century.

Under Street 2 of College Street (Fig. 37, Trench V) was a large medieval pit (Pit 2) which contained late 11th to early 12th century pottery. Street 1 contained 11th century pottery (TF 41B) and a trodden layer below it (layer 31) contained 10th to 11th century pottery (TF 41A). Layer 31 sealed Pit 1. The presence of these pits, as well as the absence of good street surfaces earlier than the 11th century, may suggest that College Street was creation of the 11th century. Street 1 of College Street is contemporary with the first Abbey Gate of Period 1 (see below).

In contrast to the College Street evidence, there were five good street surfaces pre-dating the Period 1 Abbey Gate, which were recorded just in front of the gate (Fig. 37, Trench I, Streets 1 to 5). The earliest of these contained 10th century pottery (TF 41A).

It is likely that these five early streets belonged to 'Little Abbey Lane', which skirted the Abbey Wall. The Abbey Gate here is outside the Roman defences, so this suggests that the Roman city wall in this area had gone by the early 11th century. The evidence also suggests that College Street, and by analogy St. Michaels lane, were not created until the later 11th century, when gates were made into the Abbey Precinct: until then the Abbey was inaccessible from the market (Westgate Street).

Period 1 The Abbey Gate of Period 1 (construction levels: Period 1A) was a simple entrance through the Abbey Precinct wall (Wall 1): a tooled doorjamb was bonded into Wall 1.

Wall 1 survived to a height of 1.2m and was 0.82m in thickness. It had a rubble core and was faced with untooled and irregular courses of lias and oolitic limestone. The offset foundations were of similar rubble construction as the core.

Plate One *Site 12/77;* King Edwards Gate, looking west.

Period 1: dating
Wall 1 cuts levels (Period 0) which contain late 11th century to 12th century pottery: Layers covering the Period 1 construction levels (Period 1B) contained 13th to 14th century pottery. This gives a date range for the first wall and gate of the early 12th to 13th century. The Abbey was walled in 1104–13, perhaps for the first time (Hart, 1863, p.13), and another wall was built in 1218 (Hart, 1863, 82–3, 25) althought this later structure, being built over land of St. Oswald's, was almost certainly on the N. side of the precinct. (Heighway forthcoming, a)

Period 2 The wall and gateway were rebuilt (construction levels: Period 2A). Two courses of the E. jamb of the new gate survived, 0.65m W. of the Period 1 jamb, which suggests that the gateway was narrowed. There was a leaded socket within the rebated jamb which contained the broken shank of the door hinge. The gate jamb was of one build with the Period 2 Abbey wall (Wall 2).
  Wall 2 had a mortared stone rubble core and was faced either side with courses of lias limestone.

Period 2: dating
The offset of Wall 2 cut layers accumulated against Wall 1: these contained fourteenth to fifteenth century pottery, indicating that the Period 2 wall and gate were constructed in the early 15th century, and that the Period 1 walls and gate were in use until then.

Period 3 A large gate with a gate passage and tower on the W. side replaced the simple Period 2 abbey gate. The excavation recorded the gate passage: the W. tower still stands, incorporated into an 18th century house.
  The Period 3 gate passage widened from about 4m at the entrance to about 6.5m in the gate passage.
  The interior was originally faced each side with tooled oolite blocks of various sizes. The foundations were offset on mortared and lower, unmortared stone rubble foundations, bedded on a footing of estuarine clay (IV (44)).
  The inside of the entrance passage was cobbled with lias setts, packed with brown sand (Street 13).
  The construction trenches for this gate (Period 3A) produced a sherd of a TF 52 jar, fifteenth to sixteenth century.
  The standing portion of the gate, very weathered and patched, can still be seen, and is of 16th century date. The *Memoriale*, compiled after the Dissolution and probably accurate for its own recent history, states that the gate was 'beautified' in the time of Abbot Parker, 1514–44. (Dugdale, ii, 1846, p.563, Fosbrook 1819, p.92).

The complete gate-house appears on Kip's 'Prospect' of Gloucester :1712). It was demolished before 1789 (see Period 4).

Street surfaces within and outside the gatehouse (period 3B) contained pottery dating to the 17th century; the latest find was a 16th to 17th-century token.

Period 4 The east Gate-house was demolished and converted into a house with brick walls and cellars. This building appears on Hall and Pinnell (1789). College street was then paved with round lias cobbles (Street 16).

Period 5 The 18th century brick building which replaced the gate was demolished to widen the road.

Records: SNBs 65 & 81; photos; drawings.

27/77   31 London Road Gloucester

Service trench.

The W. edge of a road metalling was recorded: this is thought to be the Roman road from Gloucester to 'Ermin Street'. The medieval road on this line cut this level, and was observed in site 33/76, trench VII.

Pottery: a flagon sherd, late 1st to 2nd cent.

Records: SNB 81, pp.139–143.

29/77   Heron Estate: see 98/75.

30/77   13–15 Barton Street.

Service trench in road.

Road metalling (4) at a depth of 1.4m was sealed beneath black organic street silt (3) containing domestic refuse and thirteenth century pottery.

Records: SNB 81, p.125.

31/77   Pitt Street (opposite no.6)

Service trench.

Nine medieval and post medieval street surfaces, layers (2) – (10), were recorded above dark loam to a depth of 1.75m.

The trench was partly backfilled when first observed. The contractor reported that natural sandy loam was found beneath the dark loam layer at a depth of 2.65m. This suggests that there was no defensive ditch outside the Abbey Precinct wall.

Records: SNB 80, p.2.

32/77   Barton Street, Gloucester (opposite no. 46).

Service trench.

The primary street metallings and N. ditch of medieval Barton Street were recorded at a depth of 1.1m. The silted-up ditch was sealed by a layer containing 12th–13th century pottery.

Records: SNB 80, p.5.

33/77   Cathedral: new Via Sacra route

Construction of new public path through garden of Kings School House. A trench 0.5m deep for a new wall was machined along the line of the northern Roman defences sectioned in 1964 (O'Neil 1965).

Layers belonging to the 2nd-century Roman rampart were located, as well as a medieval or post-medieval wall.

Records: SNB 80, p.9; drawings.

36/77: see 98/75

44/77   4–8 Deans Walk, Gloucester

Contractors trench on street frontage.

A 12th to 13th-century stone wall footing, with clay floors either side (Period 1) extended out beneath the modern street. The medieval levels were covered in brown loam, probably formed by cultivation (Period 2). See also site 54/73 (Hurst 1974, p. 41) where medieval pits were found on this site.

Records: SNB 80, pp. 40–44.

51/77   St. Marys Lane.

Service trench.

Successive metalled surfaces, layers (2) – (9), were recorded to a depth of 1m above the stony dark loam (10) which contained 13th century glazed pottery.

Records: SNB 65, pp.1–2.

54/77   27 Court Gardens.

11th-century pottery in a buried humus layer.

Records: SNB 80, p.70.

55/77   See Part III.

56/77   Bristol Road   SO 814 155

Service trench, W. carriageway of Bristol Rd. Cole Avenue to Tuffley Lane.

Natural clay was recorded at the average depth of 80cms. A thin clay-silt was succeeded by a substantial pitched stone and clay make-up with two fragmented limestone surfaces. Undated, probably post-medieval because of use of limestone.

1/78   Hempstead Lane (near Post Office)

Gas Main.

Record of ? medieval metalling of lane next to Manor Farm.

Records: SNB 80, pp.77–80.

13/78   Kings School, Gloucester Cathedral:

Foundation trenches for new schoolroom.

This is the area of the medieval frater, to the north of the Cloister; in the garden of Little Cloister House.

An east-west wall, Wall 1, build of oolite with sandy mortar, had associated floors (17) and (18) containing post-medieval pottery and a 17th century and clay pipe stem.

Records: SNB 89, 29–32; photos, drawings.

21/78   Matson Lane.

Road widening.

A short length of a cobbled surface, undated, was recorded in the road bank on the W. side of Matson church. Pottery ranging in date from late 11th to 18th century was found along the length of the bank extending east from Matson Church.

Records: SNB 89, p.56.

32/78   Ladybellgate House, Longsmith Street.

Renovation of building.

Collection of 16th and 17th century pottery and bones found in a layer of dark loam beneath the hall floor, which is raised above ground level. The house was built *c.* 1700.

For record of earlier tenements on the site, see site 66/75.

35/78   30 Westgate Street.

Sewer trench outside the building.

Roman floors and medieval streets were recorded. For a full description of the layers and their significance see Heighway and Garrod 1980, p.83.

36/78   Gloucester Northern Bypass

A watching brief was carried out by GADARG.

Longford, Queens Dyke   SO 830 205
1st century pottery (p.79) *Glevensis* 14, p.30.

Sandhurst Lane   SO 83392034
Roman (?) burial *Glevensis* 15, p.41.

Sandhurst Lane   SO 83012040
late Roman ditches *Glevensis* 15, p.41.

38/78   Station Road, Prince Albert site. (Figs. 38,39)

New housing (flats) development; wall trenching and 200m square basement area.

Period 1A   A linear Roman foundation, F1, of blocks of limestone, crossed the site from W. to E: the foundation was bounded on either side by a metalled area of crushed oolite.

Period 1B   Successive metallings above contained 3rd century pottery.

Period 1C   Two boundary ditched F5, F6, 1m. wide, 20m. apart, ran NS. They were undated, but cf. late RB ditched running in a similar direction on the other side of the Roman road (site 7/76, Heighway et al 1983).

Period 1D   Above Roman levels was a light greyish mottled sandy loam.

Period 2A   The remains of the stream-bed, F2, of the River Twyver could be seen below the brick culvert of Period 3; finds included leather offcuts, and 14th to 15th century pottery.

Period 2B   There were a number of pits and small linear features (Fs 3-4, Fs 7–14), some the result of gravel extraction.

38/78
PRINCE ALBERT SITE

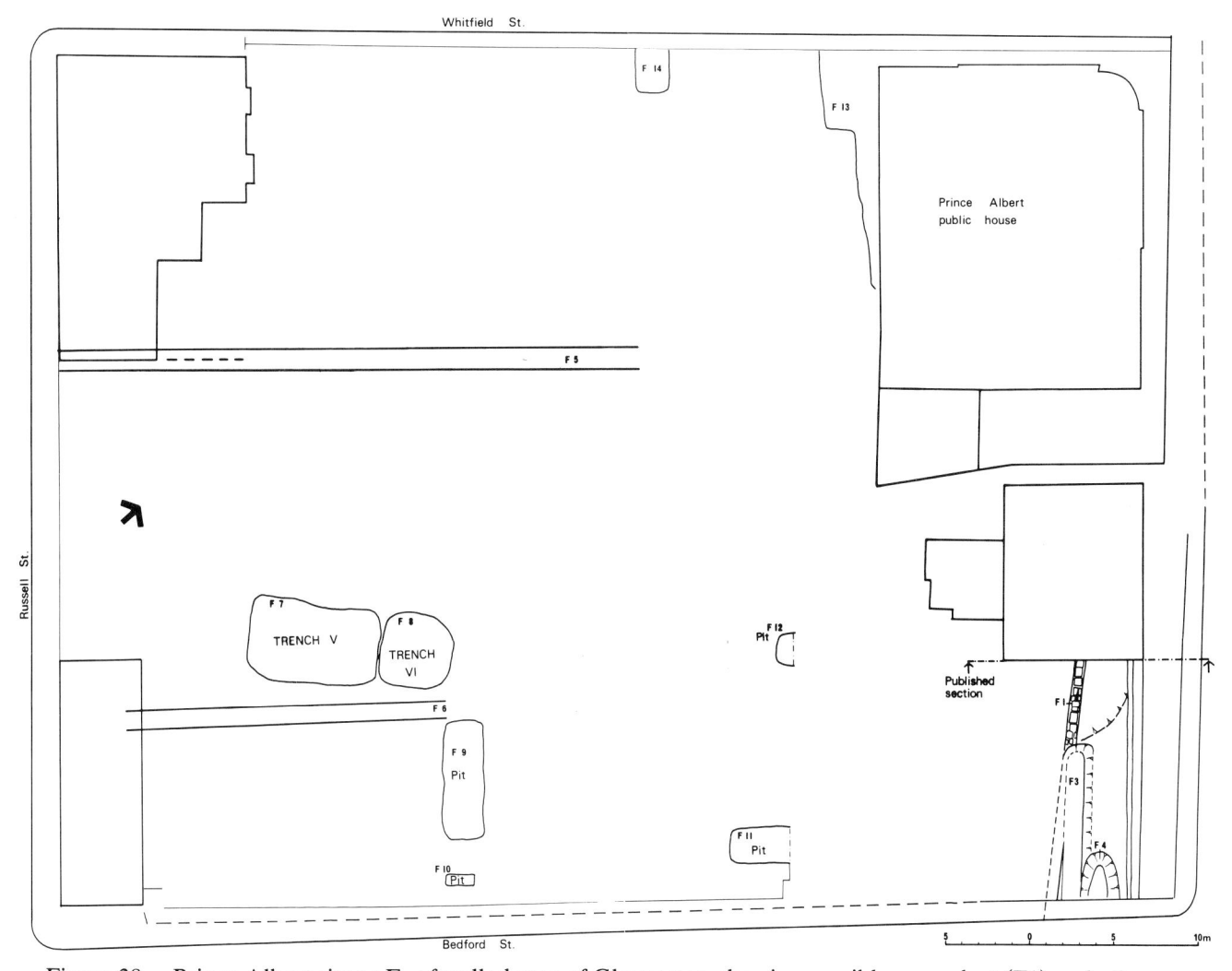

Figure 38.   Prince Albert site to E. of walled area of Gloucester, showing possible acquaduct (F1) and other Roman and later features.

38/78 PRINCE ALBERT SITE

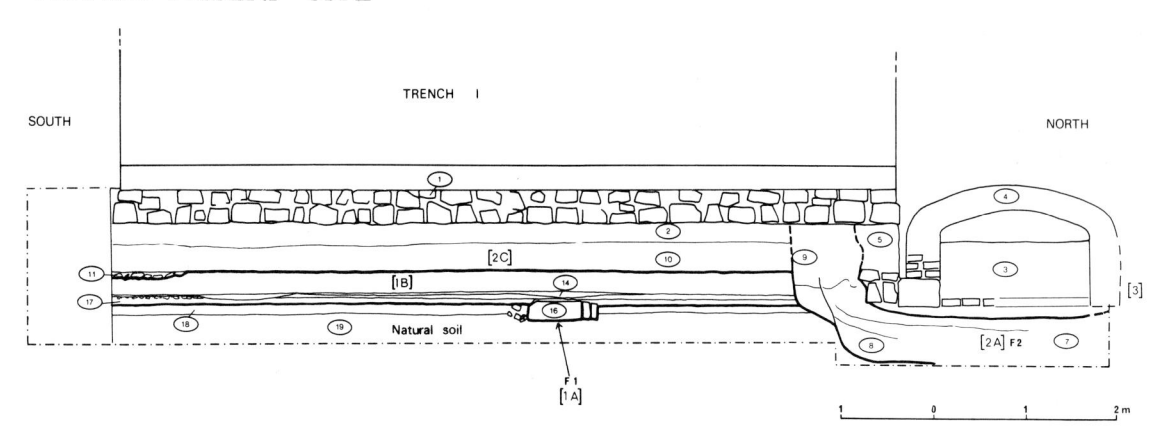

Figure 39. Prince Albert site: section as marked on Fig. 38, showing ?acquaduct (F1) and the Twyver stream (F2) beneath its post-medieval culvert. Period numbers in square brackets.

Period 2C Medieval/post medieval plough-soil.

Period 3 The Twyver was culverted in the late 19th century. The brick culvert ran parallel with Station Road.

Records: SNB 103, pp.60–65, 4 drawings.

5/79 Cathedral Crypt

A series of trenches were cut round the standing Norman columns which support the crypt.

The original floor associated with the columns was a sand mortar (5) with a lias stone rubble make-up (6), over-lying natural clay (7).
 This floor was covered by a 40cm thick make-up layer (3) and a mortar floor (2): layer (3) contained fragments of 16th to 17th century roofing tiles, as well as 13th century pottery.
 It was noticed that the columns had subsided 300mm below the medieval floor level.

Records: SNB 95, pp. 18–19.

12/79 Mechanaids Ltd. St. Catherine Street.

Three trial holes on site of proposed factory.

Period 1A (Trench II)   Five successive fine metalled surfaces overlying natural were found at a depth of 1.1m adjacent to St. Catherine Street. Finds of smithing slag and hearth lining.

Period 1B (Trench I)   To the north of these a large post pit with a posthole 30 x 34cm was cut into natural. Pottery, late 1st century.

Period 1C (Trench III)   Further north, one side of a silted ditch, containing late 1st and early 2nd century pottery (p.79), exceeded a depth of 3m.

Period 2   Over the ditch were horizontal levels of pebbly gritty loam; pottery 2nd century. Coin, unidentifiable AE3.

Period 3   Dark loams represented a period of cultivation; pottery 12th century.

Period 4   Medieval and post-medieval pits. Contained 17th century clay pipe, post medieval glass, and 18th century pottery.

Period 5   Victorian and modern.

Notes: SNB 95, pp. 23–31.

13/79   49 Victoria Street

Foundations for new kitchen extension.

Reported stone walls turned out to be a nineteenth century soakaway 1.5m square contemporary with the standing building.

Notes: SNB 95, p.32.

Finds: 2 clay pipe bowls, 1 1810–40, 1 c. 1870.

14/79   28 Pitt Street, Gloucester.

Boundary wall trench for new lock-up garages.

Period 1:   deposits of dark green charcoal-flecked loam (8) (9), containing late 1st to 2nd century pottery, tilery waste and daub.

Period 2:   Redeposited natural loam, (6) (7) 480mm. deep. Similar deposits have been recorded beneath the floor of no. 28 (site 15/79). These redeposited loams may represent a bank.

Period 3:   The levels of Periods 1 and 2 were cut by a linear feature containing 17th to 18th century pottery.

Records: SNB 95, pp.20–22.

15/79   28 Pitt Street, Gloucester.

Building trench dug 1m. below living room floor.
   A shallow pit (4) with cattle long bones, each with one broken end, cut dark loam (5), over redeposited natural sand (6), containing residual Roman red-painted wall plaster, over greenish loam (7), and pottery.

Records: SNB 95, p.33.

19/79 BERKELEY STREET

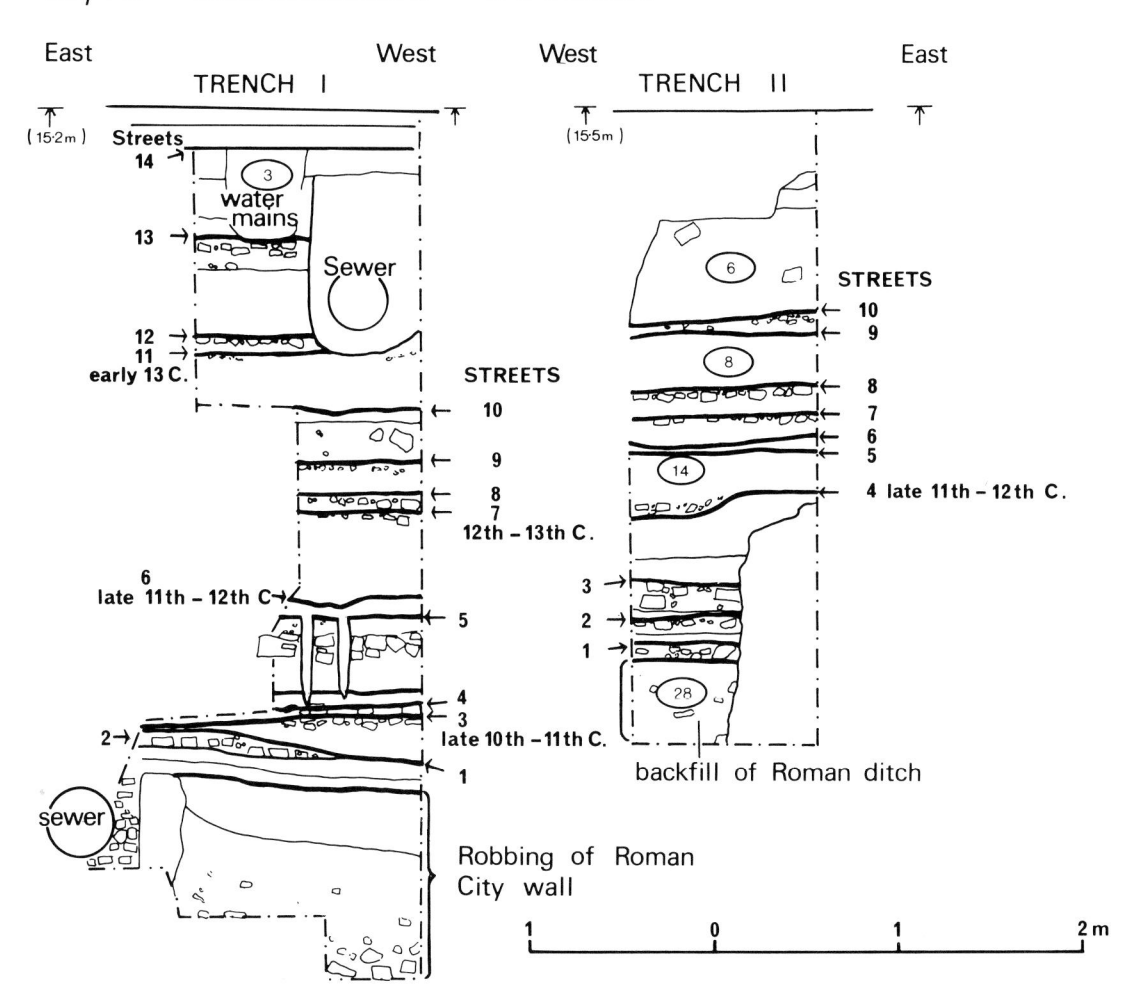

Figure 40.   Section of medieval surfaces of Berkeley Street. For location see Fig. 21.

19/79 Berkeley Street, Gloucester (Figs. 21, 40).

Two service repair trenches.

Trench I: The robbing trench of the western Roman city wall was sealed beneath 14 medieval and post-medieval street metallings. The robbing contained part of a 1st century pillar-moulded glass bowl (see p.93, No.19).

Trench II: The fill of the western Roman city ditch, containing mid to late 4th century pottery (p.81) was sealed by 10 medieval and post-medieval street metallings. The lowest street was 0.7m higher AOD than the lowest metalling in Trench I: presumably the street surfaces sloped up to Westgate Street, as they do today, although the modern rise is less, about 0.3m.

Finds were mostly from Trench I. Under Street 3 was a late Saxon decorated leather scramasax sheath (Fig.66), an upper from a Saxon turnshoe and a sherd of late 10th century to mid 11th century pottery (TF 41A). The pottery types in the street sequence (Table 3) also suggest that streets 2 to 5 may be 11th century in date, and that streets 6 to 13 continue the sequence into the early 13th century. Street 4 contained an unfinished antler bracelet. Street 5 had two stakes cut into it which produced preliminary RC date of 770 a.d. ± 80 (HAR 4187): this is certainly too early. Street 5 also sealed an iron surgeons probe (Fig.65, no.25). Street 7 contained fuel ash slag and a smithing-hearth bottom.

27/79 Barbican Way, west end.

Gas main trench, 1.8m. deep.

Successive 16th and 17th century metalled surfaces of Gloucester Quay were recorded beneath the east of the modern Quay. A polyangular wall foundation within Barbican Way was the original Clerk of Works office for the 19th century Gaol and appears on the Board of Health map, 1852.

Records: SNB 97, 22–31.

28/79 10 Lower Quay Street (Figs. 41, 42).

THE ROMAN QUAYSIDE WALL (TRENCH I)

A trial trench was mechanically dug in advance of redevelopment. Its aim was to establish the line of the Roman quayside wall, known from other evidence to run on approximately this line (Hurst 1974, p.46; Heighway and Garrod 1980). The principal discovery was a trench 6m. wide (F20) which is interpreted as the robbing trench of the Roman quayside wall.

Period 1 A Roman made-up ground level, consisting of re-deposited loam.

Period 2 Further tip lines of rubbly loam were laid down. During this sequence an irregular row of stake holes, F18, was set; it ran parallel to F20.
Dating: early 2nd century pottery; a military weapon point (Fig.68, No.9). Samian, see Fig.59A, nos.1–3.

Period 3 A post-in-trench feature, F14, was found also to run parallel to F20. F14 contained four tapering posts, D:100–120 mm., about 10mm. apart.
Both F18 and F14 may be structures relating to the Roman quayside. Samian, 2nd century; see p.84, nos. 4 and 5.

Period 4 A series of tip lines incorporating domestic and building rubbish. The tip reached a thickness of 1.5m and would have been contained behind the Quay wall, if this was already in existence. Probably this weight of material would have required a stone wall revetment. Dating: 3rd century, but all pottery could be residual.

Period 5a The remains of a construction trench, in the bottom of which was part of a mortared lias limestone structure (F 13). No helpful dating.

Period 5b Further construction tips were deposited. Date from pottery possibly late 3rd to early 4th century.
Period 5 may represent either the original building of the Quay wall, or a substantial repair or addition.

Period 6a Silt, which probably represents the build-up of river born deposits in the quay frontage. Date assumed to be 5th to 9th centuries.

Period 6b Over the river-born deposits were a series of metallings with rubble, indicating the reclamation of this area as dry land. Dating: pottery late 11th century; a late Saxon hooked tag (Fig.68, No.5).

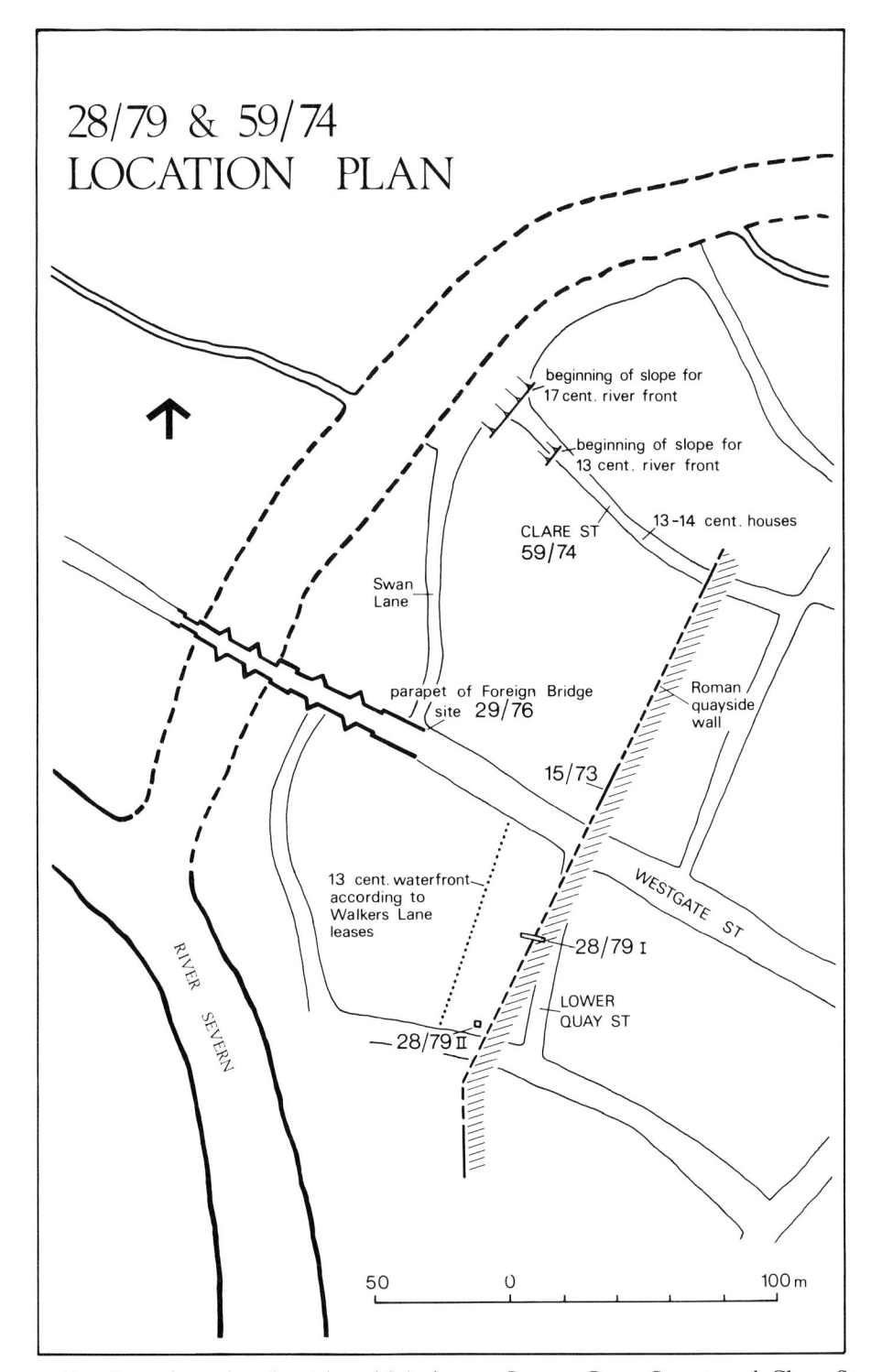

Figure 41. Location plan for 'riverside' sites at Lower Quay Street and Clare Street. Streets shown are medieval. Drawn by J. Williamson.

Period 7A   F20 is a trench 6m. wide and of unknown depth, assumed to represent the robbing of the Roman quayside wall. The robbing included a large block of tooled oolite, similar to the upper part of the oolite build observed at the Westgate flats. Site 15/73). The pottery indicates that the quayside wall was robbed in the late 11th or early 12th century. Remains of timber planks and posts abandoned in the robbing fill may derive from the use of shoring during the robbing process.

Period 7B   F10 was a flat-bottomed gully, 2.1m. wide, 1.3m. deep, running E/W, contemporary with F20. The pottery indicates a similar date, and the two features are lensed together. It is probably a drainage gully to the river.

A series of medieval buildings was now constructed over the robbed and backfilled quayside wall.

28/79 10 LOWER QUAY ST.

15/73 ROMAN QUAYSIDE WALL

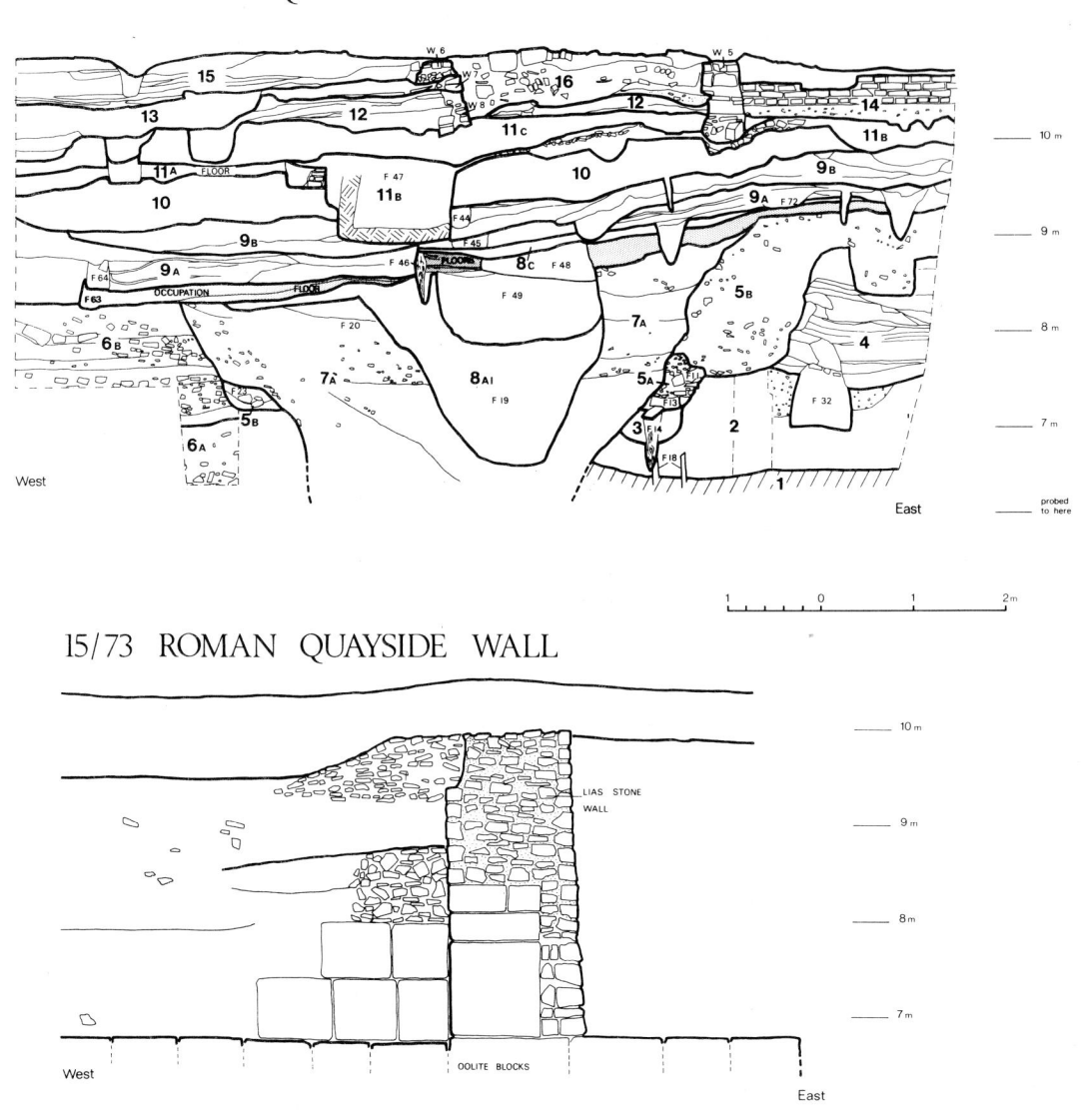

Figure 42. Section of waterfront at 10 Lower Quay Street showing robbed-out Roman quayside wall (F20) with early 12th century and later buildings above. Bold figures are Period numbers. The Roman quayside wall excavated further N. (see Fig 41) is shown at the same scale for comparison.

Period 8B Building 1: a timber building 8.8m. long, of post-in-pit construction, with two rooms front and back. It has floors of clay and wooden planks, and an open hearth in the front room. B1 was set back 2.5m. from the modern frontage, having an open area in front (8A). B1 dating from floors and occupation levels, early 13th century pottery.
Finds include a Purbeck marble mortar (Fig.70, No.21).

Period 8C Destruction of B1.

Period 9 Building 2, also with two rooms, but of post-and-sill-beam construction, was superimposed on the Period 8 levels. It had a sunken oven or furnace 1.2m. long in the front room.

Period 9A The front room of Building 2 had a clay floor; finds included a pit, F4, which contained a bronze-casting mould, bronze fragments, and dross. The occupation levels of both rooms produced smithing slag and early 13th century pottery. Secondary floors and a hearth F72, also contained smithing slag. The area beside the street which had been open in Period 8 had clay floor levels containing iron slag and charcoal; B2 in this period may have had three ground-floor rooms, making the total building length 11.3m.

Period 9B Destruction levels of 9A: these also contained early 13th century pottery.

Period 10 After the destruction of Building 2, the area seems to have been open ground for some time; perhaps there was an unoccupied plot at this point. Pottery suggests a date in the 15th or 16th centuries, but the layer presumably represents the period from the mid 13th century to the 15th.

Period 11   The area was reoccupied by a building, B3, apparently of 15th century date. The building contained a large square pit, F47, which was probably for industrial use (11B). The building was destroyed (11C) perhaps in the 16th century.

Periods 11D, 11F   A long sequence visible in the south section (not illustrated) dates from about the 13th century to the 16th, but it was not possible in section to distinguish the different phases.

Period 12   Levelling and construction of stone B4 (Wall 8).

Period 13   A stone building 5 (Wall 7) dated by pottery to the late 17th to 18th century.

Period 14   A stone and brick-built building, B6 (Wall 5), fronted directly onto Lower Quay Street. This formed part of a row of terraced cottages built in the late 19th century and demolished in 1979.

DISCUSSION

The river channel, from Roman to modern times, has always moved westwards. Although Rowbotham claims that the natural flow of the river would not scour in this way, it is nevertheless true that the buried soils found west of the Roman quay wall consist of natural siltings with very little dumped rubbish. This westerly movement of the quays must have continued since Flavian times, and presumably the Flavian quay was east of the 2nd century quay described here, and would be found buried under the made ground levels of Period 2.

The site at Lower Quay Street has to be considered with the evidence recorded by Garrod and Hurst (1974, 46) on the Westgate Flats site, further north (Fig. 41, site 15/73). There a massive masonry platform was observed, at 6.75 AOD, on which was built a wall of limestone blocks. This wall had its upper courses built of smaller limestone blocks, and above this was a second phase, a heightening and thickening consisting of coursed lias stone and rubble. The layers (2) and (4) revetted by and E. of this wall contained 2nd to 3rd century pottery; they can be equated with our periods 2 and 4.

The Westgate site section was drawn in such adverse circumstances that if there were a construction trench for this wall through the made-up ground, it may not have been visible (inf. A. P. Garrod). Thus the dating of the two phases of wall is uncertain, but the platform possibly, unless all pottery is residual, dates to the early second century. At Lower Quay Street, the platform would have been lower than 6m AOD (the depth probed). Perhaps it did not exist here although it is likely that variations in the Roman topography necessitated stepped levels in the quay platform. A platform at Lower Quay Street would predate Period 2, in other words date to the early second century. It is likely that the first-phase wall, of similar large oolite blocks, was of a date with it. One might also suggest that the early 2nd century was a likely period for an ambitious scheme such as the construction of a continuous quay and quayside retaining wall.

The second phase of the wall, which was of lias stone, can be equated with our period 5, which also contained evidence of lias stone structures, and dated to the late 3rd or early 4th century. It was at this time that defensive works on the east side of the town were carried out, including the thickening of the city wall and the addition of external towers (Heighway et al 1983). It is possible that at this stage the riverside wall was strengthened to form part of the city's defences. The existence of the mortared structure F13 (5A) could indicate a tower inside this wall.

The quayside wall survived until the early 12th century. It was thus in existence and operating as a quayside retaining wall, if not a defensive wall, in the 10th century and earlier (Heighway forthcoming). The demolition of the quayside wall coincides with the building of the stone castle (Hurst forthcoming) on a new site close by; it is not unreasonable to assume that the stone for the castle was partly obtained by the robbing of the quayside wall (which is intact further north at site 15/73, more distant from the castle). Immediately the robbing was completed, the backfilled robbing was built over by housing. The rapidity with which these building sites were taken up presumably indicates flourishing property markets in the early 12th century town.

THE PIPE KILN MATERIAL (TRENCH II)

A trench excavated by Allan Peacey uncovered waste material and pipes from an 18th century pipe kiln. The material is being prepared for publication by Mr. Peacey.

30/79   St. Catherine Street (Fig. 43) just N. of railway bridge at Deans Way junction.

Service trench below E. pavement and carriageway of St. Catherine Street (ancient Wateryngstrete).

Stone wall footings, 13th century to post medieval in date, were recorded fronting onto a sunken street. The street metallings, at a depth of 1.4m, had late 17th to 18th century pottery lying on them. There was a metalling at a depth of 2m, at about 8.3m AOD under a deep layer of redeposited clay. This could represent an early metalling of road (now Deans Way) leading from nearby St. Oswald's to Kingsholm,

30/79 ST. CATHERINE ST.

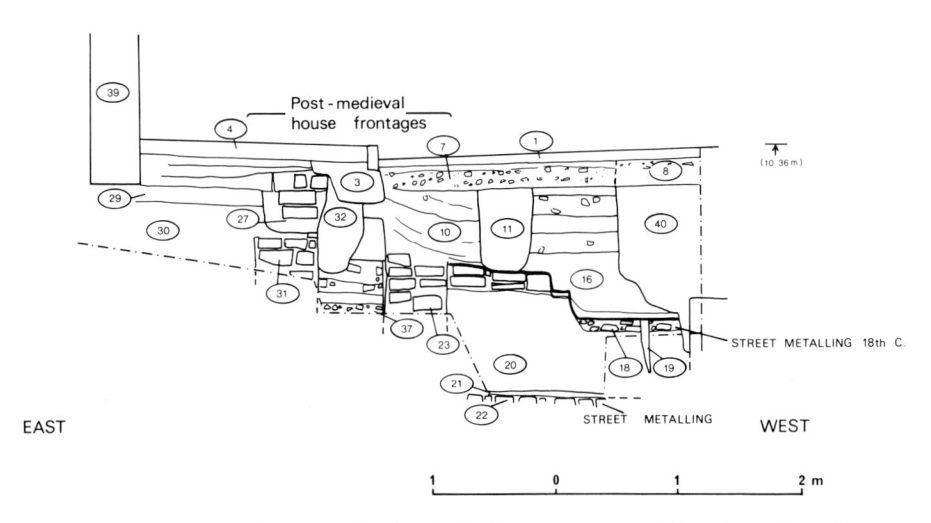

Figure 43. Record of street metalling in St Catherine's Street at Deans Way junction. The lowest metalling is undated.

but it is very low (the Roman street at St. Oswalds Priory was at c. 9.5m AOD). This 'street' may be Roman, or it may be a medieval street in a hollow way.

31/79 St. Catherine Street, near junction with Skinner Street.

Service Trench

R. Twyver, silted course, recorded beneath N. carriageway, depth 1.6m. Over the river bed was a 19th century bridge culvert, and successive street metallings.

Records: SNB 97, 41–2.

34/79 Hare Lane, under rail bridge.

Consolidation of bridge piers.

Robbed stone wall, bounded by a floor of puddled lias clay, at a depth of 1m. A destruction level above the floor was sealed by a rough stony surface containing re-used Roman debris, including late 1st to 3rd century pottery (p.79).

Records: SNB 95, pp.51–5.

43/79 Brunswick Road, Gloucester College of Art.

Service trench along N. side of main building.

A metalled area, E. of the Roman ditch was recorded, and remains of two or three inhumation burials and a scatter of 2nd to 4th century pottery sherds were noted on the spoil heap near the NW. corner of the building.

46/79 Dulverton House, Pitt Street.

Service trench 700mm deep.

The 19th century brick culvert of the medieval stream, the Fullbrook, was recorded along the S. garden boundary adjacent to the Cathedral precinct.

Records: SNB 97, pp.53–4.

Sites in 1980 and 1981 are described below in summary only, apart from a few of particular interest. Pottery and finds are not reported in full. For sites in Kingsholm, see Part III.

3/80 See part III.

7/80 Gloucester Club, Mercer's Lane. Medieval floor levels.

GLOUCESTER CATHEDRAL 1980~81

THE MEDIEVAL ABBEY

GLOUCESTER~THE ROMAN AND SAXON DEFENCES

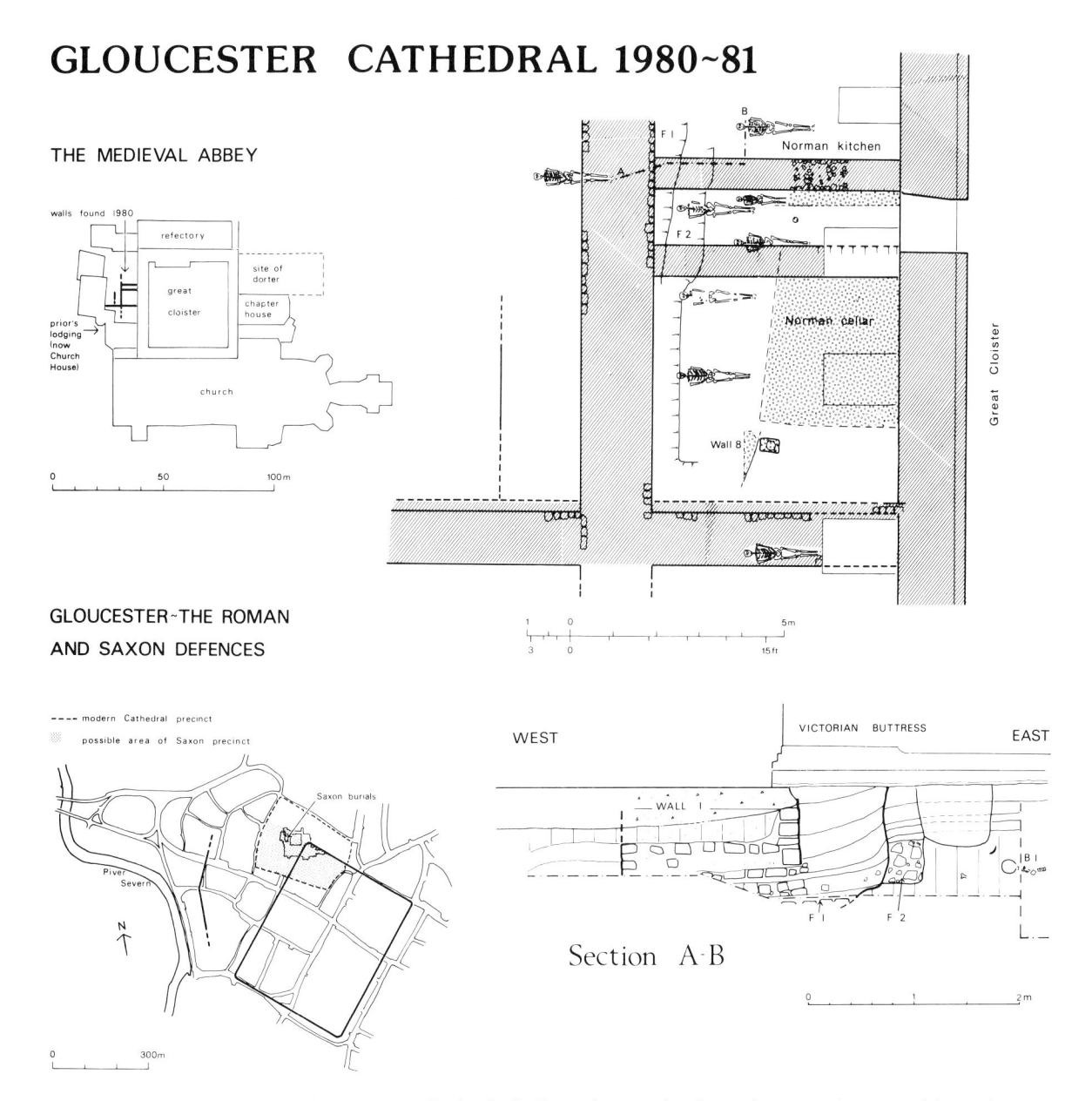

Figure 44. Church House, Gloucester Cathedral. Location and other plans to show position of Anglo Saxon cemetery outside W. wall of Roman town, and layout of Norman and later claustral buildings. Drawn by C. Guy and L. Marley.

11/80 Church House, Gloucester Cathedral (Fig. 44).

Mechanical excavation for trenches of new toilet block.

Period 1 A series of Roman tip lines, dated by pottery to the late 3rd or 4th century.

Period 2 A burial ground containing east-west inhumations of several ages. There were no overlapping burials, but the ground cut by the burials contained disturbed bones, suggesting at least two generations – about fifty years or more (see Heighway, 1980, p.217). A radiocarbon date from one of the burials yielded a date (uncorrected) of ad 970 (HAR 3971).

These burials underlie a late 11th century to 12th century building (Periods 3 and 4) which represents the late 11th century west cloister range (the present cloister is 14th century but its slypes date to the late 11th century and there must have been a late 11th century cloister and guesthouse in this position).

Pottery from the burial levels comprises only one sherd of 10th century pottery (TF 41A).

Period 3 A cellar building 4m wide with associated partition walls (Wall 8) and postholes. West of Wall 8, a floor terminated at a trench, F2, running north-south but at a slight angle to the main standing buildings. This trench presumably represents the west wall of the Norman west cloister range. Its slightly skew alignment is also shared by Church House, which has remains of 13th century date but

4/81 SOUTH-GATE

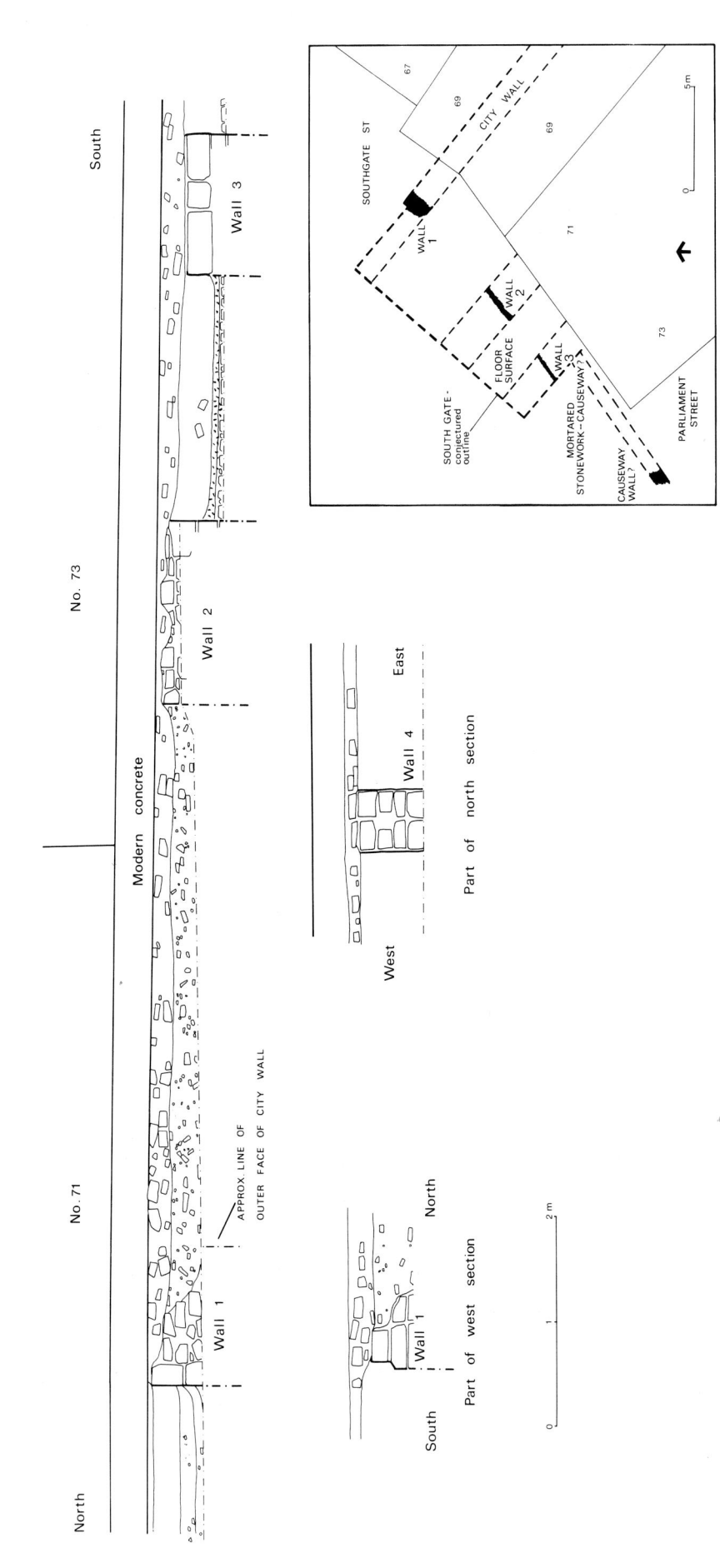

Figure 45. Section of Medieval and 17th century South Gate exposed in gas main trench. The inset shows the walls plotted onto the modern street boundaries.

could of course rest on earlier foundations. The cellar alignment, though unknown, could be similar and has been so reconstructed in Fig.44.

North of the cellar, separated from it by a wall, was an area of occupation including kitchen waste and many fish bones.

A later trench, F1, has a similar alignment to F2. It may be robbing for a second wall (Period 4?) destroyed by the walls of Period 5.

Pottery dating for period 3 suggests 11th to 12th century.

Period 4 The cellar was backfilled and a considerable sequence of floors laid over it. Dating: pottery 12th and 13th century.

Period 5 A number of walls of masonry in orange mortar appeared to be bonded into the Great Cloister wall and therefore to date to the 14th century.

Period 6 19th century external buttresses of the cloister, and other Victorian features.

One of the most interesting points to emerge from this record is the evidence of the early alignment of the claustral buildings. This alignment is not that of Serlo's church, begun in 1089, and it is possible that it reflects the alignment of the pre-Norman church constructed in 1058. This implies of course that the 1058 church occupied the same site as the Norman one.

13/80 Queens Street. 2nd century rampart, Flavian clay ovens, medieval streets. See Heighway et al 1983, for similar deposits.

14/80 St. Catherine Street. Post medieval brick culvert.

15/80 Barnwood Court. Post-medieval brick culvert.

19/80 3 Hare Lane, Kings Arms. 12th century Abbey wall. 13th century building.

21/80 Great Western Road, Gloucester Hospital. Roman pottery.

25/80 Southgate Street, Royal Hospital. Roman street, 12th century street ditch, 13th century pit.

26/80 The Quay, Shire Hall Car Park; new printing works. 19th cent. gas works.

27/80 78 Worcester Street. Brick culvert.

34/80 Gloucester Cathedral, Church House Garden. 14th century walls. TBGAS 100, 263.

34/80 Gloucester Cathedral, Church House Garden. 14th century walls.

37/80 St. Mary de Lode church. 19th century fill.

39/80 3 Hare Lane, Kings Arms. St. Peters Abbey Wall.

40/80 Cathedral, College Green. Post medieval and modern metallings.

4/81 outside 71–3 Southgate Street.

Gas main trench.

The walls of the medieval and 17th century South Gate were recorded in a trench 350mm wide. (Fig.45).

Wall 1, aligned on the City wall, was a foundation of oolite stones, with oolite chamfered offsets, and greensand facing stones above. Green sandstone as facing-stone is used in late 11th century work at St. Oswalds Priory and in the 12th century Foreign Bridge. Wall 1 may be of medieval build and the gate, if of similar plan to the N. and E. gates (see Heighway et al. 1983) would have had an internal tower.
Walls 2 and 3, oolite wall footings in orange mortar, represent the 17th century South Gate, of which there are several illustrations, and which stood forward of the city wall (see, for example, a painting by R. Curzon, dated 1888, in Gloucester Folk Museum).

Wall 4, on a N.S. alignment, may represent a post-medieval causeway wall similar to Wall 14 at the East Gate (Heighway et al. 1983).

10/81 49 London Road. Roman street surface. TBGAS 100, 262.

11/81 Cathedral, 2 College Green. 2 inhumations of Abbey cemetery (possibly post-medieval).

13/81 St. Luke Street. Victorian Church.

14/81 ST. NICHOLAS CHURCH
Sewer connection

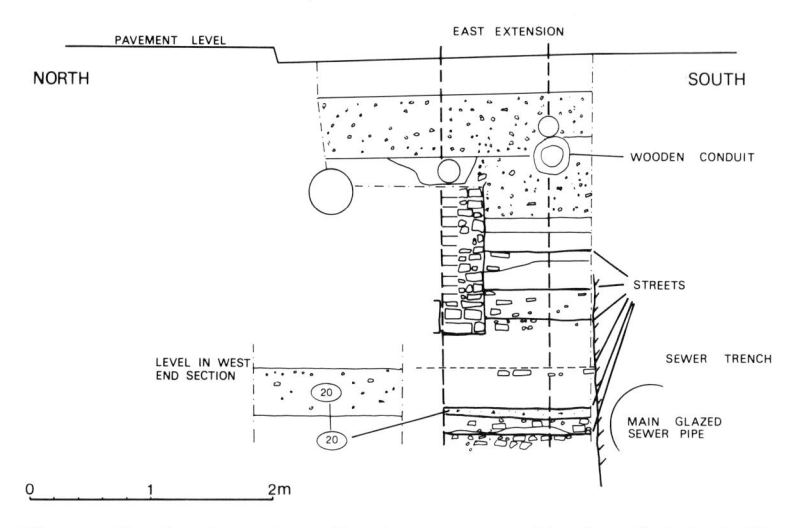

Figure 46. Section of medieval streets outside St. Nicholas' Church.

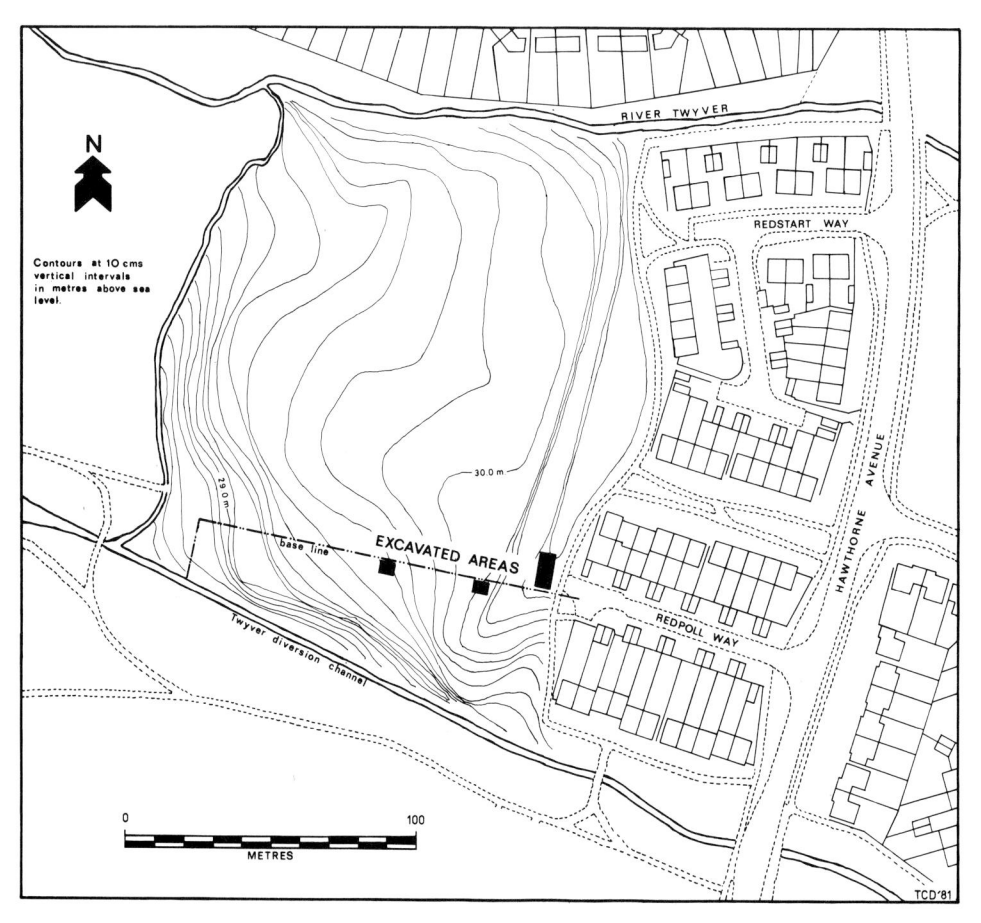

Figure 47. Saintbridge: location of further area excavated in 1981 (site 26/81). Drawn by T. Darvill.

14/81 Outside St. Nicholas, church (Fig.46).

At the bottom of the trench was a good street surface metalled with stone and re-used Roman building materials. Over this was a series of worn street surfaces, interspersed with thick layers of rapidly-accumulated organic material. These organic levels were sealed by a street level associated with a wooden water conduit (17th century: see site 42/74). A mortared lias stone wall footing faced with 65mm bricks, aligned E–W, may be the remains of a 17th-or 18th-century culvert.

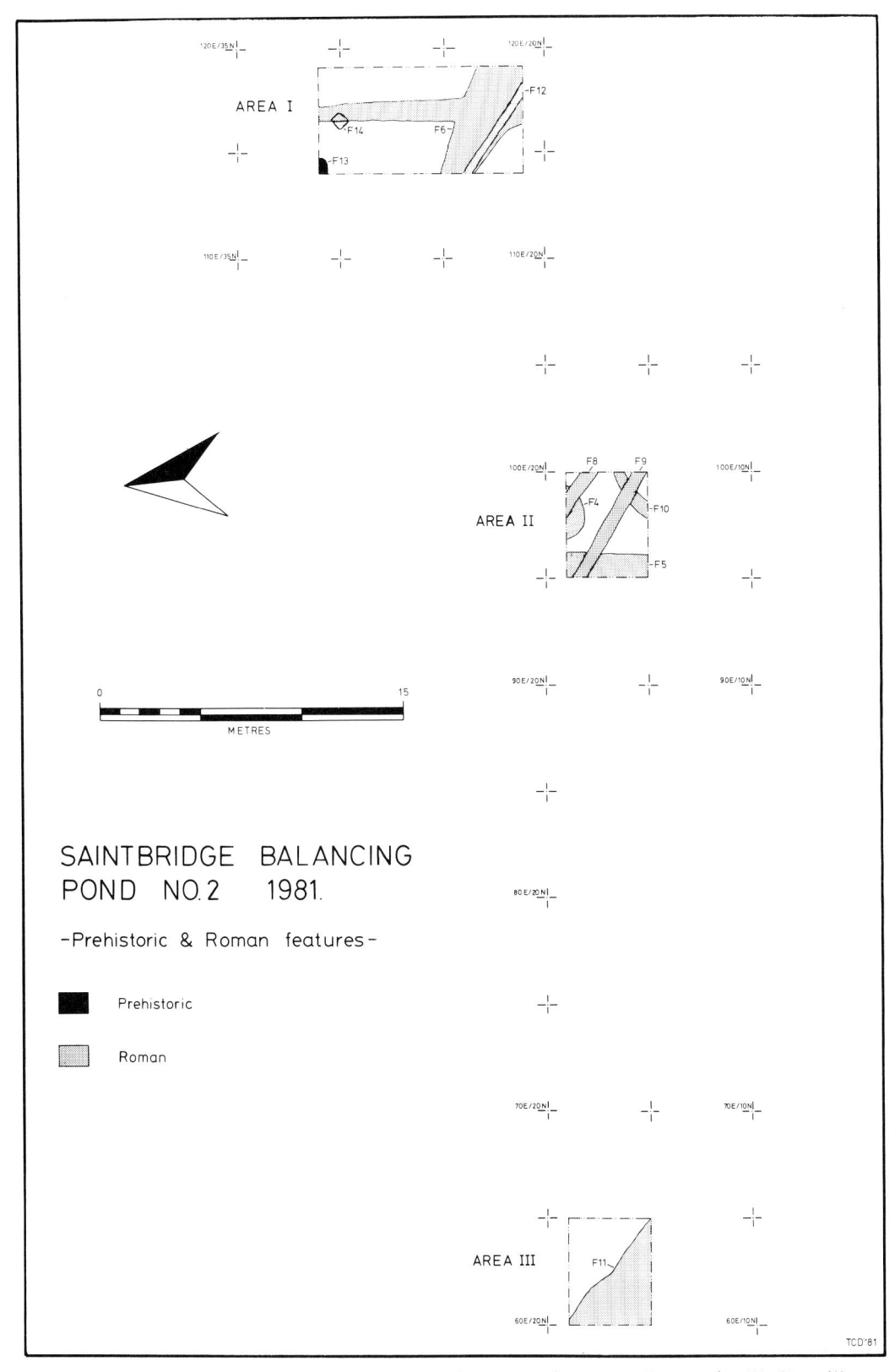

Figure 48. Saintbridge 1981: prehistoric and Roman features. Drawn by T. Darvill.

The footing was bounded along its length by a large timber beam.

There was no adequate dating evidence for the earliest street in this sequence. The sequence, however, with its metalling of re-used Roman material, and organic layers above, is similar to that in another observation in Northgate Street (Heighway et al, 1983, site 67/75) where the metalled street was thought to be 10th or 11th century.

15/81 91 Westgate Street. Photographic record of building.

16/81 162 Barnwood Rd. Roman and medieval pottery; 2nd century ditch.

17/81 Bus depot, London Road.

Excavation 485m square, 1.4m deep, for alternations to depot.

Until the 2nd century, the site was open ground. In the mid to late 2nd century it was occupied by a building consisting of at least two rooms with mortar floors, with a courtyard area to N. and E. In the courtyard was an octagonal oolite stone well-head. The area E. of the courtyard was open ground. This open area was metalled over in the late 3rd or 4th century.

The well-head will be exhibited in the forecourt of the new depot.

19/81 Horsebere Brook, Longford. SO 841 213 Roman pottery.

26/81 Saintbridge, Balancing pond (Figs 47, 48) SO 852 167.

Rescue excavation by Tim Darvill for Gloucester City Museum, in advance of construction of balancing pond. A full report is in preparation.

This site represents an extension west of site 98/75, *q.v.*

Three trenches, I–III, were dug by hand. The only evidence of prehistoric settlement was found in I, a shallow pit F13 containing three prehistoric potsherds. All three trenches contained extensive evidence of Roman ditches and pits, which had severely disturbed all deposits down to natural subsoil. All these features can be interpreted as the ditches of a field system.

Medieval cultivation had been similarly destructive.

The site attests to the high value of this farming land which has been intensively used by successive farming groups.

32/81 11 Barbican Road. Castle ditch, backfill of sunken upper fills. TBGAS 101, 192.

33/81 50–52 London Road. Roman inhumations. TBGAS 101, 192.

34/81 1 Berkeley Street. Roman defences(?), medieval floors. TBGAS 101, 192.

35/81 Derby Road. Negative evidence.

PART 3 THE KINGSHOLM FORT, GLOUCESTER

Observation of building works has produced further information about the fort or fortress at Kingsholm.

It was recognised long ago that the earliest Roman occupation at Gloucester was at Kingsholm, about half a mile N. of the present town (Green, 1942, 40).

This early settlement may have been either a fort or a fortress. Green (1942) suggested a fortress for the II Legion, Richmond (1962) an auxilliary fort with the XX Legion quartered later on the site of the fortress at Gloucester. Webster (1970) proposed that Kingsholm was an auxilliary fort, then later a legionary fortress for the XXth, with the II Legion still later based at Gloucester.

Whatever the status of the military establishment (henceforth described as a fort), it is likely, as Green suggested (1942, 41) that it owed its position (rather low-lying in relation to the present town) to a convenient crossing place of the River Severn.

The Kingsholm fort was replaced in the 60's by a fortress at Gloucester.

Excavations at Kingsholm in 1972 confirmed the existence of timber buildings of two phases. These buildings were dismantled in the mid 60's AD; there were pits of discarded stores (Hurst 1975, 267–94). The known alignment of these buildings provides the alignment of the fort.

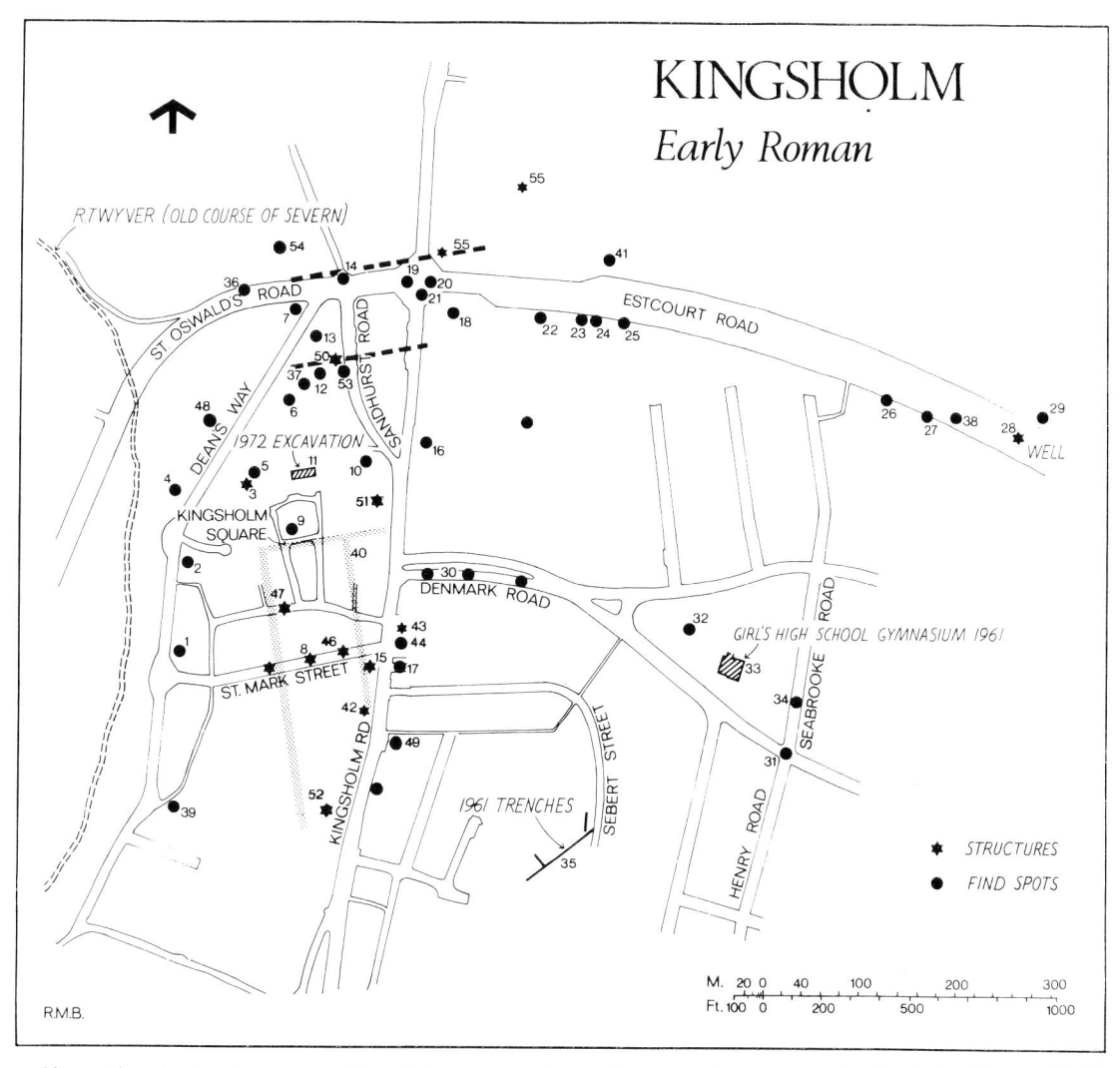

Figure 49. Kingsholm, the area of the 1st-century fort or fortress. 1st-century finds. After Hurst 1975, with additions. The very heavy dashed lines indicate two possible lines for a N. military defence ditch (sites 5/81, 9/83).

The position of the fort defences is still uncertain. The recent discovery (in 1983) of a 'V' ditch on the fort alignment may indicate the N. defence (site 9/83); another likely defence ditch further S. (site 5/81) had superimposed 1st-century buildings of a 'military' character. The implication of the evidence from these last two sites is that there were two superimposed forts at Kingsholm, the first being smaller. However, much more information is needed. First-century buildings can be plotted (Fig. 52); at the moment it is not possible to tell whether these are inside or outside the fort. A rule-of-thumb may be to assume that post-in-trench buildings are 'military', other constructions, such as simple sill trenches, being outside the fort. On this basis the S. limit of the fort is somewhere between site 4/78 (Fig. 49, no. 43) and site 22/81 (Fig. 49, no. 52). The E. limit of the fort has probably been destroyed by 19th century gravel quarrying. The W. limit would have been aligned on the river. The Twyver stream today runs in a wide channel which probably represents the old river course and thus the W. limit of the fort. Taking the most northerly of the two fort limits marked on Fig. 49, it has to be said that the size of the 'fort' is much closer to that of a fortress.

The clay bank recorded by Charles Green (1942, 46) is probably a field bank, covered by a made-up ground from the levelling of the Rugby ground (Hurst 1975, 279–80), fn 10, No. 39).

The Kingsholm fort site was used in the late Roman period as a cemetery. During the 1972 excavation, an unusual burial was recorded. It was of a man with iron knife and belt buckle whose body had been placed in his own mausoleum. Other observations have added to the extent of the cemetery. Burials were aligned on the Roman street.

The Kingsholm Roman cemetery was at least in part and in its later stages, of high status. This may be of significance in view of its later position as the site of a late Saxon palace (Heighway 1983).

The following gazetteer continues the numbering and the maps used in Hurst 1975. The sites are described in a separate section below.

GAZETEER (continued from Hurst 1975, p.279)

Early Roman (Fig. 49).

40	negative evidence for defences	Site 5/76
41	1st century pottery	Site 30/76
42	1st century road metallings	
	1st century timber building	
	1st century finds	Site 52/76
43	1st century pottery	
	1st century timber building	Sites 55/77 & 4/78
44	1st century pottery	Site 12/78
45	1st century pottery	Site 25/79
46	1st century floors;	
	1st/2nd century building	Site 12/80
47	1st century metalling	Site 18/80
48	1st century pottery	Site 30/80
49	1st century pits (Vicus).	Site 2/81
50	1st century timber buildings on earlier ditch.	Site 5/81
51	Buildings	Site 20/81
52	Buildings	Site 22/81
53	Finds.	Site 25/81
54	1st century pot.	Site 20/78
55	1st century pits and ditches.	Site 9/83

Late Roman (Fig. 50) (continued from Hurst 1975, p.283)

36	Inhumations	Site 4/78
37	Inhumations	Site 12/78
38	Finds	Site 25/79
39	Inhumation	Site 40/79
40	2 Inhumations	Site 3/81
41	Burials	Site 20/81
42	Burials	Site 9/83

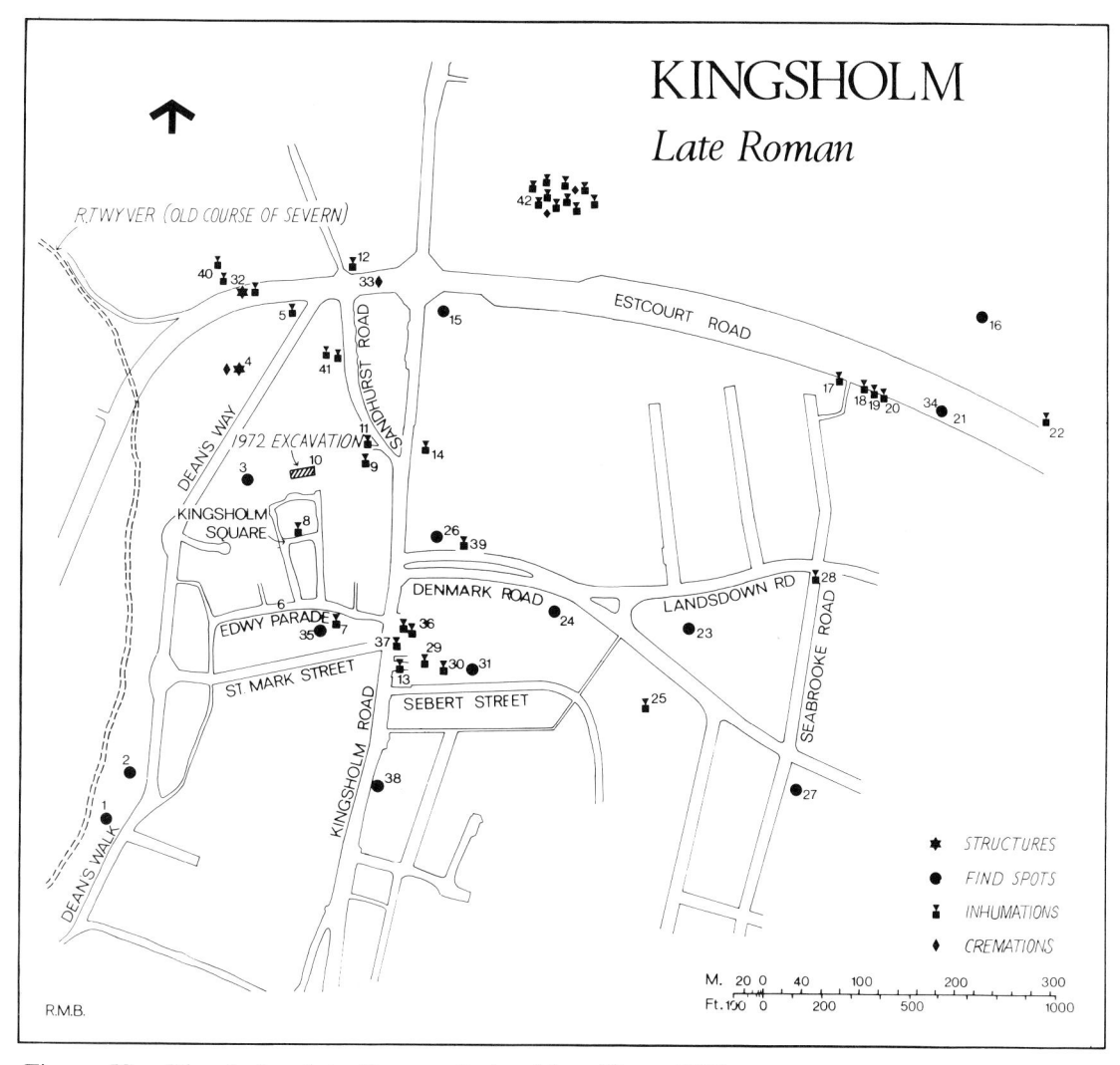

Figure 50. Kingsholm, late Roman finds. After Hurst 1975.

57/74   9-11 ST OSWALDS RD.

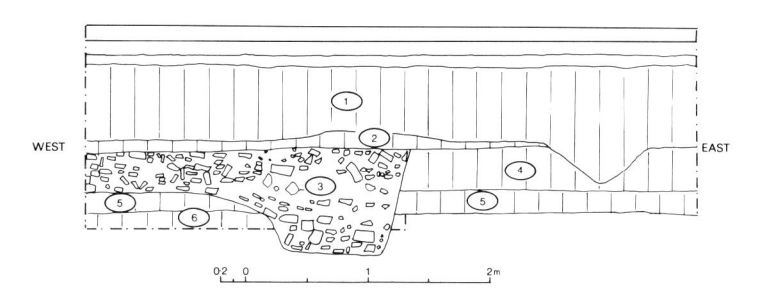

Figure 51.   Section of Roman levels in St. Oswalds Rd.

THE SITES

57/74   9–11 St. Oswald's Road (Fig. 49 No. 36 & Fig. 50 no. 32).

G.P.O. trench 15.5m. long.

A flat-bottomed feature was recorded in section; it contained small angular lias fragments and mortar lumps mixed with brown loam (layer 3). This may be a robbed wall.

Pit (7) (not on section), cutting natural sand (6) and (5), contained animal bone, unpainted wall plaster, and mid 1st century pottery including Claudian samian. (p.86, no.17).

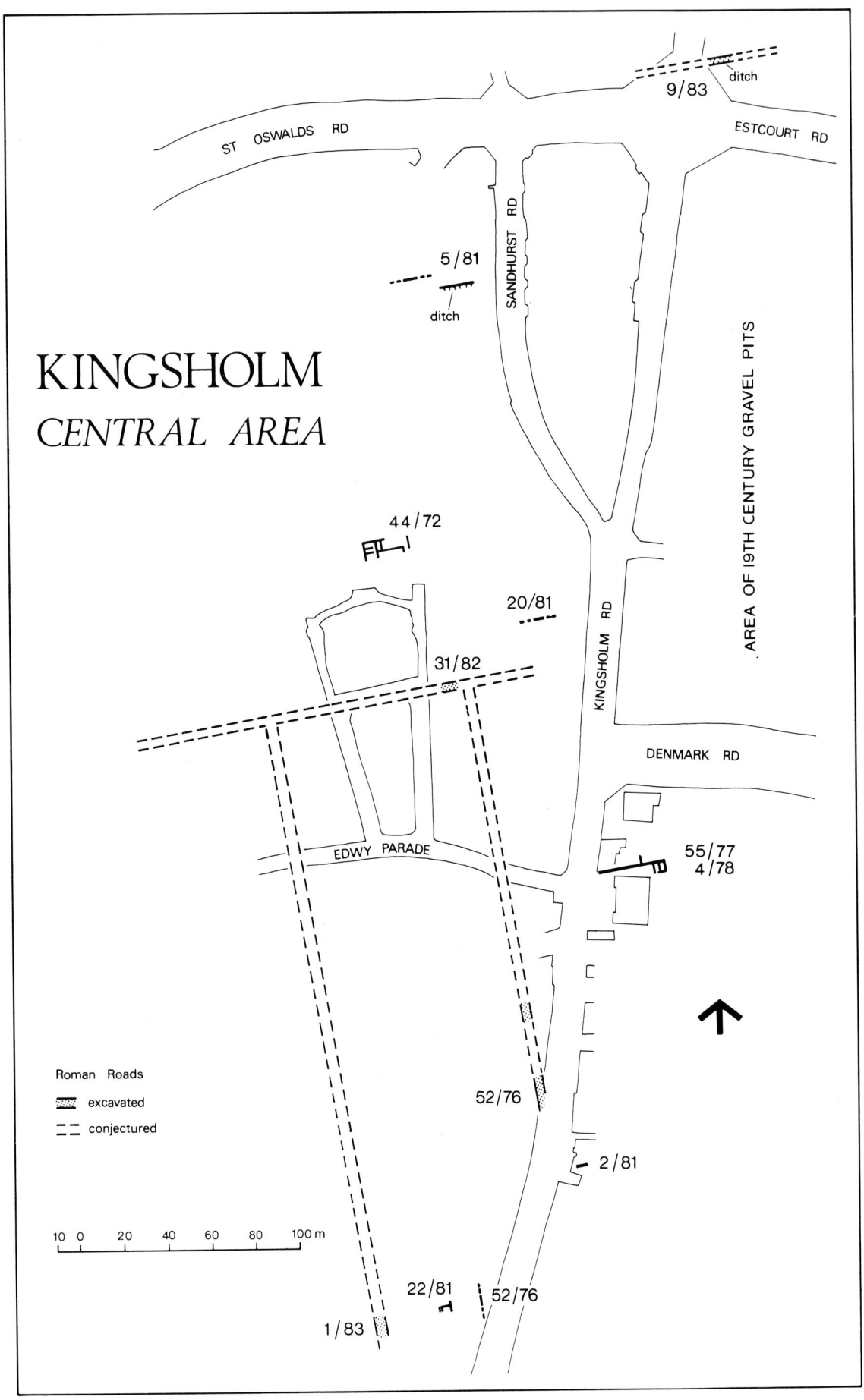

Figure 52. The central area of the Kingsholm fort or fortress: plan of 1st-century buildings and ditches. Positions of streets projected from 1982–3 evidence (not published in detail). Drawn by J. Williamson.

A human skull and bones were found on the spoil tip.

The bones were probably some of the many late Roman burials already recorded in this area of Kingsholm (Hurst 1975), and it is possible that the robbed wall represents another mausoleum, one of which was found at Kingholm (ibid., p.274).

16/75   Estcourt Road (Fig.49, no.38).

Excavation of new bus lay-byes and G.P.O. trenches.

Summary: Hurst 1975, p.279, no.38.

Trench I (outside no. 98)
Seven loam-filled features cut into natural gravel included modern service trenches, post-medieval pits F1, F5, and three pits with Roman pottery, F2 (2nd century), F3 (late 3rd to 4th century), F6 (?1st century). The pottery indicates a settlement contemporary with the fort at Kingsholm (p.77).

Trench II (outside no.85)
19th century pit.

Records: SNB 41, pp. 29–37; photos.

5/76   23 Kingsholm Road (Fig. 49, no.40)

Insertion of new main sewer.

A continuous section was recorded (by momory, since the owner refused permission to draw the section), from the rear of the property through the house and front garden into the W. carriageway of Kingsholm Road.

Under the medieval and modern black loam (4) was a layer of gravel (5) and clay (6); layer (5) contained one sherd of Roman pottery. Below this was natural clay (10).

This evidence established that the defences of the first-century fort (see Hurst 1975) are not on this line.

Records: SNB 58, pp. 59–65.

30/76   Kingsholm, Estcourt Road, W. of no. 15 (Fig. 49, no.41)

Machining of site and digging foundation trenches.

Next to 15 Estcourt Road was a pit filled with brown loam (3) containing 1st century amphorae sherds.

Notes: SNB 58, 67–9.

52/76   Kingsholm; Rugby Ground. (Fig. 49, no.42).

Construction of new wall on Kingsholm Road frontage; foundation trenches 0.8m deep. Structures described here were amplified later (22/81, 1/83) and information from these last two sites included on the plan, although no detailed report is given.

Period 1A 1–4   Successive gravel metallings were recorded 6m W. of Kingsholm Road; these may represent the Roman street leading south from the 1st century Kingsholm fort.

Period 1B   A pebble surface (1B 1, 2) bounded by a 0.4m wide wall slot represented a building of late 1st century date. Pottery indicates that the building was contemporary with the Kingsholm fort and was destroyed at about the time of the building of the Gloucester fortress. The style of construction (beam-slots rather than post-in-trench) indicates a civilian rather than a military building; presumably part of the *vicus*. The building was destroyed (1B 3) and re-occupied (1B 4).

Period 2   Mortar floors were found containing 2nd century pottery and some wall-plaster.

Period 3   Post-Roman loam accumulation.

Period 4   Two robbed stone walls were post-medieval.

Period 5   Modern.

Records: SNB 58, pp. 109–129.

55/77   76 Kingsholm Road (Fig. 49, no. 43)

Forecourt extension; machining of topsoil.

Loam 1.6m thick containing medieval and Roman pottery, covered the remains of a bunter pebble surface II (3) embedded on a make-up of redeposited sandy loam II (4) above natural.

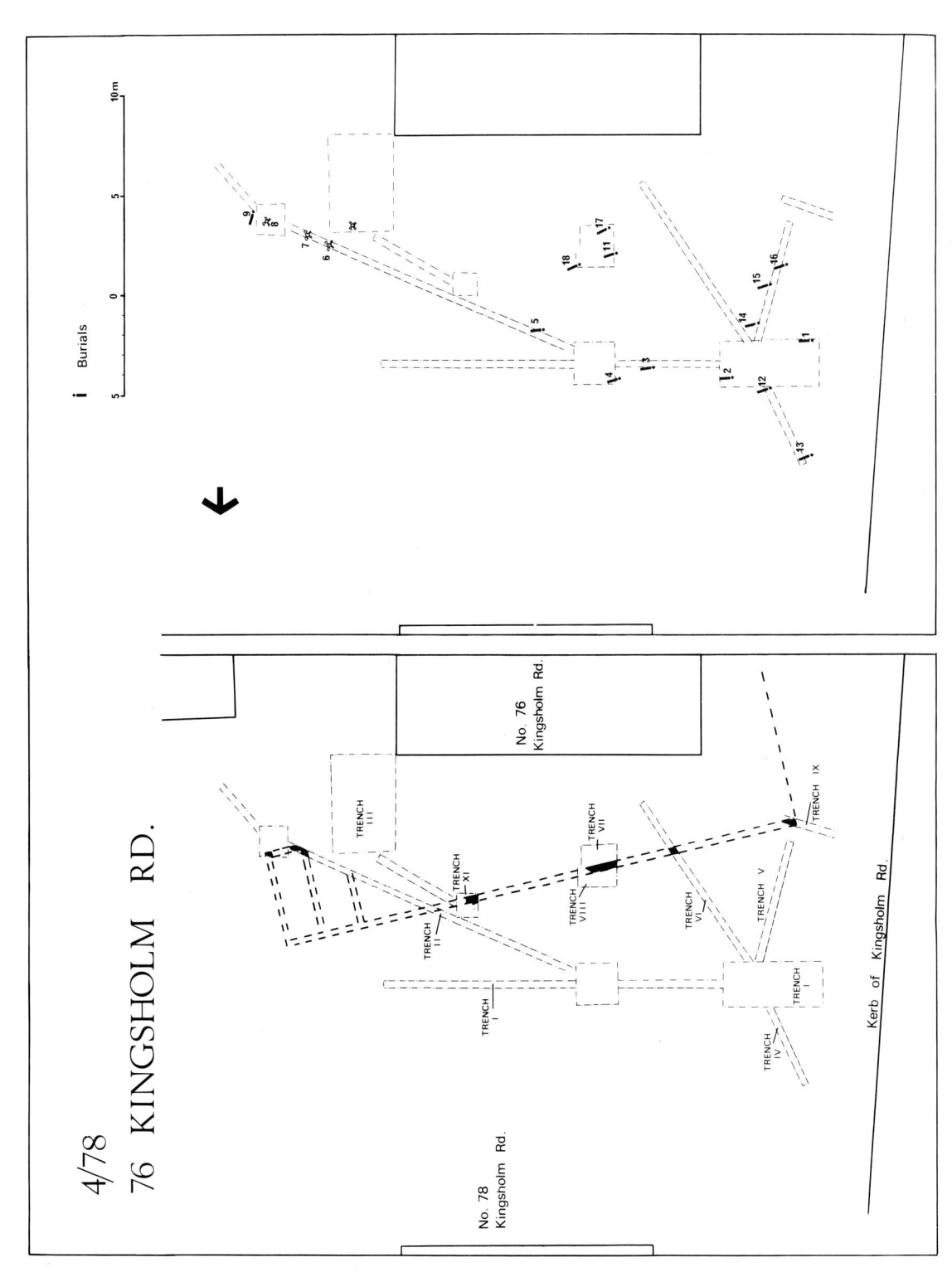

Figure 53. 76 Kingsholm Road, plans of 1st-century timber building and late-Roman burials. Drawn by L. Marley.

See 4/78 for more details.

Records: SNB 80, pp. 71–3.

4/78 76 Kingsholm Road (Fig. 49, no. 43, Fig.50, no.36)

Construction of new display and parking area.

Period 1A   Part of a 1st century Roman timber building with post-in-trench foundations, 27m long and 4.8m wide. At one end, internal partitions spaced several pockets of white painted plaster indicated replacement of vertical wall posts. Samian pottery: pre-Flavian.

Period 1B 1   The outside of the building was occupied by a metalled area resting on natural. (noted in site 55/77, q.v.)

Period 1B 2   Silt over this metalling.

Period 2   The site was later occupied by a Roman cemetery: 18 shallow inhumans of second to fourth century date were recorded. The burials were aligned with heads to the west, on the same axis as the Period 1 building. Iron nails indicate burials in wooden coffins.

Period 3   The side of the Roman and medieval street was recorded across the front of the site.

Period 4   A layer of loam c. 80cm thick represented post-Roman cultivation. This contains pottery from the 11th century onwards.

Records: SNB 89, pp.2–20; drawings.

12/78 74 Kingsholm Road (Fig. 49, no. 44, Fig. 50, no. 37)

Kitchen extension, foundation trenches.

Period 1:   A group of 1st century pottery from a pit (8), and some pottery from layers cut by the burial.

Period 2:   A shallow inhumation burial aligned N/S (layer 5).

Period 3:   Loam representing cultivation (layers 3,4).

Records: SNB 89, pp. 26–8.

20/78 'Brickland', Sandhurst Lane, land to the W.   SO 830 203 (Fig. 49, no.54)

Gas main trench.

Scatter of Roman pottery indicating settlement dating to period of Kingsholm fort (p.79).

Records: SNB 89, pp. 45–6.

25/79 34 Kingsholm Road (Fig. 49, no. 49; Fig. 50, no. 38).

Trench in back garden, 1m deep.

Finds of Roman and medieval pottery: no structural features.

Records: SNB 97, pp.32–3.

33/79 Edwy Parade, Junction with Kingsholm Road.

Service trench, 0.9m deep.

A gravel metalling 200mm thick lay above natural loam; over the metalling was dark loam settled by modern street levels.

Records: SNB 95, 50.

40/79 46–8 Denmark Road (Fig.50, no. 39)

Builders trench.

A shallow inhumation, laid prone with head to W., at a depth of 1.2m.

3/80 28 Deans Way.

17th–18th century wall.

12/80 St. Mark Street, Kingsholm (Fig. 49, no.46)

1st century floor levels, 1st/2nd century building, medieval metalling.

18/80 Edwy Parade, Kingsholm (Fig. 49, no.47)

1st century metalling; medieval pits.

30/80 99 Deans Way (Fig. 49, no.8)

Claudio-Neronian mortaria.

2/81 46 Kingsholm Road (Fig. 49, no. 49)

1st century pits contemporary with Gloucester fortress. Vicus. TBGAS 100, 263.

3/81 13 St. Oswalds Road (Fig. 50, no. 40)

Two Roman inhumations. TBGAS 100, 263.

5/81 17 Sandhurst Road. (Fig. 49, no.50)

Excavation for construction of rear extension; Trench I; also trench II cut in back garden.

Period 0   Fine estuarine silt deposit.

Period 1   A slope-sided feature, at least 3m wide and 1m deep (see Fig 54, Section A) was recorded. There was no dating evidence, but as no turf or humus layer was observed over the ditch backfill, the ditch is probably not prehistoric, and can be assumed to immediately pre-date the Roman building constructed on top of it (see Period 2). The ditch is aligned on the Kingsholm fort.

Period 2   The Period 1 ditch was sealed by spreads of clay and wall plaster, which were similar to construction spreads in Trench II. A timber building of post-in-trench construction was recorded in both trenches. Charcoal-flecked occupation layers associated with the building also sealed the Period 1 ditch. The floors of this (probably military) building were of clay, and a clay hearth was associated with them. A small rubbish pit cut a primary floor surface, and contained an amphora handle stamped -SEMPOLY, also a spear head (Fig. 65, No.31) and a rectangular bronze mount (SF 22).

Period 3   A loam deposit overlay Pd 2 occupation suggesting that the Pd 2 building was being demolished and its posts dug out. Over this was a clay destruction level, from demolition of Period 2 walls, containing a spear head (Fig.65, no.30) and pottery.

Period 4   A number of pits and postholes seem to suggest that the period 2 building was rebuilt; at least some of the building was put to industrial use.

Period 5   Destruction of Pd. 4.

Period 6   Post-Roman loam accumulation.

20/81 35 Kingsholm Road (Fig. 49, no. 51; Fig. 50, no. 41) (Fig. 52).

Prehistoric flints and pot.
Claudio/Neronian buildings.
Late Roman burials.

22/81 Kingsholm Road, Rugby Ground. (Fig. 49, no.52)

Pre-Flavian timber building;
Roman masonry building.

25/81 15 Sandhurst Road (Fig. 49, no. 53)

Pre-Flavian & Flavian pottery;
Claudian copy coin.

27/81 72 Deans Way (see Fig. 50, no. 3)

Roman building.
Coin Edward Confessor.

29/81 Kingsholm Road, Toll House.

Pit or ditch; date unknown.

30/81 Kingsholm Road, St. Oswald Road Junction.

Negative evidence.

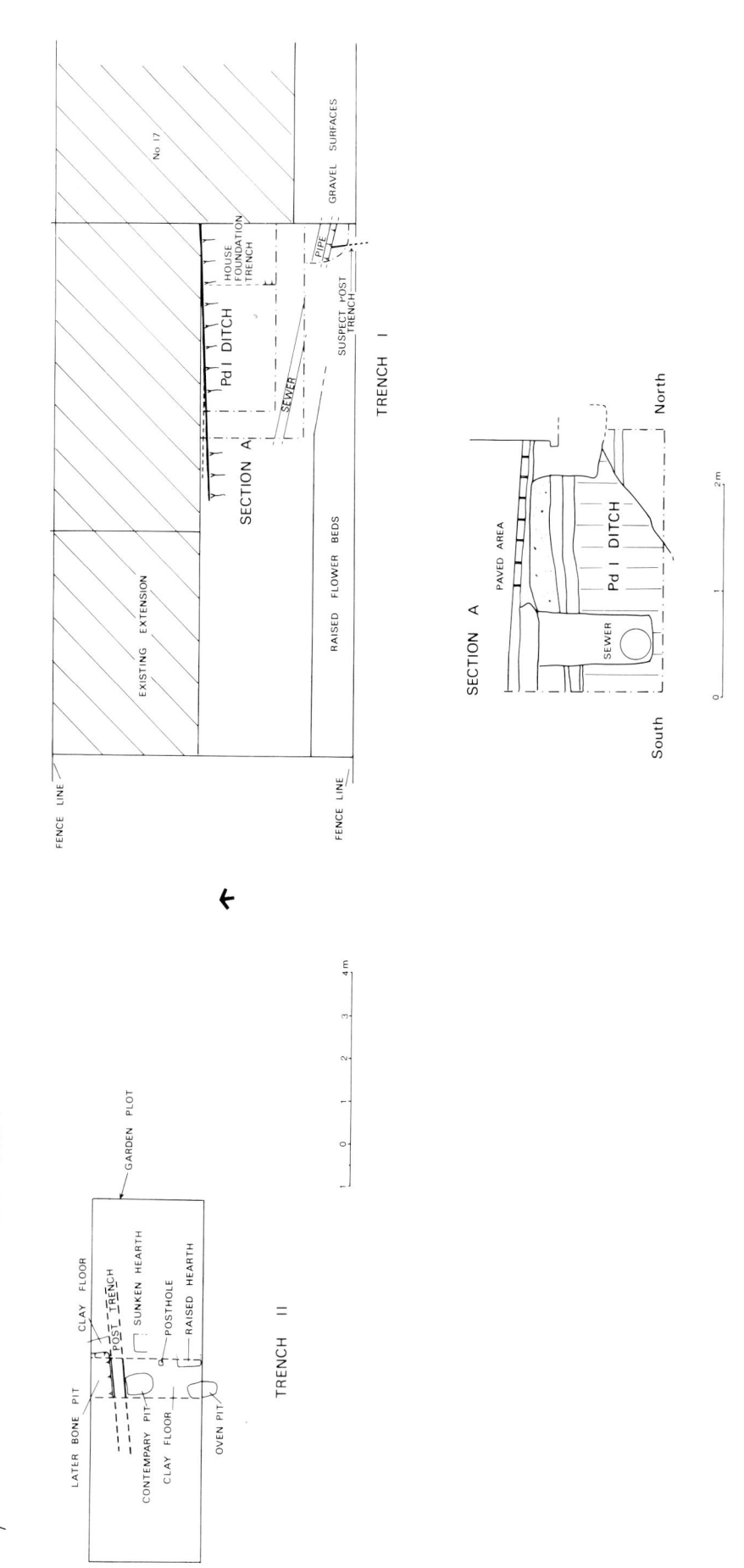

Figure 54. 17 Sandhurst Road, 1st century site. Plans and sections. For location see Figs 49 and 52. Drawn by L. Marley.

36/81 5 Denmark Road.

Negative evidence.

9/83 Gambier Parry Lodge, Tewkesbury Road. (Fig 49, no. 55; Fig. 50, no. 42)

Though outside the scope of this report, the discoveries on this site are so important it was felt they merited inclusion here. The conclusions are based on A. P. Garrod's interim report, and work still continues at the time of writing.

Prehistoric

A few Neolithic and Bronze Age flints have been made, but no prehistoric features discovered.

Roman building

Remains were found of a mid to late 1st-century building 10m long with a graded pebble floor and wall sills or wall trench. The building is located between two parallel Roman ditches 18m apart. The building was 90m E. of the Tewkesbury Road frontage. Provisional dating: mid to late 1st century.

Roman burial ground.

Concentrated at the centre of the site, extending E. from the Roman building, were 125 burials dating from the early 2nd to the 4th centuries. They respect or follow a Roman ditch. Most of the burials are inhumations, laid supine in coffins; but there are seven crouched burials and seven cremations. A few of the burials contained personal jewelry and pottery vessels. Five additional inhumations were recorded in more scattered positions. A tombstone recovered in the burial ground depicts a standing male figure dressed in a Gallic coat with possible military-style cape. The inscription reads: DIS MANIBUS. L. VALERIUS AURELIUS. VET LEG XX. The name JULIUS at the bottom of the broken stone is part of the name of the heir. (Inf. J. Wild and M. Hassall).

The orientation of the Roman building and of its ditches; also other ditches and the inhumations in the burial ground; are all similar and are parallel to or at right angles to the line of 'Ermin Street', the earliest military road to Kingsholm. (Tewkesbury Road itself has not yet been shown to have been a Roman road.) An exception to these alignments is a pit or ditch 3.5m wide at the junction of the Tewkesbury and Escourt Roads: this ditch is on the alignment of the early Roman military complex (fort or fortress) at Kingsholm (See Fig. 52). Finds include Claudio-Neronian pottery and Republican and Claudian coins.

Roman pits and gravel pits

A number of pits or ditches with excavated sand and gravel levels missing extend E from the Tewkesbury road for about 100m. These contain much Claudio-Neronian occupation refuse, including important groups of pottery.

A Celtic decorated copper alloy harness piece, and five silver quarter staters have been found on the site by users of metal detectors. These are assumed to have derived from the mid-1st-century pits.

PART 4: THE SITES BEYOND THE DISTRICT BOUNDARY

26/74 Stenders Hill, Mitcheldean (Fig. 8) SO 65921841

Part of a mortared stone vaulted structure, probably a lime kiln, was recorded.

Records: SNB 31, 8–10; photos.

27/74 Silver Street, Mitcheldean (Pl.II) SO 66481800

The exposed surface of a metalled road was photographed. The road was buried by a steep bank and hedge so is unlikely to be post-medieval. It is not the known Roman road from Ariconium to Lydney (Margery 1957, p.64), though it runs parallel to it, on more low-lying ground.

Records: SNB 31, p.11; photo

Plate Two Roman road in Mitcheldean: site 27/74.
View south from north end of Silver Street.

62/75 Field Court, Quedgeley SO 804 138

New housing estate

Field Court Farm is a moated site. The building is an early fifteenth century hall with a cross-wing of the late sixteenth century. The building is threatened with demolition and has been recorded by Patricia Borne (Museum Buildings Record; Glevensis 13, p.11). The manor is known from the 12th century (Pugh 1972, p.183). The manor house of the 12th century was presumably on the moated site; the moats had been filled by 1967 (ibid p.184).

Observations of sections cut through the moat were made. The moat was roughly rectangular and the house stands within it. A section through the W. side of the moat showed a shallow profile with a deep 'V' towards the middle. The deeper part could not be excavated, but it was less than 2m wide.

A section through the N. side of the enclosure ditch suggested a similar profile.

No dating evidence. Some unstratified Roman pottery was found (2 Severn Valley ware sherds: TF 11B).

Records: SNB 41, pp.69–71; photos; plans.

93/75 Glasshouse, Newent

Finds of pottery from 17th and 18th century kiln site. See Vince 1977 and site 84/74.

75/76 Dymock church.

Trenching all round wall for damp-proofing.

Trenching was complete when the following observations were made:-
a) A straight-joint still visible in the N. transept had earth and rubble foundation to E. stone foundations to W.
b) These earth and rubble foundations stop on the N. chancel wall where there is a door-jamb or pilaster strip.
c) A possible straight-joint was observed in the foundations between the N. Transept and nave wall.

Records: SNB 55, p.36 ff: photos.

23/77 Poulton Priory, Nr. Cirencester.

A record of the graveyard of Poulton Priory, near Cirencester, was made by Tewkesbury Archaeological Centre under the directorship of Alan Hannan. These records are now at Gloucester Museum Excavation Unit.

Records: SNB 67 (box file); photos.

24/77 Stow on the Wold church.

Trenches for dry areas.

The trench-digging was watched by Alan Hannan, who recorded by sketches and photographs several decorated stones (?12th century). These have now been moved to the interior of the church.

Records: photos; drawings.

35/77 Castle Tump, Dymock

Road works cut through part of the site of the motte and bailey castle.

Several agencies besides the Gloucester Museum watched the works here, and other records therefore exist.

Trench 1: machining of new driveway to rear of Castle Tump Cottage to new barn. No archaeological features.
Trench II: Cutting back of W. side of motte for new retaining wall. Tip lines sloping south recorded; apparently a deliberate post medieval levelling.
Trench III: the cutting back of the area to the south of the motte, perhaps the bailey. Observed by the unit only once; photograph taken. The 'bailey' seemed to consist entirely of natural red sandstone, with several large 18th and 19th century rubbish pits cut into the surface.

Records: SNB 80, pp. 24–6; photos; drawings.
Finds: Unstratified:- SF 1 iron object; SF 2 red sandstone mortar, found in garden; pottery; clay pipe stems.

50/77 Prinknash Park   SO 135 877

Scatter of handmade bricks 6 to 8cms thick observed in an area saturated with fired clay fragments and charcoal.

19/77 Bourton on the Water church

Section drawn of construction trench of Victorian wall.

Records: SNB 39, p.149.

22/78 Whaddon church

Extensive contractors' excavations in chancel due to subsidence beneath floor.

The church has a 13th century nave and chancel, but was restored in 1855, and the chancel in 1880. (Verey, 1970, p.402–3).

The excavation showed that subsidence was due to a large 18th or 19th century pit which had probably once contained one or two coffins. The chancel arch and chancel step were clearly also Victorian. The foundations of the chancel pier were cut deeply into natural soil. There was no evidence of any earlier building, although the excavation did not at any point abutt the N. or S. walls of the chancel. All medieval floors had gone, presumably when the 1880 restoration took place.

Records: SNB 84, 156–7.
Plans: Sections 1 and 3
Finds: Clay pipe stem and Victorian button from construction trench of chancel pier.

22/79 Whaddon   SO 8336 1407

Mechanical levelling of field.

Summary: Glevensis, 14, p.28.

Finds of 13th and 14th century pottery and bones: one sherd Roman pottery. The finds suggest that Whaddon Green once had buildings around its perimeter.

Records: SNB 95, pp.42–4.
Finds: pottery, Welsh slate. SF 1 I (2) flint.

PART 5 THE POTTERY

THE PREHISTORIC POTTERY by T. C. Darvill

35/74 Squires Gate, Longlevens

This small group of 19 sherds seems to derive from one vessel. No rim or base pieces are present. The sherds represent about 10 sq.cm. of pot surface. The fabric is dark brown on the exterior with a black core. Macroscopically oolite and limestone rock fragments are the main temper. The inside of the pot shows lime scale.

One sherd was thin-sectioned by S. Sofranoff (slide N216, Dept. of Archaeology, University of Southampton). Microscopic examination showed a liberal scatter of rock fragments which were up to 2.5mm across. Some of these were of limestone while other were calcite re-crystalised around oolites. There was also a scatter of angular quartz grains up to 1mm, a little white mica and some iron oxide stains. These were set in a fine-grained anisotropic groundmass of undistinguishable clay minerals. The clay was in general well mixed.

With no diagnostic feature of form it is rather difficult to put this pottery into any particular tradition. The appearance and fabric suggest a place in the late Neolithic – perhaps in the Peterborough series.

65/74 Robinswood Hill Barracks

A group of prehistoric pottery comes from F3 layer (14): in both form and fabric it resembles late Iron Age material. There are four rim sherds of which one is from a large storage jar. The other three rims are from small cooking pots. The remaining sherds were all body fragments and none display any decoration.

The fabric is generally dark, mostly brown/black and has oolite tempering. There are also many voids in the fabric. The sherds are very abraded and give the impression of being residual.

98/75 Saintbridge

A preliminary sorting on the basis of fabric and typology reveals two groups of prehistoric pottery. Within the remaining Roman and medieval pottery assemblages there remain sherds which could be prehistoric, but are best regarded as being indigenously produced wares dating to after the Roman conquest. It should also be pointed out that present knowledge of prehistoric wares in the Cotswolds and lower Severn Valley is poor; partly because of a lack of intensive study and analysis.

From macroscopic examination it is possible to distinguish two groups of Neolithic and Iron Age date. Each of these groups came from different parts of the site.

?Neolithic

The putatively Neolithic assemblage consists of about 40 sherds, comprising three types.

Of most significance is the single, unabraded decorated sherd (Fig. 53, A) recovered from phase R7. This sherd, which is about 30mm x 40mm, has a buff/light orange outer surface whilst the core and inner surface is grey/black. The fabric is liberally scattered with fossiliferous shell tempering and small black rock fragments, which are unrecognisable macroscopically, but both are up to 1.5mm ∅. There are a few voids and a scatter of sub-angular quartz sand. The decoration consists of two deeply incised lines running horizontally, with two similar lines below them set obliquely at an angle of about 60° to the lower horizontal line. A fifth line is almost vertical, but is less deeply incised and does not connect with any of the other lines. The sherd is about 7mm thick, and most probably comes from near the top of an open mouthed deep bowl. The cultural affinities of this sherd probably lie with the grooved ware, or Rinyo-Clacton, ceramic tradition of the late Neolithic (see Smith 1974, 119). Incised lines were commonly used to build up geometric motifs and bands of ornament on late neolithic vessels, and parallels for the decoration visible on this sherd can easily be found among the large collection of pottery from Durrington Walls in Wiltshire (*cf*. Wainwright and Longworth 1971, P223, P230, P231). Certainly, relatively thin walled vessels with fine fabrics are present in most grooved ware assemblages. However, it is extremely difficult to judge cultural affinities from a single bodysherd, and it must be admitted that other interpretations are possible (eg. a late Bronze Age/early Iron Age date).

Four sherds of Beaker ware. These are very fragmentary and do not display any characteristic beaker decoration. The fabric, an orange/red exterior and red/black core and interior surface is however diagnostic. The two sherds from Roman Burial 2, have a soft fabric with some voids in it, along with a little shell, very occasional limestone fragments and some iron oxide stains. The other two sherds, from Post pit 31, are smaller, c. 10mm ∅, but are very similar. It is obviously not possible to place these fragments into any of the groups defined by Clarke (1970).

An assortment of very small fragments of shell and oolite tempered wares. These display considerable variation in colour and firing conditions; but this is to be expected with earlier prehistoric pottery. The sherds in this class come from the fill of Roman Burials 1 and 2, although it seems likely that they are derived from an old land surface which has been cut by the grave slots. All the sherds were bodysherds; none were decorated. A neolithic date is most likely, but positive ascription to a particular period is not possible.
Despite the fact that these three types of putatively neolithic pottery derive from different layers (although Burial 2 contained two beaker sherds and some of the plain wares of the third group) they may all originate from a single activity complex. This would be consistent with the evidence available from other sites.

The two beaker sherds from Post Pit 31 derive from one of three Post Pits found and, although not in direct association, the possible grooved ware sherd comes from Pit 28 and Hearth 29 nearby. Despite the fact that grooved ware is frequently found associated with henge monuments, over 54% of recorded finds come from essentially domestic sites (Wainwright and Longworth 1971, 249). At a number of such sites both grooved ware and beaker wares have been found together, although whether they were used together on any particular site is open to debate.

If the identification of grooved ware pottery at Saintbridge is correct, then its presence is of some interest as the Cotswolds and lower Severn Valley have hitherto formed a void in the known distribution of this class of pottery (Darvill 1978). This is highlighted on Fig. 16 of I.F. Smith's treatment of the Neolithic (Smith 1974, 118). Recent finds have been published from The Loder's and Roughground Farm, Lechlade (Jones 1976), and to the north, the nearest occurrance of grooved ware is at Barford, Warwickshire (Oswald 1969).

The collection of flints recovered from Saintbridge (see below p.93) serves to reinforce the possibility that an earlier prehistoric settlement existed on the site. The available evidence suggests a small occupation site dating to the early second millennium b.c. Its location on a well drained terrace would be appropriate, and further investigation is desirable.

Iron Age

From layer (40) (Medieval plough soil) comes a group of sherds, of the same fabric and probably from the same pot, which seems to be of middle iron age date. The fabric has a hard black outer surface with a dark red-brown core. It is heavily tempered with quartzite, up to 2mm ∅. The rim of the vessel has slight interior bevelling and there is one lug/handle also from the vessel. This is well made with a tapered hole in it, possibly for passing a string through for suspension or to secure a perishable lid. More could perhaps be said if the vessel could be restored, if that is possible. There are two similar lugged vessels from Period 1 – iron age B – at Salmonsbury, Bourton-on-the-Water, Glos., although the rims are different (Dunning 1976, nos. 8 and 9 on Fig.13 p.383) and Dunning states, "This form of handle appears characteristic of western second B pottery on the Cotswolds", (1976, 95), although he cites no further examples.

ROMAN AND MEDIEVAL POTTERY by C. Ireland

The Roman Pottery

Very few of the Watching Brief sites did not produce any Roman pottery at all. It is very common on sites in the city and its urban environs to find quantities of Roman residual material in later contexts. Sites within the city itself on which this is absent may possibly be of some interest as negative evidence for Roman occupation. In most instances the residual pottery occurred as common types, predominantly Severn Valley wares and Black Burnished ware. It is not proposed to discuss this in any detail, and any material of this kind is noted in the pottery summaries (microfiche I). The most useful aspect of the residual pottery occurs when particularly early or late types are represented which, when plotted onto distribution maps, contribute to the general pattern of settlement areas at any given period. Several sites produced stratified material which is of relevance to the study of ceramic trends in the locality of Roman Gloucester. These are dealt with in a chronological sequence below.

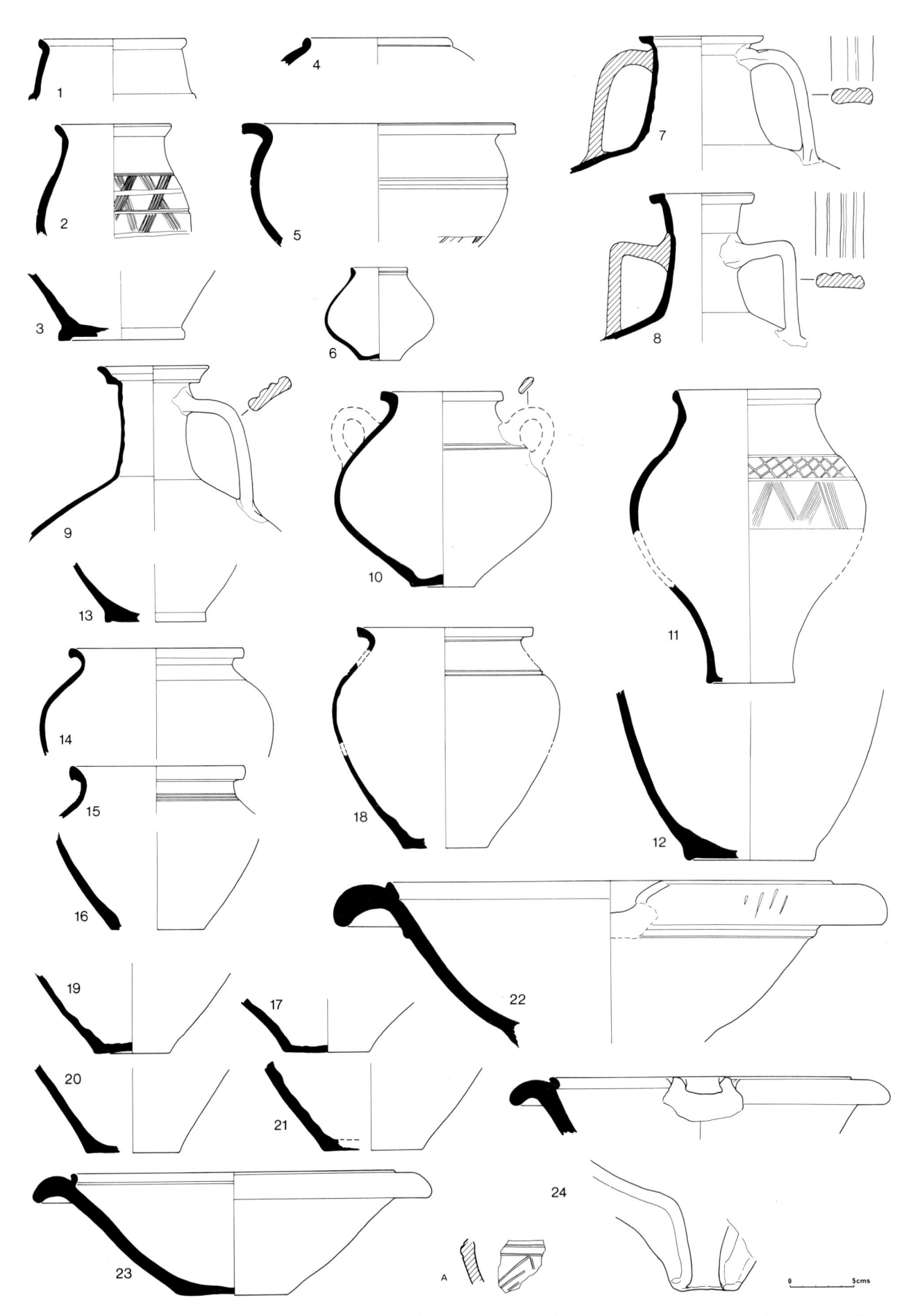

Figure 55. Prehistoric and Roman pottery, drawn by L. Marley. Nos 1–25 are stratified in the earliest (1st-century) phase of various sites at Kingsholm. For full catalogue, see Microfiche II. Type Fabrics: nos 1 and 2, TF 11D. No. 3, TF 20. No 4, TF 17. No 5, TF 39. No 6, TF 36?. Nos 7–10, TF 24. Nos 11–13, FT 11D. Nos 14–17, TF 39. Nos 18–21, TF 213. Nos 22–24, TF 9S. No 25, TF 17. A: Neolithic grooved ware from Saintbridge, site 98/75. For a brief index of Type Fabrics, see p.87–88.

Early Roman: Kingsholm

The main excavations at Kingsholm are to be the subject of a forthcoming report by Henry Hurst and the pottery will be reported on by M. J. Darling. A brief summary and discussion of the pottery types and their relationship with other sites in the west has already been published (Darling 1977).

Five Watching Brief sites produced stratified early Roman material: 57/74; 30/76; 52/76; 4/78; 12/78. Two of these sites produced evidence of timber buildings with associated pottery from occupation and destruction; three sites produced pits containing discarded material similar to those noted in Hurst 1975, indicating the abandonment of the fort. The pottery from either type of feature is not essentially different and the most representative group comes from the pit on site 12/78 which contained 23 separate vessels (Fig.55).

Considered as a whole, the stratified groups give some indication of the proportions of fabric types current during this period. It should be pointed out, however, that, unlike pits examined on the other major sites in Kingsholm, these groups do not contain any early fine wares, although odd sherds did occur on the sites in other contexts: About 50% of the vessels represented were in the typical 'local' fabric and its variant (TF 24; TF 36) which produced flagons and honey jars predominantly, and a gritty jar fabric (TF 213) which produced distinctive cooking jars. The flagon fabric is also known at Usk and Cirencester (Darling 1977, 62), and a few sherds have been noted at Dodder Hill, near Droitwich (Helen Rees pers. comm.) which would seem to imply a fairly wide distribution. At least 5 mortaria were recovered in this fabric from the pit on site 12/78.

Severn Valley wares were present and accounted for about 9% of the total. The vessel types include storage jars, wide mouth jars, a butt-beaker and a carinated cup sherd. The fabric types are an early variant which had a vesicular appearance (TF 11D) and a charcoal tempered variant (TF 17). This industry appears to have been supplying vessel types not produced in the repertoire of the local industry. A hard grey gritty ware (TF 39), however, was also producing cooking jars and accounts for about 18% of the assemblage. Other coarse wares were supplied by 'native' type industries (TF's 2 and 21) which never seem to have occupied a very important part of the market. The only fine wares to be represented in these groups are Samian ware (11%) and a single sherd of an imported flagon (TF 211) which is otherwise a common component of assemblages at Kingsholm and Cirencester, although in small quantities. (Rigby 1982, fabric 21).

Site/Phase	Flagons 24	211	Butt beaker 11D	Carinated cup 11D	Beaker 36?	Fine cups and bowls 8	Honey jar 24	Amphora 10	Storage jar 11D	17	Cooking jars 11D	213	39	4?	Bowls 39	Native jars 2	21	Mortaria 9S
52/76 1B	6	1				5		2		1	1		8			1		
4/78 1A	6			1		2								1	1		1	
37/74 PIT	14					1					1					1		
30/76 PIT								2										
12/78 PIT	2v		1		1	1	1		2			5	5					5
	28	1	1	1	1	9	1	4	2	1	2	5	13	1	1	2	1 1	

TABLE 1. Watching Brief Sites. Stratified Groups: Kingsholm

The pottery from two sites within Kingsholm Rugby Ground has been examined (52/76 & 22/81). The evidence from the 1981 site, which is not covered in the site reports on the watching briefs (1974–1979) is included in this discussion since it serves to amplify the evidence from the 1976 site. A large timber building, or perhaps two timber buildings, back to back, was represented by a series of timber sill slots. A single slot was noted in the 1976 site, but the 1982 site revealed considerably more of the same building. The earliest

Figure 56. Minor sites: early Roman pottery. Drawn by L. Marley. No. 25, site 65/74, F3, TF 17. No 26, site 65/74, F3, TF 11D. No 27, site 98/75, R2, TF 4. Nos 28–39, 98/75, R2, TF 11D. Nos 40–42, 98/75, R2, TF 23. No 43, 98/75, R2, TF 20. No 44, 33/76, XI, TF 2. No. 45–6, 33/76, XI, TF 11D. No 47, 33/76, XI, TF 17. No 48, 33/76, XI, TF 201. No. 49, 33/76, XII, TF 17 (butt beaker). No 50, 33/76, XII, TF 20 (stopper). No 51, 33/76, XII, TF 11D? (bowl). No 52, 33/76, XIII, TF 11A (bowl). No 53, 33/76, XIII, TF 19C (jar).

pottery was recovered from what is probably a destruction horizon (1B 3). This phase included pottery types which are characteristic of material from the Kingsholm fort, comprising sherds of Kingsholm type flagons TF 24, gritty jars TF 213, early Severn Valley ware variants TF 11D and pre-Flavian to Neronian or early Flavian Samian. The Samian suggests that the destruction of the buildings was contemporary with or later than the construction of the Gloucester fortress. A pit which cut into the building levels (22/81) contained a high proportion of Gloucester products, including white slipped flagons, grey ware jars, as well as Kingsholm-type gritty jars and early Severn Valley wares. Similar proportions of fabrics were recovered from the occupation and destruction of timber buildings of the Gloucester fortress (Hurst 1972 period 1b). An indeterminate feature, probably earlier than the pit, contained a single Gloucester type jar sherd, an imitation TN platter similar to examples from Usk (Green 1979, 106f), a Kingsholm type flagon base and a rare example of a lamp in Lyon ware (Wheeler 1930, Type I). The latest Roman horizon is represented on the 1976 site by a loam layer (3) period 1B 4 containing Trajanic Samian and a mixture of Gloucester and Kingsholm type products.

At present very little is known of the ceramic sequence in this area following the disuse of the Kingsholm fort. The evidence of pottery described above suggests that there was some overlap between certain 'Kingsholm' products and wares probably produced specifically for the Gloucester fortress, and later the *colonia*. This pattern is repeated in Period 1b levels in the Gloucester fortress. Previously it was considered that the Kingsholm-type products were all residual, but it is possible that this is not the case.

Early Roman: Robinswood Hill Barracks (65/74), ditch F3.

This is a small group of pottery from the fill of ditch F3 (see Fig.56). Despite the small quantity, the group is of interest because of the characteristically early fabrics and vessel types present. The carinated vessel in an early Severn Valley ware variant (TF 11D), the handmade storage jar in Charcoal tempered ware (TF 17), and the native jar base (TF 34) can all be paralleled amongst the assemblages at Kingsholm (Darling 1977, Fig. 6.9, 28) and in period 1a (Hurst 1972) at the legionary fortress (op.cit, Fig. 6.10, 2 and 18). There is comparable material at Usk (Greene 1973) and Cirencester (Rigby 1982) and a possible 'native' settlement at Beckford (H. Rees pers. comm.).

Early Roman: The Heron Estate housing development (98/75), period R2.

This group is of interest because of the large quantity of vessels (see Fig.56), some of which were almost complete and gave the appearance of having been smashed in situ; they were all from a single deposit. The excavator comments that only a sample of the material visible in the deposit could be removed in the available time. Over 70% of the vessels were of Severn Valley types. 54% comprised vessels in the early vesicular variant (TF 11D), including at least 6 tankards similar to Webster's (1976) type 38, with straight sides, grooved rim and lattice decoration applied between grooves applied at the top and base of the handles. Webster attributes these vessels to the mid to late 1st century (op cit, 30), and the wide-mouth jars from the group would also fit in with this, as similar jars are known from period 1a at the legionary fortress (Darling 1977, fig.6.10, 7–8). The remaining Severn Valley wares are coarse storage jars (TF's 17 and 23) and include a large portion of a base which has had a hole cut through the middle (no.40).

Large fragments of an oven dome in a coarse variant of the grog-tempered fabric (TF 2) used for small 'native' jars and larger storage jars at Kingsholm and in the military levels of the legionary fortress were found in association with the group. The domestic nature of the deposit probably accounts for the small quantity of finer wares; a single Samian vessel and two flagon sherds, one of which is non local, the other probably Kingsholm local fabric.

On the present evidence from excavations in the legionary fortress, the presence of 2 BB1 jars (Gillam 1976, type 1) would indicate an early 2nd century date for the group. However, comparable early BB1 has been noted at Usk (Darling 1977, 62) and Exeter (Bidwell 1977) in 1st century contexts. It may be possible, therefore that this group could be contemporary with the period 1 legionary fortress, rather than the early colonia.

Early Roman: sites in the Kingsholm area.

Two sites are of particular interest, as they give some indication of the distribution of occupied areas possibly contemporary with the fort at Kingsholm. 98, Estcourt Road (16/75; Hurst 1975, 279, no.38) produced a pit containing a grog-tempered native jar and a sandy grey ware sherd in a fabric which is found at Kingsholm and in the military levels of the legionary fortress. A second site in Sandhurst Lane (20/78) produced a scatter of 1st century pottery.

The pit in Estcourt Road forms part of a group of find spots in this area, which is over 500 metres from the central area of Kingsholm where the 1972 excavation took place. The group includes a 1st century well

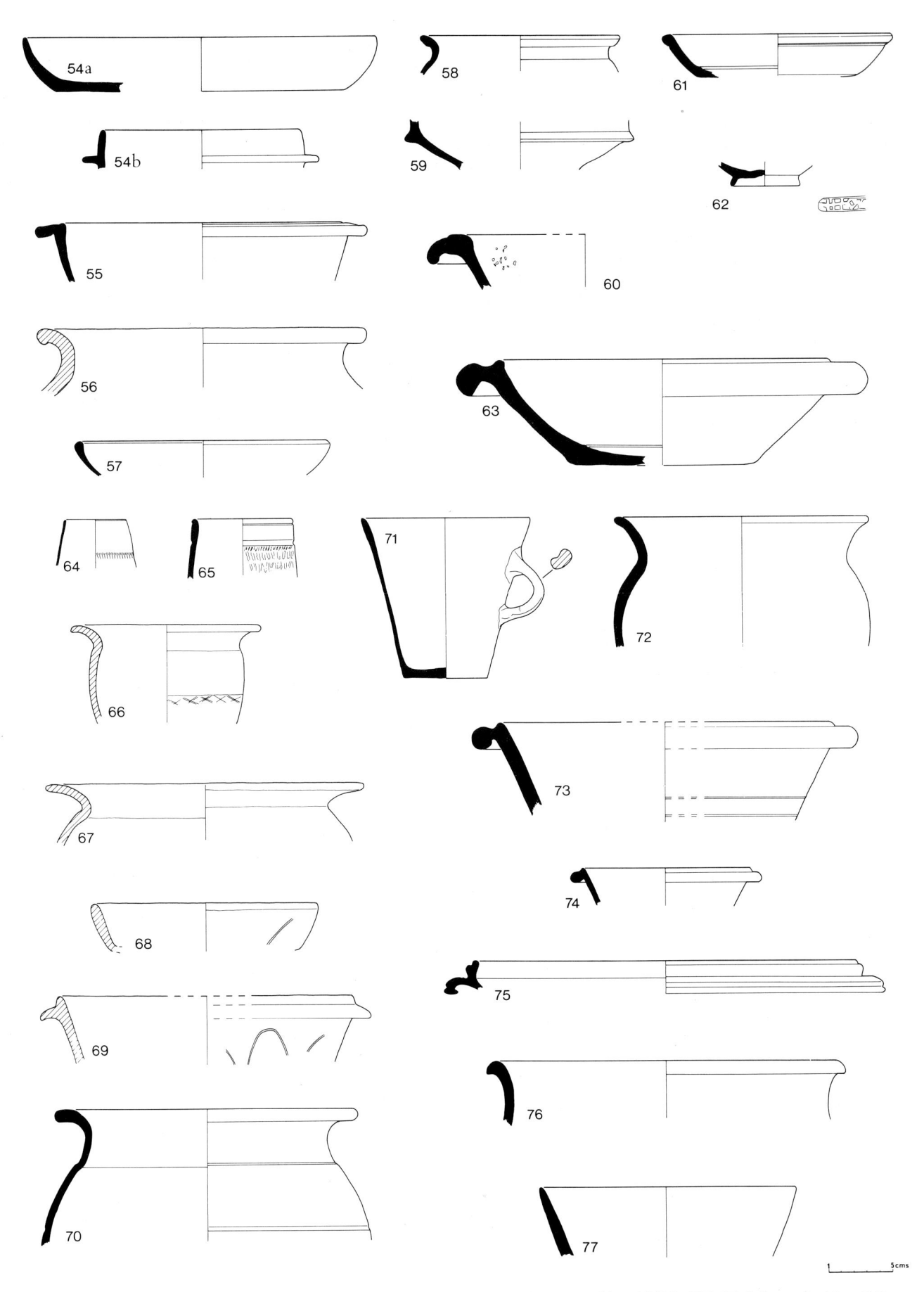

Figure 57. Minor sites, Roman pottery, drawn by L. Marley. No 54a, 80/76, TF 35 (platter). No. 54b, 80/76, TF 35. No 55, 12/79, Pd. 1C, TF 11A. No 56, 12/79, Pd 1C, TF 17. No 57, 12/79, Pd 1C, TF 202. No 58, 14/79, Pd 1, TF 11A. No 59, 14/79, Pd 1, TF 3. No 60, 14/79, Pd 1, TF 9. No 61, 14/79, Pd 1, TF 12E. No 62, 38/74, Pd 2, TF 20. No 63, 38/74, Pd 2, TF 9C. No.64, 65/74, F1, TF 12B. No 65, 65/74, F1, TF 20. No. 66/9, 98/75, R6, TF 4. No 70, 98/75, R6, TF 5. No 71, 98/75, R6, TF 11B. No 72, 98/75, R6, TF 19A. No 73, 98/75, R7, TF 5. No 74, 28/76, R 2/2, TF 5. No 75, 28/76, R 2/2, TF 9A. No 76/7, 28/76, R 2/2, TF 11B.

(Green 1948), and a Claudian coin (Hurst 1975, 279). The relationship with the Kingsholm site is unclear, and the area does not lie on a known Roman road. The existence of a 'native' settlement close to the military site at Kingsholm was set forward by Green (op cit).

To the north of Kingsholm along Sandhurst Lane occupation can be deduced from spreads of pottery (20/78; 36/78, see Glevensis 14, 30) which includes early Severn Valley wares and Kingsholm wares, unlike the sites in the Estcourt Road area, which produced few 'military' looking vessels.

Early Roman: The Vicus.

A number of sites produced evidence for occupation from the late 1st century in the area to the north and north-west of the legionary fortress, presumably indicating the presence of a substantial vicus. These include the sites revealed along the Northgate St. to London Road sewerage scheme (33/76), in particular trenches XI, XII and XIII, located at the junction of Northgate St. and Worcester St. These 3 trenches can be considered together, since they produced finds from an early occupation deposit visible in all 3 areas, representing occupation on the site of the road which is now Worcester St. in the late 1st century. Contemporaneity with occupation within the legionary fortress is perhaps indicated by the presence of Gloucester products, which are normally present in contexts associated with the destruction of legionary buildings (Hurst 1972, period 1b; Heighway et al 1983 period 1). On a sherd count basis these are slightly less in quantity here than early Severn Valley wares which is the reverse of the proportion in period 1b. However, there are few occupation deposits from within the fortress with which to compare contemporary occupation outside in the vicus (Garrod pers. comm.). In the fills of pre-fortress ditches (Hurst 1972 period 1a), thought to have been filled during the construction of the fortress, there are no Gloucester products, but a large quantity of early Severn Valley wares and Kingsholm products (Darling 1977, fig.6.10). It is as yet unknown exactly when the production of pottery for the fortress at Gloucester began.

An interesting vessel from trench XIII represents a Lower Rhineland-type form in a 'local' fabric (TF19c) tempered with metamorphic rock fragments (Fig. 56 no.53). Alan Vince comments that this probably indicates a source in the Malvern Region. Significantly, the only products from this region of this date which have been recognised by Peacock in his paper (1967) are 'native' type jars. Other vessels in this fabric (which differs in firing and manufacture to the latter) have been recognised in Gloucester. A second jar sherd came from 33/76 trench XII, and a base sherd from Hare Lane (34/79). Reeded rim bowls with sloping flanges have been noted at the Cross site (Hunter 1981, Fig 5, 11, period 2) and St. Oswalds Priory (41/75, unpubl). Mortaria with Flavian rim forms have been noted at the North Gate site (1/74 unpubl), and New Market Hall (Hassall and Rhodes 1974, Fig 23, M22, unstrat). Shouldered jars have been noted at the East Gate site (Heighway et al 1983 no.286) and St. Oswald's priory (41/75 unpubl. unstrat.). Further work is required to understand the distribution of this small, probably Flavian, industry.

Further to the west, 3 sites produced material indicative of late 1st or early 2nd century occupation: Catherine St. (12/79); Pitt St. (14/79) and Hare Lane (34/79) Catherine St. produced a ditch-like feature (period 1C) which contained material of late 1st century date, including Gloucester products, early Severn valley wares and a TN platter of form 31 (Rigby 1973). TN is rare in Gloucester, and it is perhaps interesting that this particular example does not come from either of the two military occupied areas in Gloucester (Fig.57 no.57). This feature was sealed by loam levels containing Dorset BB1, probably indicating an early 2nd century date.

Pitt St. produced a group of pottery (Fig. 57 nos.58 to 61) which represents a range of products produced in Gloucester, and similar to types found at the College of Art kiln site (Rawes 1972), with the exception of the red-slipped bowl (TF 12E, no.61). To date most of the red slipped vessels have occurred as residual material, making their dating a matter of hypothesis (Heighway et al 1983). An early 2nd century date has been suggested, but an earlier date may be possible. The contexts from which the Pitt St. vessels were recovered appear to be redeposited loams and may not represent deposits in situ (Garrod pers. comm). The original location and the date at which they were redeposited remains unclear.

The Hare Lane site produced material which can be dated between the late 1st and 3rd centuries, including Gloucester products, some Kingsholm products, and an early Malvernian jar base (TF 19C: cf.33/76).

To the north of the city's defences two sites produced ceramic evidence for the 1st–3rd centuries. At the Norris's garage site (77/74) only one 2nd century BB1 vessel was stratified, but the residual material suggests that the site was used between the late 1st and late Roman periods. The Prince Albert site (38/78) produced little material, and that mainly of 3rd century date.

Late Roman

Comparatively few sites produced stratified ceramic evidence of the late Roman period. Fabrics which tend

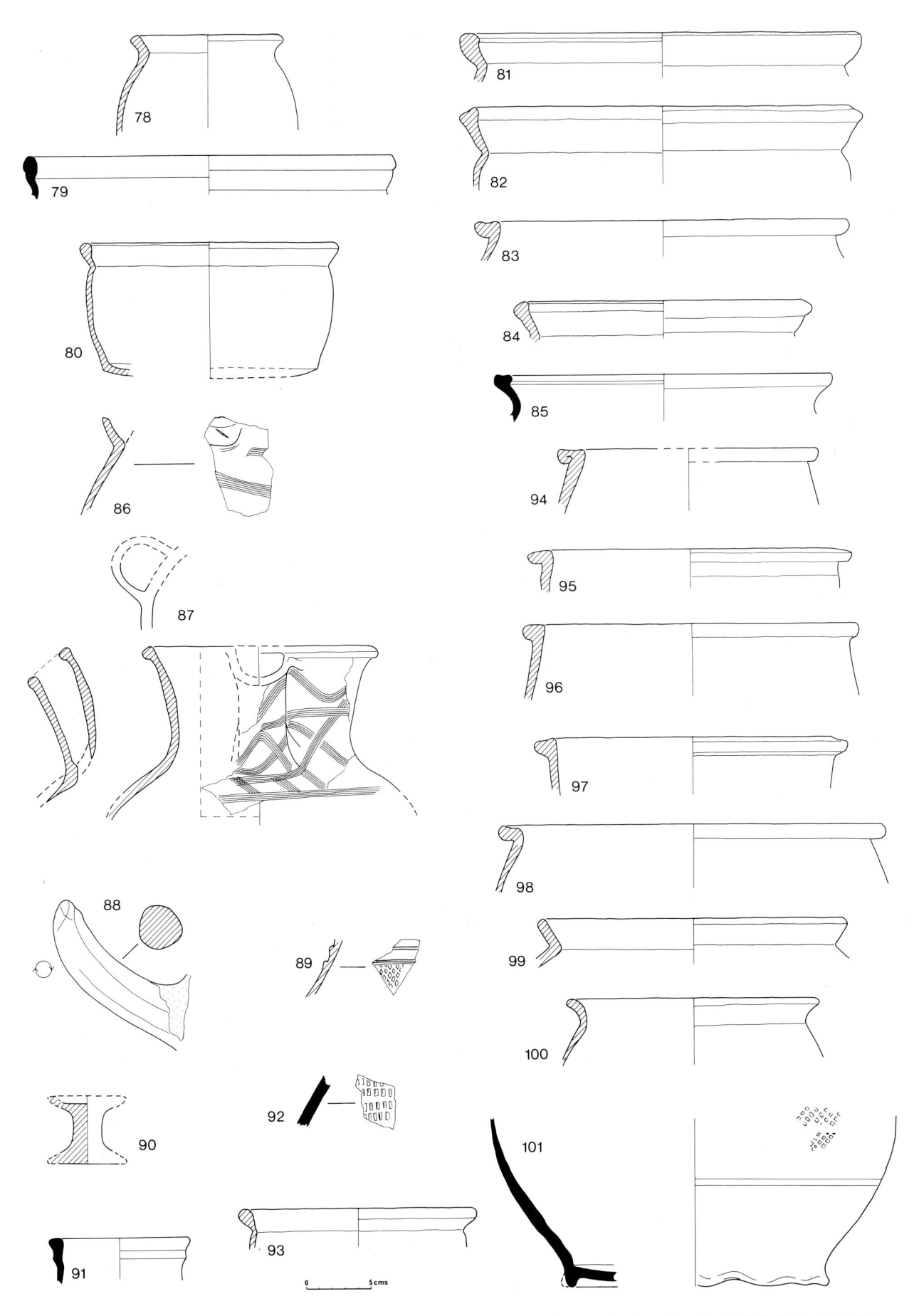

Figure 58. Minor sites, late Saxon and medieval pottery. Drawn by L. Marley. No 78, 25/76, Pd 1, TF 41A. Nos 79–82, 59/74, Pd 3, TF 40. Nos 83–5, 59/74 Pd. 3, TF 41B. Nos 86–7, 59/74, Pd 3, TF 44. No 88, 59/74, Pd 3, TF 52 (skillet?). No 89, 59/74, Pd 3, TF 53 (jug). No 90, 59/74, Pd 3, TF 83 (lamp). No 91–3, 59/74, Pd 3, TF 90. No 94–5, 19/79, Streets 3–4, TF 41B. Nos 96–8, 19/79, Street 5, TF 41B. No 99, 19/79, Street 7–8, TF 41B. No 100, 19/79, Street 8–9, TF 90. No 101, 19/79, Street 12–13, TF 90.

to be characteristic of the late period in Gloucester from the 3rd century onwards, particularly TF's 5 and 22 and later colour-coated wares, were poorly represented, even as residual material from within the city walls. The only sites which produced stratified evidence were:30, Westgate St. (57/77; 35/78; Heighway and Garrod 1980) where from periods 4 and 5 fabric types indicative of a date between the late 3rd and late 4th century or later were present, and Berkeley St. (19/79) where a group of late fabrics indicative of mid to late 4th century date were included in the fill of the late Roman city ditch. Other sites were located outside the city defences and probably represent rural settlements.

Just outside the northern defences 2 sites in Market Parade (77/74; 37/74) produced late fabric types as residual material (including late Roman shell-tempered ware, TF 22) indicative of late 3rd to late 4th century occupation. To the north of the city in Estcourt Rd. (16/75), a pit containing late 3rd century material may be associated with the late Roman burials in this area (Hurst 1975, 283,34). The remaining sites to the south of the city appear to represent rural settlements, but with identical sources for the majority of the pottery.

On the Robinswood Hill Barracks site (65/74) there were a number of ditch features which were apparently filled over a period of time, the latest date from the pottery being the late 3rd century for the latest ditch F1. The absence of any later types would imply that the area possibly ceased to be occupied by the early 4th century. Further to the east, the extensive site on the Heron Estate development (98/75; 45/74) produced evidence for occupation between the mid to late 3rd century and the late 4th. The area of metalling R5 and a single burial (RB2) could be dated to the late 3rd century. The fills of the ditch features and the pits, however, would appear to be the latest features on the site and contained fabrics characteristically of mid to late 4th century date. To the south west of the city, near Quedgeley (28/76), evidence for some form of late Roman occupation and industrial activity was recovered. The pottery from the 1st phase Roman features (excluding loam layer (4) and Ditch 3) contained pottery of late 3rd to 4th century date, with no diagnostically very late 4th century material. The loam layer and the Ditch 3, however produced late 3rd to 4th century material (in addition to 4 sherds of possible late Saxon material; see below).

The Saxon Period

Ceramic evidence for this period is rare, particularly for the immediate post-Roman period, and is uncommon even from the 10th century, when a local industry was producing limestone tempered wares. None of the Watching Brief sites produced evidence for the early or middle Saxon period. However, a single site near Quedgeley (28/76) produced several sherds of pottery which may correspond to wares in late Saxon levels at 1, Westgate Street (Heighway, Garrod and Vince 1979, 165–7). These were recovered from contexts post-dating the late Roman occupation (see above p.32) and indicate rather friable sherds of TF's?41A, 47 and 45, which probably give a date somewhere between the 9th and 10th century. Evidence for occupation within the city between the late 10th and mid 11th centuries is provided by finds of Gloucester Late Saxon Ware (TF 41A). A few of these were finds of residual pottery, for example in period 8 at the 30 Westgate St. site (57/77), but fortunately the majority were in primary contexts and are, therefore, useful for dating. two sites in Berkeley Street (25/76; 19/79) produced sherds of this pottery which has proved useful in establishing the topography of the city in this area during this period. A rim (Fig.58 no.78) similar to vessels from the 'waster' pit on the 1, Westgate St. site came from the lower fill of the city ditch (25/76) and a similar rim was recovered from the silt levels between streets 3 and 2 (19/79). Similarly at the King Edward's gate site (12/77) on the opposite side of Westgate St. from the above sites, the earliest street surface (Street 1) contained 4 late Saxon sherds.

The Medieval Pottery

The increase in the supply of pottery to the city in the second half of the 11th century can be demonstrated by the appearance of Gloucester Early Medieval ware (TF 41B). This is the most common type of pottery until the early 12th century when the range of fabrics and vessel types widens significantly (see Vince in Heighway et al 1983; Vince 1981). Small quantities of other wares are present during the late 11th century, such as Sand and Limestone tempered ware (TF 43), and rarely a glazed vessel (TF 51). When these types are plotted onto distribution maps (Figs.4 and 5), an increased use of pottery is perhaps demonstrated rather than any significant widening of trade or occupation areas. From the evidence of street sections it would appear that Gloucester Early Medieval ware is still present by the early 13th century, but this may be residual material, and evidence from larger sites suggests that it had ceased production sometime in the mid 12th.

A number of pottery types are characteristic of the 12th century. Types which appear by the early 12th are Malvernian cooking pots (TF 40); and other cooking pot fabrics TF's 44, 48, and 91; tripod pitchers: TF's 44, and 52. These can be divided typologically into early and late types and are therefore useful for dating a number of contexts. These include the construction and abandonment of the celler at 30, Westgate St. (57/77), which contained early 12th century types; the occupation levels which overly the street metallings in Westgate St. (35/78), the loam levels below Clare St. metalling (59/74) and, the construction of the Foreign Bridge (29/76).

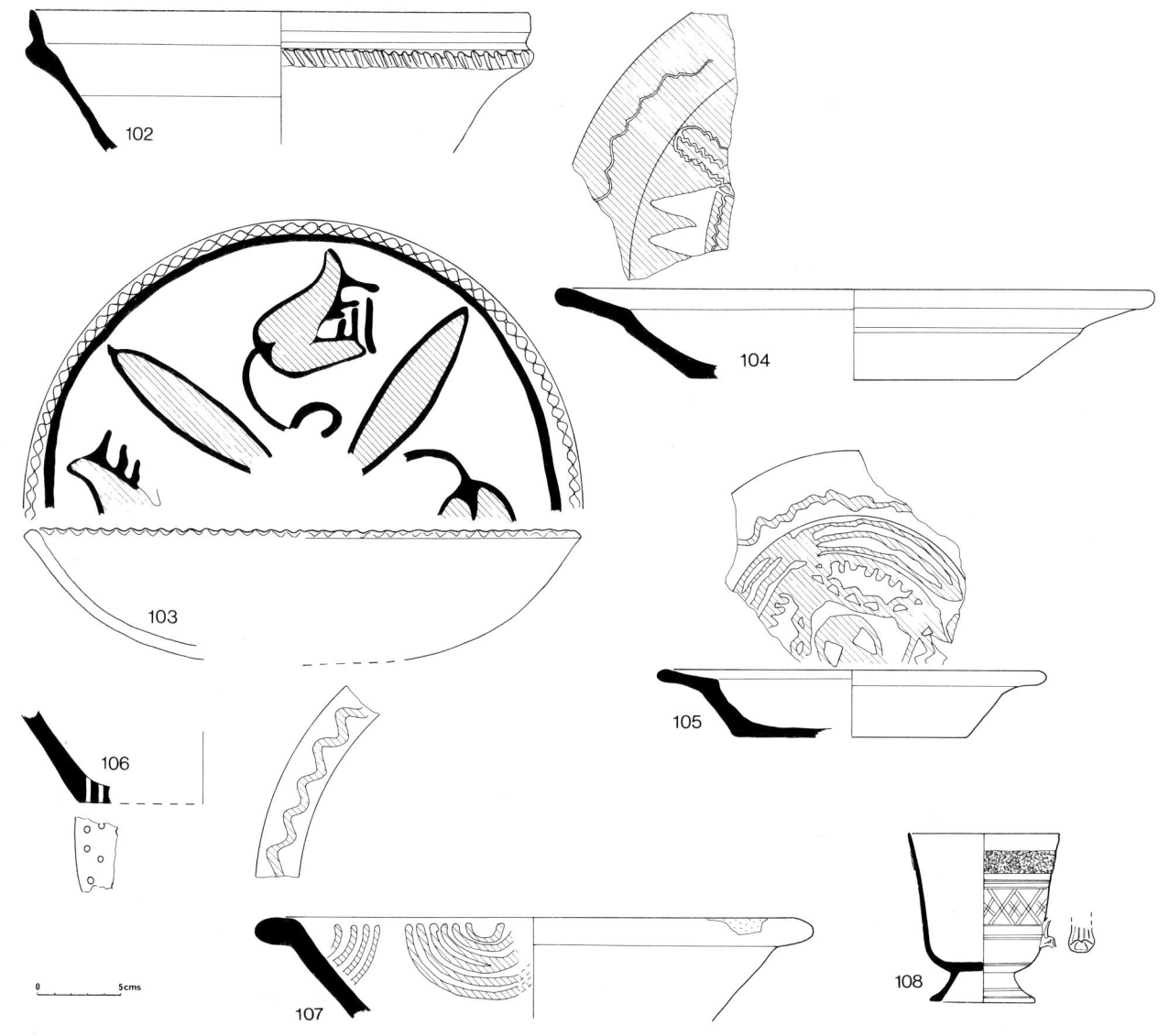

Figure 59. Minor sites, post-medieval pottery. Drawn by L. Marley. No 102, 58/74, TF 52. No 103, 78/75, TF 72. No 104/7, 12/79, Pd 4, TF 54 (Newent Glasshouse wares; plate, dish, collander, and bowl). No 108, 35/78, Pd 10, TF 121 (cup). No. 109: see p.88.

The early to mid 13th century is ceramically characterised by the appearance of glazed jugs in TF's 53 and 90. Some late tripod pitchers are also present and some of the cooking pot fabrics continue into the 13th century. The metalling of Clare St. (59/74) produced an interesting group of pottery dated to this period, (Period 3) including a sherd from a Shrewsbury type pitcher (TF 108), which is uncommon in Gloucester, and an Oxford/Brill type lamp (TF 83; Fig.58, no.90), which is apparently present rather earlier than jugs in the same fabric. A similar lamp was present in an early to mid 13th century context at the Hamel, Oxford (Mellor 1980, Fig.11, 1). The later metallings of Berkeley St. (19/79) produced types of this date, and no later types were apparent. At Lower Quay St. (28/79; see below) early 13th century levels (periods 9A & 9B) produced 5 sherds of Ham Green cooking pots (TF 53) which are otherwise uncommon in Gloucester. A single rim was recovered from an early 13th century phase at 1, Westgate St., (Vince 1979, period 7C, Fig.10, 146).

In the later Medieval period the number of fabric types increases, with the majority of industries producing jugs; few cooking pot fabrics are apparent at this time. Cooking vessels are produced in TF's. 44, 52 and 110; jugs and other glazed wares in TF's 44, 52, 54, 79, 83, 92 and 99. With the exception of TF's 79 and 99, which can be considered to be very late medieval types, the others could belong anywhere from the late 13th to 15th century, with few typological variations to aid dating. Contexts which contained material of this type include the layers over the construction levels for the Abbey Gate (12/77: period 1B). Here the presence of a bottle or small jug base in Oxford late medieval ware (TF 83) would suggest a 14th rather than late 13th century date (Mellor 1980, 176). Layers accumulated against Wall 1 contained pottery of late medieval date including late medieval jug fabric TF 99. Material of this general date, including 14th to 15th century types, was recovered from the fills of features associated with gravel extraction at the Prince Albert site (38/78).

	10th–late 11th			Early 12th–Early 13th						Late 13th	
	Cooking Pots					Pitchers		Jugs			TOTALS
	41A	41B	41C	40	91	44	131	53	90	52	
12/77 Street 1	1	1									2
Street 3–4		4									4
Street 8									1		1
Street 10				1							1
Street 12										1	1
25/76 II(6)	1										
II(5)		1									
19/79 Street 3	1										1
Street 3–4		4									4
Street 5		10									10
Street 6–7		1									1
Street 7–8		1									1
Street 8–9			1		1						2
Street 9–10		1									1
Street 10–11		1		1		1	1	1			5
Street 11–12						1			1	1	3
Street 12–13					1	1		1	1		4

TABLE 3 King Edwards Gate (12/77) and Berkeley Street (29/76, 19/79): distribution of pottery types in the street sequence.

Fabric Type	Context	Cooking pots				pitchers		jugs			lamp	TOTAL
		41B	43	40	90	44	52	53	90	108	83	
Black organic loam	(33) (46) (64) (28)	8	1	2	1	2						14
Building	(26)	1										
Road Surfaces	(40) (43)	4		2		4	3	4	4	1	1	23
Buildings	(63) (60)			1				2				3
	(27)			1					1			2
TOTAL		13	1	6	1	6	3	6	5	1	1	

TABLE 4 Clare Street (59/74): medieval pottery sequence: Period 3.

	41A	41B	41C	40	42	49	110	52TP	90	44	54	83	52	50	99	60	68C
0	2	12	1			1											
1A													1				
1B					1		1	1	2	9	2	1	10	3			
2A		1								1					1		
2B													1				
3A			1				1	4					1				
3B												1	1			1	1

TABLE 5 King Edwards Gate (12/77): medieval sequence

The Post-Medieval Pottery

Many sites produced pottery types of the 18th and 19th centuries in the latest levels. There are one or two large collections of 19th century material (e.g.77/74 and 74/75) which have not been studied in detail. There were few collections of earlier material, although this did occur as residual material in many instances. Few sites showed any ceramic continuity from the late medieval period. This may be due, in part, to the long life of the Malvern Chase industry whose products are the most common between the 15th and early 17th centuries to which undiagnostic sherds can only be given a broad date range. Period 11F on the Lower Quay Street site (28/79) produced a collection of material derived from occupation of buildings over a period of time spanning the medieval period and into the early 16th century (see below p.89).

Two groups which can be attributed to the early 17th century are of interest. A small group from the loam layer above the early metalling of Quay Street (58/76) can be paralleled with that from the fill of a culvert at the North Gate site (Heighway et al 1983, Period 8C2), which contained a similar Malvern Chase vessel types and a similar range of fabrics. The other, much larger, group came from the levelling of ground for the construction of a building in the 17th century at Lower Quay Street (28/79, see below) which represents a large quantity of Malvernian vessels smashed as unused vessels (see Figs. 61 and 62), possibly brought in by river.

SAMIAN WARE (decorated and stamped) by Felicity Wild

List of all Samian identifications in Microfiche I.

Site 28/79: 10 Lower Quay St.

Period 1

    Form 37, Central Gaulish, showing Cinnamus' ovolo 2. *c*. A.D. 150–170 (Not illustrated).
1. Form 37, Central Gaulish showing overlapping impressions of an ovolo, possibly that used by potters such as Attianus and Austrus. Probably *c*. A.D. 130–160 at the latest. (I (153))
2. Form 37, Central Gaulish, in the fabric of Les Martres-de-Veyre, showing a basal wreath of the bud (Rogers 1974, G31). This appears on a bowl in Stanfield's Ioenalis style, Rogers' potter X.12 (Stanfield and Simpson 1958, pl.40, 462). This sherd probably also shows the same figure (0.660). *c*. A.D. 100–125. (I(156))
3. Form 37, South Gaulish, with zonal decoration showing lion (0.1417) in scroll. The leaf and general decorative scheme was used by Frontinus (Knorr 1952, Taf. 25A) who also used the lion. *c*. A.D. 70–90. (I(157))

Period 3

4. Form 37, Central Gaulish, in the fabric of Les Martres-de-Veyre. *c*. A.D. 100–125. (I(79))
5. Form 33, Central Gaulish, stamped TIBERI.M (die 1c) by Tiberius ii of Lezoux[b]. This is probably one of Tiberius' later dies, which was used on forms 15/31, 18/31R, 31 and 38. He also made form 27 and probably 80, and one of his stamps occurs at Benwell. *c*. A.D. 150–170.
   Form 18/31R, Central Gaulish, stamped [TAR]VAGIM (die 2a) by Tarvacus or Tarvagus i of Lezoux[a]. All the other stamps from this die are on the late Antonine forms 79 and possibly Lud. Tg. This is on a late example of form 18/31R, which is almost 31R. Mid- to late Antonine. (I(150))

Other sites

33/76

6. Form 33, Central Gaulish, stamped BORILLIOF (die 5b) by Borillus i of Lezoux[a]. This die occurs twice at Newstead. His other dies also occur in Scotland, in the Aquincum hoard and on 18/31R and 27, though also on 79 and 80. *c*. A.D. 150–180.
7. Form 37, Central Gaulish. Two joining fragments of bowl showing part of the advertisement stamp AD[VOCISI] of Advocisus of Lezoux. Panel decoration shows cupid to left (0.504)?; Mercury on mask (0.538) and cupid to right (0.508) over leaf (Rogers 1974, H.189) *c*. A.D. 160–190. (XII(42))

5/78: St Mary de Lode Church

8. Form 29, South Gaulish, showing part of the lower zone with a wreath of ivy leaves, poorly impressed. The leaf is very close to that on a bowl illustrated by Knorr (Knorr 1919, Taf. 91F), though may be slightly shorter. The same leaf occurs on a bowl from Period IA at Fishbourne (Dannell 1971, fig.126, 2) there dated to *c*. A.D. 40–55. Claudio-Neronian. (IV(116))

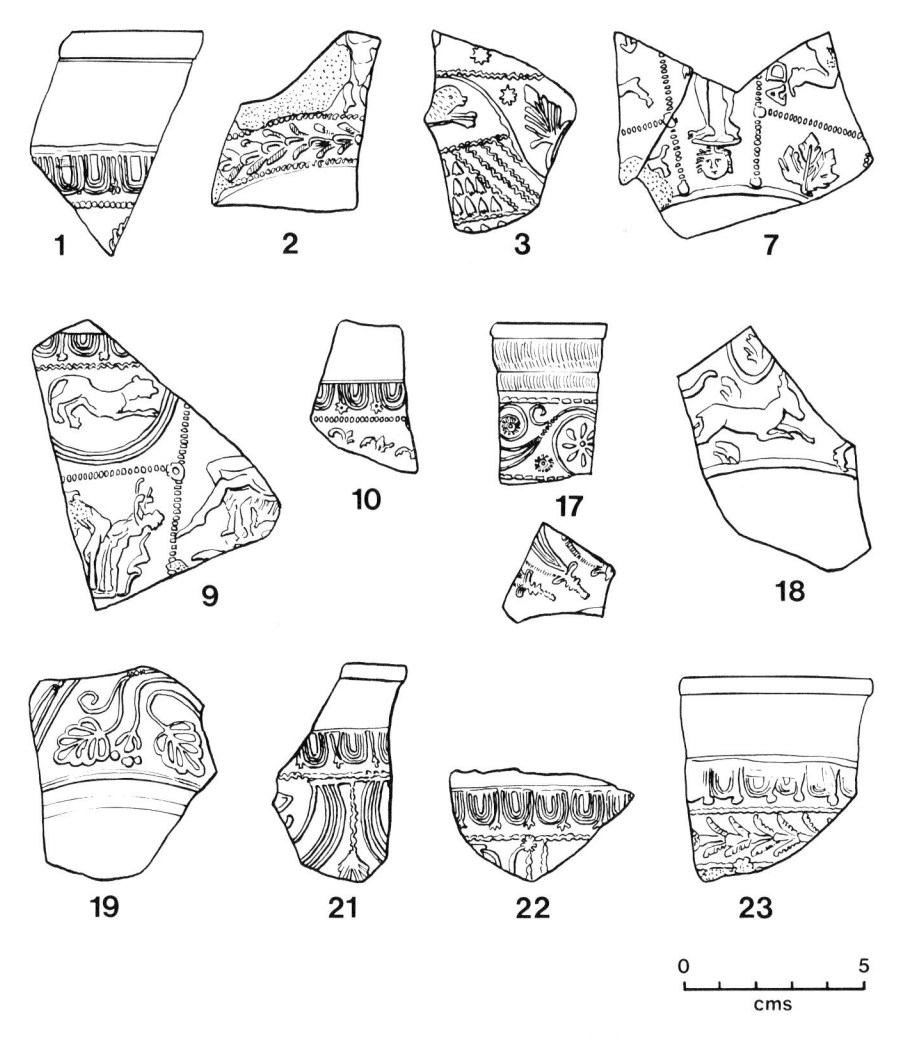

Figure 59A. Samian pottery. Drawn by Felicity Wild.

34/79 Hare Lane

9. Form 37, Central Gaulish, showing panel decoration with panther (0.1518) in festoon over erotic group (O.B, reduced), and seated Bacchus (0.571). The borders, junction motif, panther and group were all used by Criciro, the Bacchus by his slightly later associates Divixtus and Advocisus. *c.* A.D. 135–170. (I(13))

25/79 34 Kingsholm Rd.

10. Form 37, Central Gaulish, probably in the fabric of Les Martres-de-Veyre. The ovolo was used on bowls in Stanfield's Donnaucus style, and later, at Lezoux, by Attianus. The acanthus tips also occur on Donnaucus-Ioenalis style (Stanield and Simpson 1958, pl. 41, 481), and the date is likely to be *c.* A.D. 100–125. (I(1);u/s)

38/74 Kings Walk

11. Form 27, South Gaulish, showing an illiterate stamp (Illiterate 69), assignable on form and fabric to La Graufesenque. This stamp always occurs on form 27. The only dated site at which it has been recorded is Chester. Probably Flavian. (II(22), SF 5, Pd.2)
12. Form 31, Central Gaulish, stamped CROBISOM (die 1a) by Crobiso of Lezoux[b]. There is a graffito beneath the base. Crobiso's work includes a fairly high proportion of form 27 and this stamp occurs at Bearsden and Bothwellhaugh, but also at Halton Chesters, where it could presumably be either late Hadrianic or mid-Antonine. *c.* A.D. 135–165. (II(35) SF1, not phased)
13. Form 18/31, Central Gaulish, stamped CA[RATIMA] (die 1a) by Caratus ii of Lezoux[b]. There is little evidence for the date of this stamp. Others belonging to Caratus were used on form 27 and occur in Antonine Scotland, however, so the period of the stamp is likely to be *c.* A.D. 135–165. (II(35)SF2)
14. Form 33, Central Gaulish, stamped [CINT]VSMVSF (die 6a) by Cintusmus i of Lezoux[b]. This is one

85

of Cintusmus' commoner stamps, used on bowls from moulds of Cinnamus, and present at Castlecary, Newstead, in the Verulamium Period IID fire and in the Aquincum hoard. *c.* A.D. 150–175. (II(35) SF 3)

15. Form 31, Central Gaulish, stamped MARTIM (die 1d) by Martius iv of Lezoux[b]. Occurrences at Chesters, Malton and in the Brougham cemetery suggest a date *c.* A.D. 155–185. (II(35) SF 4)

57/74: 11 St Oswalds Rd

16. Form 27, South Gaulish, stamped [SA]LVETV (die 5g) by Salvetus i of La Graufesenque[a]. This particular stamp occurs in Period I at Valkenburg ZH and so is likely to be Claudian or early Neronian. *c.* A.D. 40–55. (I(1), SF 1, u/s)
17. Form 29, South Gaulish. Two fragments, one of upper zone showing scroll, one of lower, showing volutes, probably from the same bowl. The large rosette in the upper zone was used by Licinus and Primus. A scroll on a bowl by Licinus (Knorr 1952, Taf. 45A) shows a similar tendril binding and small rosette. The volute is typical of the Claudian period. A similar, though not quite identical, zone of volutes was used by potters such as Albinus (Knorr 1919, Taf. 1A) and Daribitus or Senicio (Knorr 1952, Taf. 21F), and occurs in Period IB–C at Fishbourne (Dannell 1971, fig. 127, 8) where a date of *c.* A.D. 40–55 is suggested for it. A Claudian date seems probable. (I(7), Pit)

7/76: Wellington Street Car Park (see Heighway et al. 1983)

18. Form 37, Central Gaulish, showing freestyle decoration with stag (0.1723) and the leaf-tip space filler used by Attianus and the early associates of Cinnamus, such as Paullus. The stag has been recorded on work in the style of Cinnamus, and a date *c.* A.D. 140–160 seems probable. (III(37), Pd 1B)

52/76: Kingsholm Rugby Ground

19. Form 29, South Gaulish, showing lower zone with leaf scroll. The bud motif was used by a number of Claudio-Neronian potters, and appears in the first pottery shop at Colchester (Hull 1958, fig.74, 16). The leaf is possibly that used by Melus and Mommo. A very similar scroll, with the bud but a different leaf, occurs on a bowl stamped FELICISMA (Knorr 1952, Taf.32B). The general connections suggest a date *c.* A.D. 55–75. (Ii(18), u/s)

80/76: Castlemeads

20. Form 29, South Gaulish, showing rim and upper zone with triple festoons containing stirrup leaves. Insufficient remains to suggest the work of a particular potter. The piece is likely to be Neronian or early Flavian. (I(6))
21. Form 37, South Gaulish, slightly burnt, showing a trident-tongued ovolo above triple festoons with stirrup leaves. The ovolo is probably that used by Mommo and Vitalis ii. Vitalis used the triple festoon with stirrup leaf, which appears on a bowl with this ovolo in the London Museum (No. 6690L). *c.* A.D. 75–100. (I(6))
22. Form 37, South Gaulish, showing ovolo with trident tongue curving to the left, over panel decoration. The ovolo was used by M. Crestio, and the date is likely to be *c.* A.D. 80–100. (I(6))
23. Form 37, South Gaulish, showing ovolo with tongue ending in a blob, above a horizontal wreath of trifid leaves. The ovolo occurs on bowls in the style of M. Crestio, who also used the wreath in a similar position beneath the ovolo (Knorr 1952, Taf. 19H). *c.* A.D. 80–100. (I(6))

I should like to thank Miss Brenda Dickinson for supplying the notes on the potters' stamps. The potter and die numbers will appear in her and Mr. B.R. Hartley's forthcoming Index of Potters' Stamps on Samian Ware. According to their notation, the letter (a) after the kiln site denotes that the die in question has been recorded there, the letter (b) that other dies of the same potter have been recorded there.

LIST OF FABRIC TYPE NUMBERS USED FOR GLOUCESTER POTTERY

A fuller description of most fabric types is in Heighway *et al* 1983, Appendix B1 and B2 (microfiche). A complete description of all fabrics is in Excavation Unit File No. PFG/2 (Roman) and PFG/3 (post-Roman). The following is a list of the type-fabrics mentioned in this report including those in Microfiches I and VI.

TF number   Name of ware or source

Roman fabrics

1A	Oxford parchment
2	Grog-tempered 'native'
3	Mica-coated, local
4	Dorset Black-Burnished
5	Micaceous grey
7	Local white-slipped flagons
8	Samian
9	Mortaria
9A	Oxford white
9B	Local
9C	Kent/Gaul
9D	Mancetter/Hartshill
9I	Rhineland?
9S	Kingsholm
9X	Oxford red colour-coated
10	Amphorae
11A	Local micaceous (= 3A, 7, 9B, 207B)
11B	Severn Valley, fine micaceous
11C	Black burnished, ? local
11D	Early Severn Valley
12	Colour-coated
12A	Oxford
12B	Nene Valley
12C	New Forest
12D	local
12E	Gloucester Red-slipped Samian copies
12G	A red colour coat, ?Wilts.
12H	Lyons
12I	Lezoux, 'Black Samian'.
12J	Central-Gaulish 'Rhenish'
12K	Moselle 'Rhenish'
13	Oxfordshire fine white
15	White-slipped flagons (= 9/0)
17	Charcoal-tempered, ?local
18	Malvernian 'native'
19A	Malvernian Severn Valley
19B	Malvernian Coarse
19C	Early Malvernian Wheel-thrown
20	Miscellaneous sand-tempered
22	Shell-tempered
23	Coarse Severn Valley
24	Kingsholm flagon
25	TF 11A with added sand
26	'Fine' Grey
31	Native, shale & limestone tempered
34	Native calcite-tempered
35	Late 1st century coarse
36	TF 24 with added sand
39	Sandy grey
201	'Belgic' black-burnished
202	Terra nigra types
205	?N. Wilts grey burnished
206	Wheelthrown black-burnished
207	Roughcast beakers
208	Poppyhead beakers
210	Fine white painted
211	Imported white
213	Kingsholm gritty

TF number	Name of ware or source	TF number	Name of ware or source
Post-Roman fabrics		69	Cream ware
40	Malvern Chase cooking pot	70	N. Devon earthenware
41A	Gloucester Late Saxon	71	Transfer printed
41B	Gloucester Early Medieval	72	Moulded slip
42	Miscellaneous unglazed sand tempered	73	'embossed' slip
43	Sand and limestone tempered	74	Iron glazed
44	N. Wiltshire oolitic-limestone-tempered	75	Black glazed Kitchen
45	Shell-tempered	77	Whieldon (Agate)
46	Organic-tempered (grass tempered)	78	Staffs brown-bodied hollow
47	Flint-tempered	79	Late medieval jug
48	Bath fabric 'A' (Cheddar Fabric 'J')	80	Ashton Keynes
49	Quartzite-tempered (Hereford Fabric A8)	81	Saintonge
50	Miscellaneous glazed	82	Fulham stoneware
51	Stamford	83	Upper Thames (Oxford Fabric AM)
52	Malvern Chase glazed	90	Worcester jug
53	Ham Green	91	Worcester cooking pot
54	Fine micaceous red earthenware	92	Bristol Redcliffe
55	Yellow glazed cream bodied earthenware	94	Westerwald stoneware
		95	Early English stoneware
57	Donyatt	96	Later English Stoneware
58	Staffs cream bodied hollow	97	Stroat
59	Surrey–Hants border wares	98	Oxford Tripod pitchers (Oxford Fabric Y)
60	Cistercian		
61	Staffs Black glazed	99	Late medieval jug
62	Tin glazed	103	Cranham earthenware
63	Miscellaneous flower-pot	105	Martincamp
64	Staffordshire Wheelthrown plates	106	Coleford
65	Tudor Green	107	Merida
66	Porcelain	108	?Shrewsbury type
67	White salt-glazed	109	Scratch marked
68	Early German Stoneware	110	Sandy limestone tempered
68A	Raeren	120	Wedgwood black basalt
68B	Köln	121	Nottingham stoneware
68C	Frechen	125	Black-glazed red earthenware

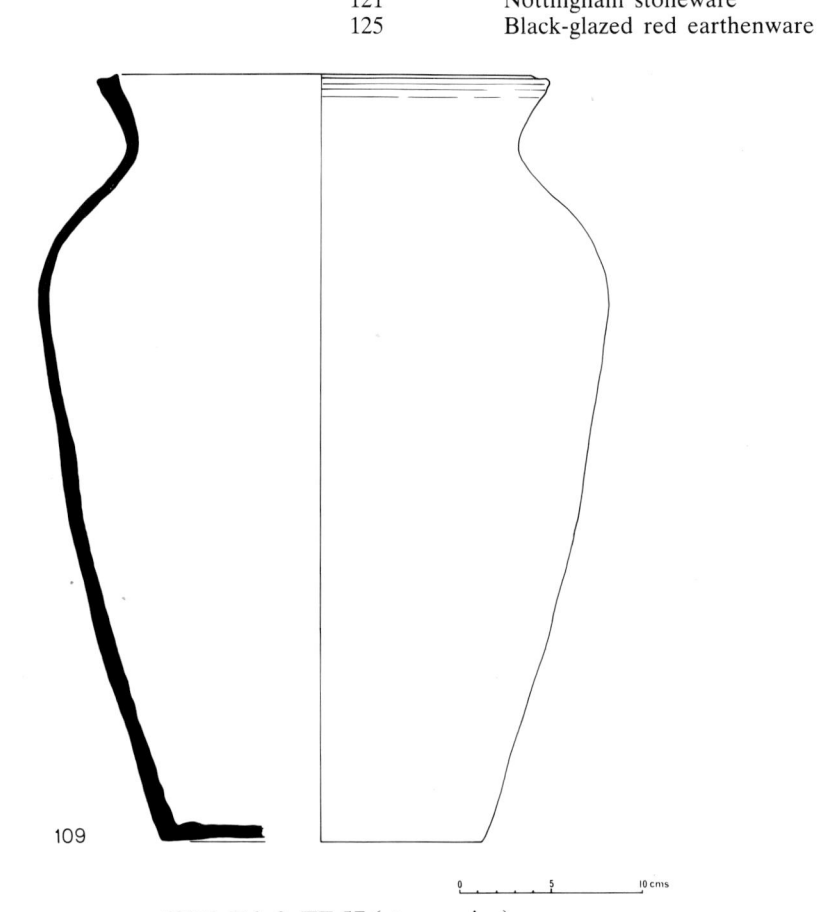

109

63/76, Pd. 3, TF 57 (storage jar)

PART 6   THE POTTERY FROM 10 LOWER QUAY STREET by Caroline Ireland

The pottery from this site has been dealt with seperately since the quantity involved and the complexity of the stratigraphy equates the site with a major excavation. The same system of pottery classification to that used for the other watching brief sites and major excavations in the city, has been used (see Ireland 1983, Vince 1983, Goudge 1982).

The Roman Pottery

Periods 1 to 5 produced material which could be attributed to the early 2nd to the late 3rd or 4th centuries. Pottery of late 1st century date was present as residual material, and indeed, the early 2nd century pottery from Periods 1 and 2 was present in a redeposited loam sandwiched between 2 groups of loam layers containing late 2nd to early 3rd century material. The earliest loam level in Period 1/2 contained late 2nd century Samian and Dorset BB1 (see lists in Microfiche VI). The uppermost levels of the redeposited loam are probably not much later than this. The complex series of tip lines and pits which comprise Period 4 produced pottery which appears to span the 3rd century. Period 3, however, contained a Dorset BB1 flanged bowl with a low head, probably indicative of a 3rd century date. It is possible that much of the pottery in Period 4 is residual. Period 5, the Quay Wall construction, contained little pottery. All the types present were late Roman, but possibly only late 3rd to early 4th century. The absence of shell-tempered ware could suggest a date before the mid 4th century.

A small grey-ware crucible (below, p.102, no.25) was used for casting gold.

The Medieval pottery

Periods 6 to 11 produced pottery from the late Saxon to the late medieval periods. No certain late Saxon contexts producing pottery were noted, and it is probable that this material is residual. There is a continuous sequence of pottery from Period 6 to Period 9, spanning the late 11th to the early 13th centuries. From Period 10, late medieval types are present, characteristic of the 14th or 15th centuries, and in Period 11 a sequence of pottery throughout the late medieval period, into the early 16th century, is apparent. It would therefore appear that a phase of pottery from the mid 13th to 14th century is missing, but this can probably be accounted for in the group of accumulated occupation layers in Period 11F, and a single sherd in Period 9A. The range of fabrics and vessel types, and the proportions of these in each period, does not alter significantly the pottery sequence as already known from other sites. There are several unknown fabrics, and this can probably be explained in terms of the riverside location, and reflect a wider sphere of influence for pottery sources, although it may not necessarily represent extensive trade.

In the period summaries (Microfiche VI) residual Roman pottery is excluded.

The Post-Medieval Pottery

Period 11 includes a sequence of pottery from the late medieval into the post-medieval periods. Period 12 comprises a group of material possibly dumped in this area and used to level the site for the construction of Building 4. Period 13 contained late 17th to 18th century material and is the latest described (in Microfiche VI) in this report. Periods 14–17 are effectively modern.

Editors Note

Mrs. Ireland had to resign her post as Pottery Researcher before this report was complete in detail. It has been considered more cost-effective to give her work as completed here, rather than attempt to have it completed by another hand.

Bronze-casting mould

The semi-circular base of a bronze-casting mould came from Period 9A (early 13th century). The mould material is organic-tempered clay, similar to that used in another casting mould found near the East Gate (Heighway et al 1983, p.212). The mould diameter is about 70mm.

Graffito: identified by Mark Hassall (Fig.62A).

]DII˙]dii, or]d(a)e: in either case a personal name in the genetive. If inverted IICI[, or IILI[, ECL[, ELI[but these forms are less likely. Scratched into a sherd from a jar in TF 11A, local micaceous ware (Period 4, probably residual).

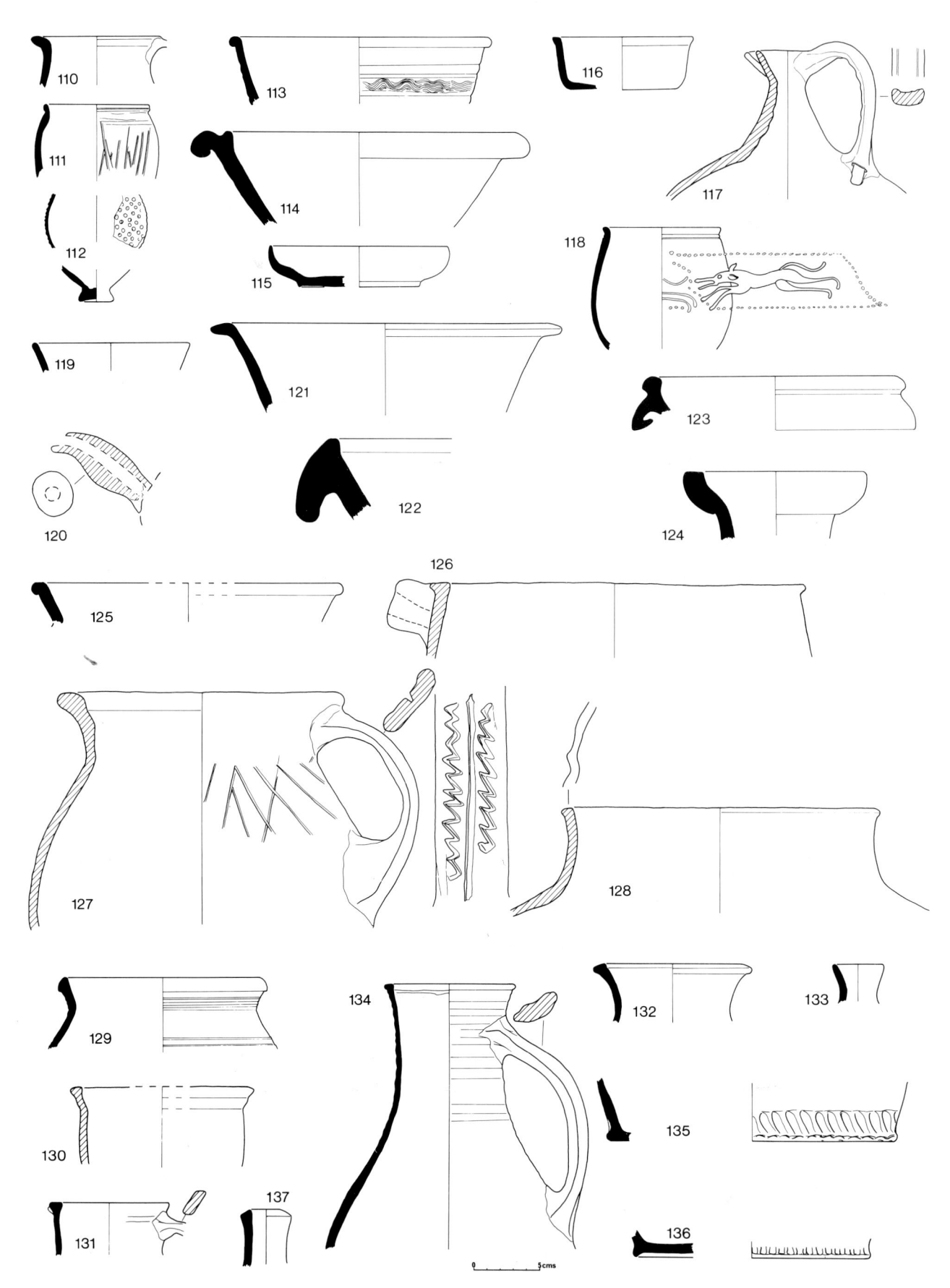

Figure 60. Site 28/79, Lower Quay Street. Roman, medieval and post-medieval pottery. Drawn by L. Marlet. *Period 1*: No 110, TF 11A or 7. No 111, TF 11A. No 112, TF 208 (poppy-head beaker). No 113, TF 26. No 114, TF 9C. No 115, TF 11B. *Period 3*: No 116, TF 11A. *Period 4*: no 117, TF 4. No 118, TF 12B (hunt cup). No 119, TF 12 (beaker). No 120, TF 7. No 121, TF 19. No 122, TF 91. No 123, TF 9A. *Period 5B* No 124, amphora. *Period 7A*: no 125, TF 41? No 126, TF 41B. *Period 8B*: No 127, TF 50 (pitcher). *Period 9A*: No 128, TF 53 (jug). *Period 9B*: No 129, TF 53. No 130, TF 41B. *Period 11A*: No 131, TF 65 (jug). *Period 11F* No 132, TF 44 (jug). No 133, TF 52 (flask or bottle). No 135, TF 54 (jug). No 136, TF 54 (jug). *Period 11D*: No 134, TF 52 (jug).

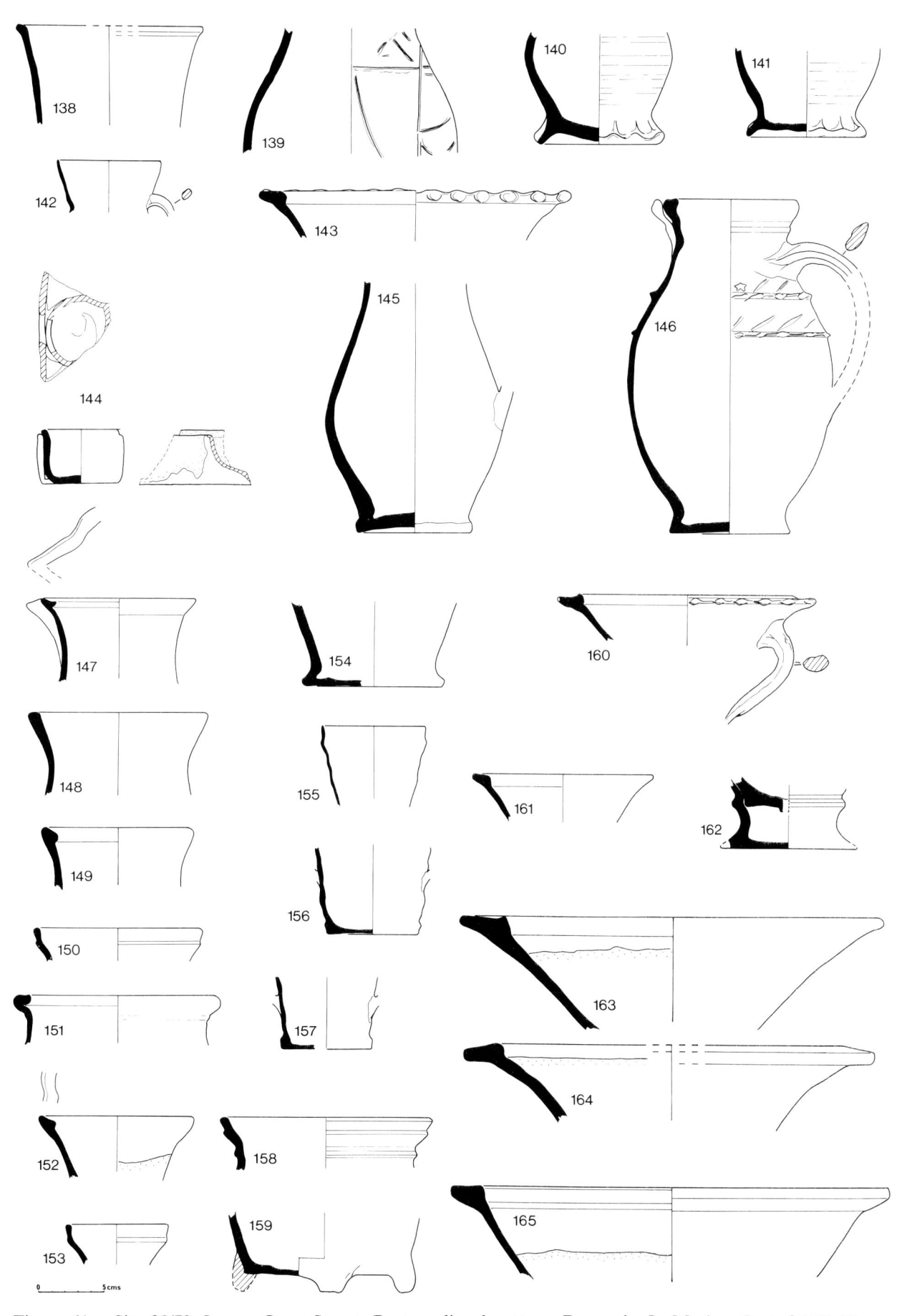

Figure 61. Site 28/79, Lower Quay Street. Post-medieval pottery. Drawn by L. Marley. *Period 11F*: Nos 138–9, TF 99? Nos 140–141, TF 68A (drinking pot). No 142, TF 60 (cup). No 143, TF 52 (bowl or chafing dish). No 144, TF 92 (inkwell set). No 145–6, TF 52 (jugs). *Period 12*: no 147–154, TF 52 (jugs). No 155–7, TF 60 (cups). No 158, TF 52, jar. No 159, jTF 52 (footed vessel). No 160–162, TF 52 (chafing dish). Nos 163–6, TF 52 (bowls). Nos 167–70, TF 52 (spouted bowls). No 171, TF 52 (bowl). No 172, TF 52 (dish). No 173, TF 52 (bowl). No 174, TF 52 (dripping dish).

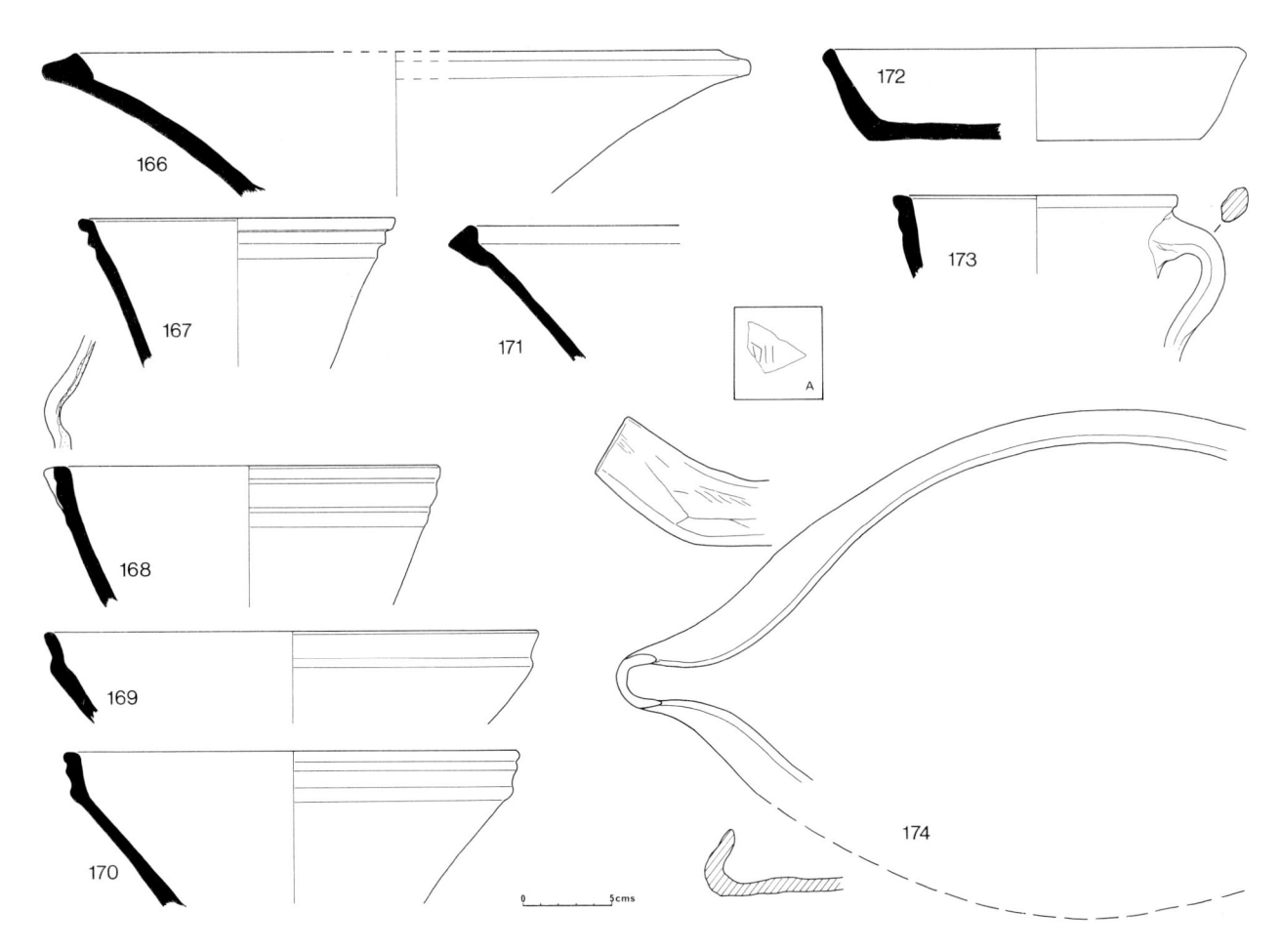

Figure 62. Site 28/79, Lower Quay Street. Post-medieval pottery. Drawn by L. Marley. *Period 12*: nos 166–174, TF 52. Drawn by L. Marley.

PART 7 SMALL FINDS FROM MINOR SITES (excluding Lower Quay Street, 28/79)

Only dateable finds in primary contexts, or finds of particular interest, have been described and illustrated here. A full list of small finds and contexts is Microfiche V. The date against each context is the date of that context.

Bone

1. Pin, L: 175mm. Possibly a beating pin for use in weaving. *cf* 11th century examples in Heighway, Garrod and Vince 1979, p.203. (Site 59/74, Clare Street, Period 3, 12th to 13th century, SF 1).
2. Horn or antler bracelet, ? unfinished. (19/79, Berkeley St., Street 4, 11th century, SF 1).

Copper Alloy: personal ornaments and dress fittings

3. Bow brooch. (65/74, Robinswood Hill, F3, 1st century, SF11)
4. Buckle (37/74, U/S, SF 2)
5. Penannular Brooch. D: 26mm (16/75, Estcourt Road, F6, 1st century, SF2)
6. Zoomorphic buckle. A well-known late Roman type: Hawkes and Dunning (1961), Type IIA. (98/75, Saintbridge, Pit 20, R1, late 4th century, SF4).
7. Finger ring. D:20mm. (98/75, U/S, SF2).
8. Buckle. W:25mm (28/76, Quedgeley, Building 1/2, 3rd to 4th century, SF5)
9. Fitting with two rivets. (51/76, third metalling of Portway, SF1)

Copper Alloy, other items

10. *Lid of seal box*, tear-shaped, perforated. (65/74, Robinswood Hill, F1, 3rd century, SF 2).
11. *Disc.* D:40mm. (65/74, F1, 3rd cent., SF1).
12. *Tweezers.* L:56mm. (59/74, Clare St., Period 3, 12th–13th century, SF2)
13. *Rim of vessel*, either a plate, or bowl with flat rim. The rim diameter of the vessel was about 20mm. (29/77, Saintbridge, U/S, SF8).
14. *Tweezers.* (4/78, Period 1A, 1st century, SF1).
15. *Military fitting* (2/81, VI(4), SF1).
16. *Fragment of bow brooch* (2/81, VI(7), SF2).
17. *Double Hook.* (5/81, 6, Roman, SF19)

Flint by A. Saville.

Prehistoric flints occurred on the Robinswood Barracks site (65/74), occasionally from other sites, and twelve from the Saintbridge site (98/75). These are catalogued in the microfiche lists. The Saintbridge collection comprised eight unretouched flakes and blades, one bipolar bladelet core, one miscellaneous retouched flake, one large edge trimmed blade and a broken and reworked 'fabricator'. These pieces are not homogeneous nor in themselves diagnostic, but a general neolithic – early bronze age date range may be given, and they perhaps indicate several phases of prehistoric activity in the vicinity.

Glass

18. Fragments of window glass, painted. (63/76, Cathedral, 11th century, SF2).
19. *Roman vessel* by J. Price. Fragment from rim and body of large pillar-moulded bowl, blueish-green. Short shoulder, part of one broad thick rib. Wheel-polishing marks on inside surface and on shoulder outside. 55 x 44 mm. 1st century AD. (19/79, Berkeley St., robbing of city wall, 5th to 10th cent., SF8).

Gold

20. Fragment of tube. (28/76, Quedgeley, Building 1/2, 3rd to 4th century SF1).

Iron

21. Object, possibly part of a hinge. (29/76, Foreign Bridge, 12th century, SF1).
22. Stylus, one end pointed, the other broken off. L:133mm. (33/76, XIII, Worcester St., 1st to 2nd century street, SF 8).
23. Adze. (52/76, Kingsholm Rugby Ground, 1B3, late 1st to 2nd cent. SF 1).
24. Binding sheet for wooden shovel. (57/77, Westgate St., 12th century or later. SF 2).
25. Surgeons probe. (19/79, Berkeley St., under Street 5, 11th or 12th cent). (SF 3).
26. Harness ring or thumb ring. (19/79, Under Street 3, 11th cent., SF 4).
27. Awl. L:90mm. (19/79, Street 4, ?12th century, SF 6).
28. Awl or chisel. L:110mm. (30/79, St. Catherine St., above ? Roman street, SF 2).
29. Socketed point: ferrule? L:47mm. (5/81, 9, Saxon or medieval, SF 9).
30. Spear head. (5/81, 3, Roman phase 1, demolition, SF 18).
31. Spear head (5/81, 2, Roman phase 1, SF 20).

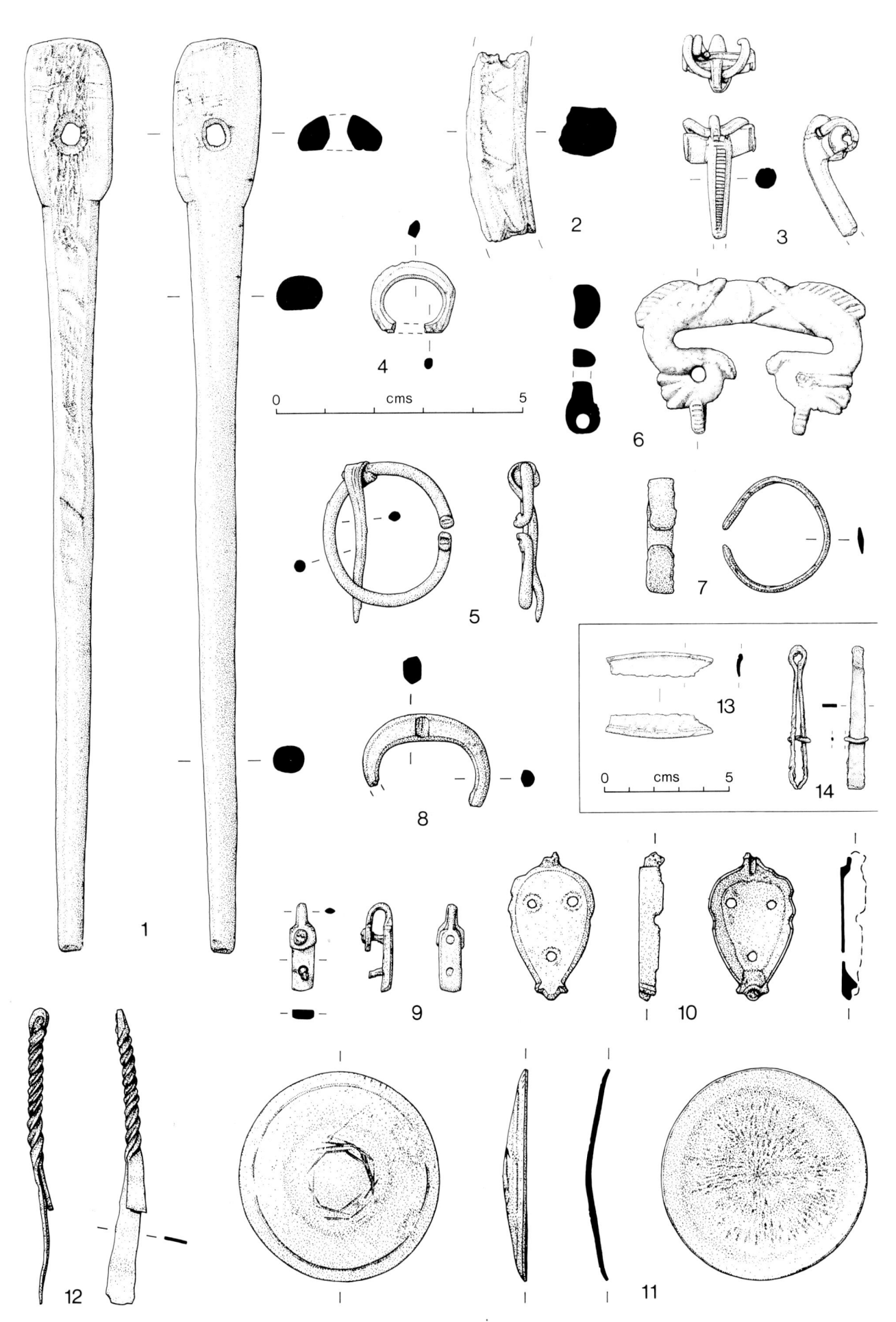

Figure 63. Small finds from Minor Sites. Nos 1 and 2, bone. Nos 3–14, copper alloy. Drawn by D. L. Owen and J. Williamson.

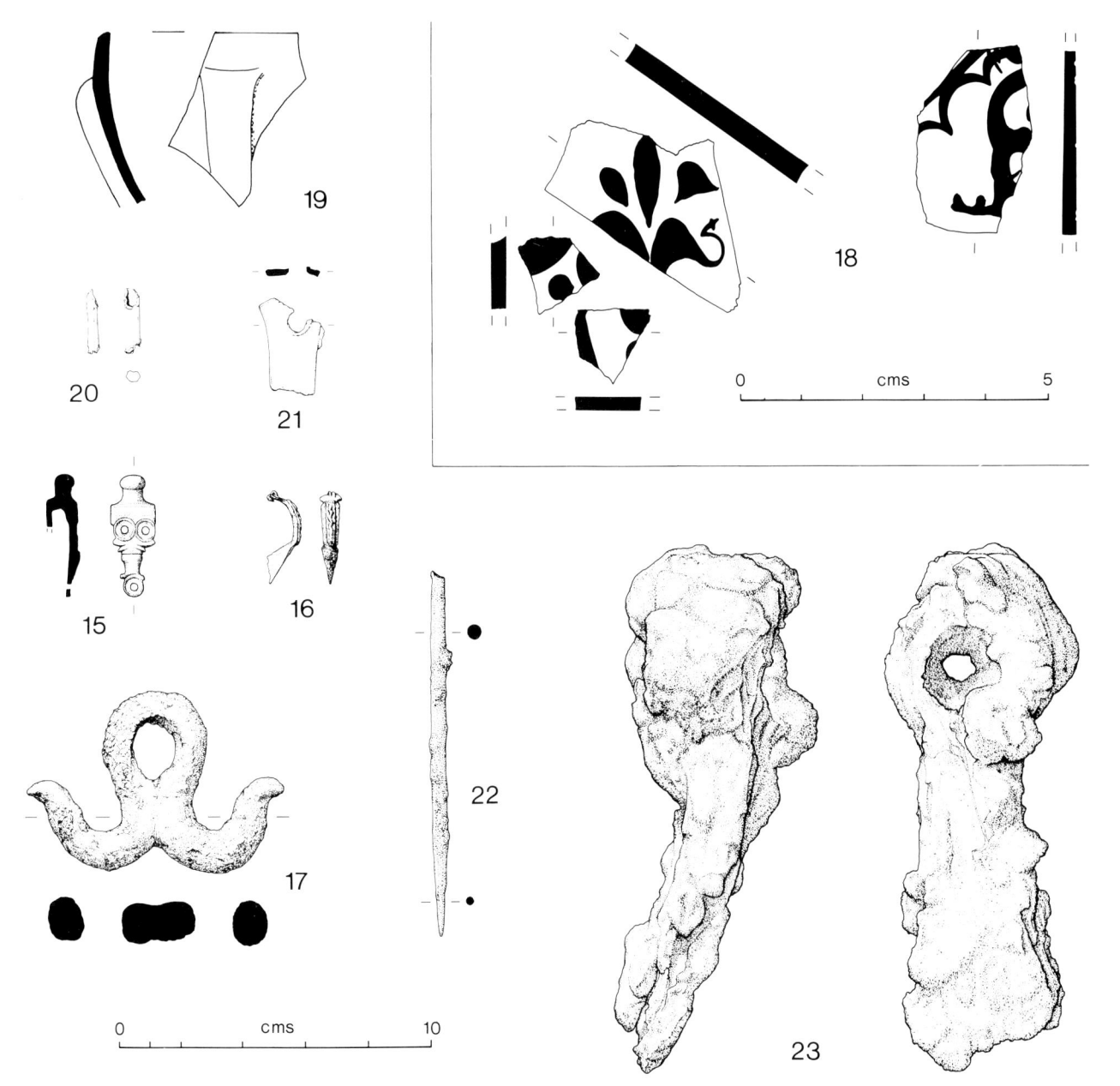

Figure 64. Small finds from Minor sites. Nos 15–17, copper alloy. Nos 18–19, Glass. No 20, Gold. Nos 21–23, iron. Drawn by D. L. Owen and J. Williamson, and Western Archaeological Trust.

Jet

32. Pin (28/76, Quedgeley, Ditch 2, late 3rd to 4th century, SF 2).

Lead

33. Hammer-shaped object, with a possible suspension loop broken off. A weight? (98/75, Saintbridge, R7, 4th century, SF 11).
34. Weight? 220 grammes. D: 34mm. (66/75, Ladybellgate House, Period 4, 17th century, SF 5).

Leather

35. Medieval turnshoe; (Fig.67) probably left shoe; the parts remaining comprise forepart of sole, and two large fragements of upper. The exact upper pattern is uncertain.
    The sole section is c. 19cm. in length; c. 10cm. across tread, and has a rounded toe shape, and fairly narrow waist. There are large grain/flesh stitch-holes around edge, S.L. 5.5mm., and lines of stitching, where repair patches have been sewn. There is also a fragment of rand: a triangular-sectioned strip of leather with large stitch-holes, S.L. 5.5mm.
    Most of the vamp area survives, although toe end is incomplete, with lasting margin having large, grain/flesh stitch-holes S.L. 5.5mm. There is the start of an opening at the centre of the throat, and also

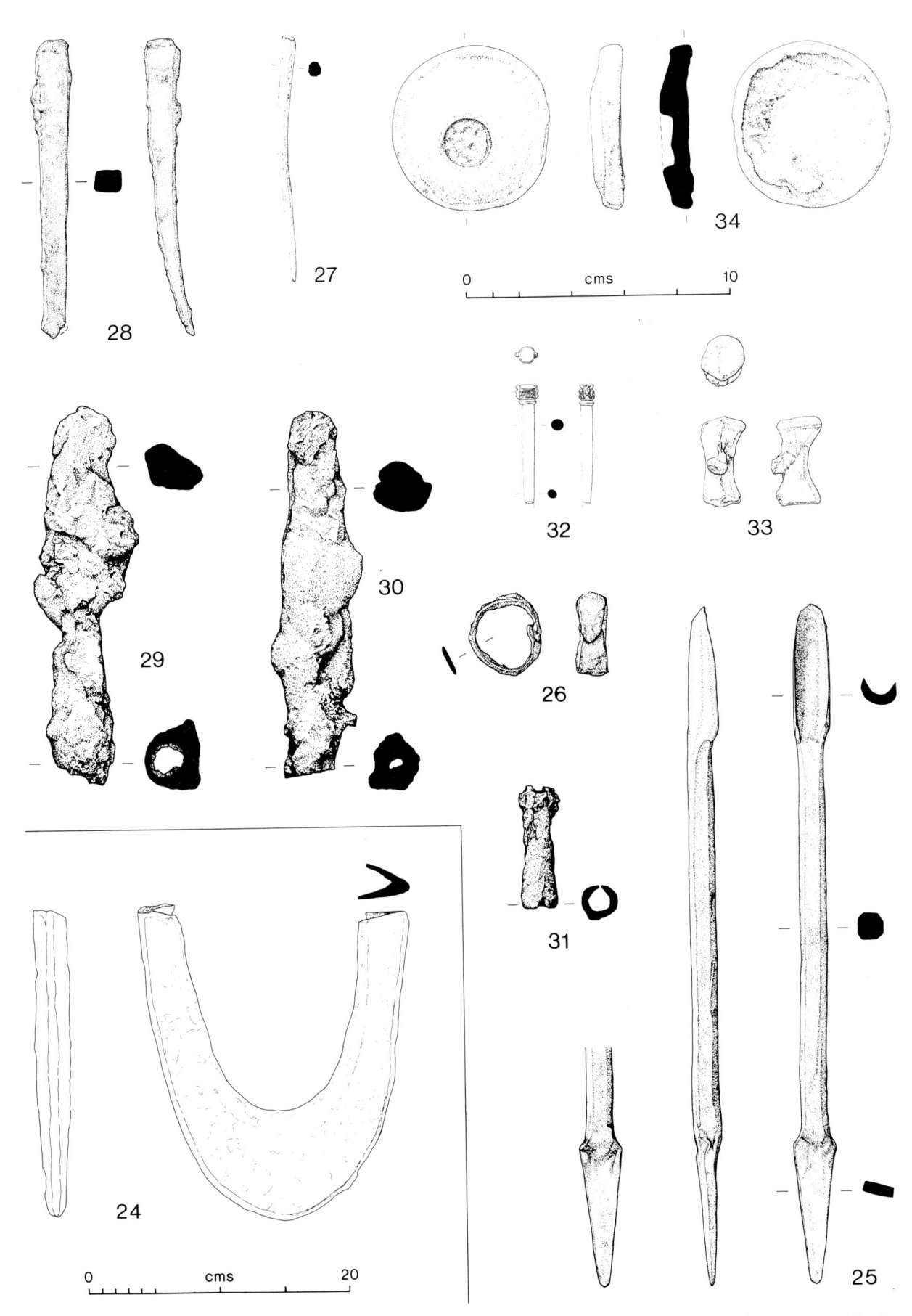

Figure 65. Small finds from Minor Sites. Nos 24–31, iron. No 32, jet. Nos 33–34, lead. Drawn by D. L. Owen.

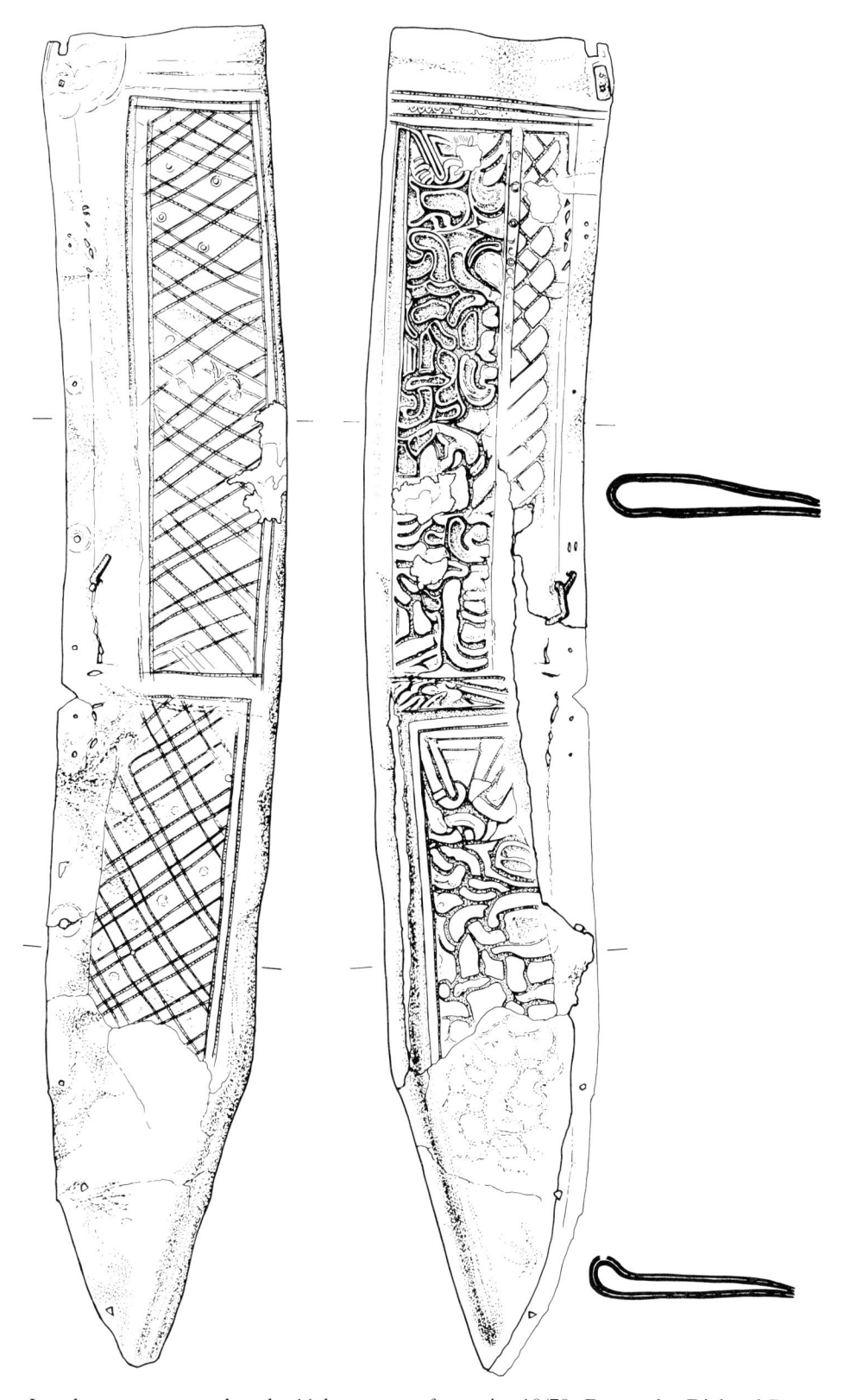

Figure 66. Leather scramasax sheath, 11th century, from site 19/79. Drawn by Richard Bryant. Scale 1/2.

a side seam, on the inside of the foot, with fine, edge/flesh stitching, S.L.3mm. This seam is matched on a smaller, joining fragment, which is dissected by the bottom of another opening, with large lace-holes, two on either side, c.15–18mm. apart.

Another fragment of upper, presumably from the same shoe, has a row of five lace holes along one edge, varying from 18 to 23mm. apart. Another edge, approximately at right-angles to this, is oversewn, and may be the top edge of the upper.

The complete shoe would have had the appearance of a side-laced, ankle boot, and would date to the thirteenth century.
(33/76, VIII, Worcester St./Northgate St.: under street 12; medieval SF 1)

36. *Leather Scabbard*. (Fig. 66). A complete leather scabbard for a late Saxon scramasax knife was preserved in the build-up over a street metalling.
It measures c.415mm. in length, and 70mm. across the throat, and is made from one piece of thick leather, folded, and riveted together down the edges. One, rectangular-headed rivet remains in situ at the top, and there are holes for others, surrounded by circular impressions on the back, spaced from 35 to 50mm. apart. At the corner of the throat, on the back, there are traces of concentric scoring, probably caused by an attachment here for suspending the scabbard from a belt. About half-way down the same side, there are two bent metal staples, which would have provided another means of suspension.
The point of the scabbard is angled, reflecting the characteristic shape of the scramasax blade, with the back edge sloping towards the cutting edge.
The scabbard has been repaired, as there are two groups of stitch holes, irregularly disposed, at c.60 and c.200mm. from the top edge, and adjacent to former rivet positions.
Both surfaces of the scabbard are decorated in the traditional style, the decoration being divided into two sections, clearly indicating the handle and blade of the knife within, and comprising rectangular panels, delineated by narrow borders of engraved lines.
On the front, the main panels are infilled with embossed interlace, crude in character, with thick, and interrupted strands giving a general impression of irregular shapes, rather than of continuous, flowing lines. At the top of each panel, the interlace becomes very angular. To the right of the upper panel, there is a narrow border of 'ring and dot' ornament, probably effected with a rough stamp. Next to this is a wider border of linear interlace, of two thick strands, giving the appearance of a twisted rope or cable.
The gap between the two main panels bears an embossed motif of obscure design. The back of the scabbard bears two panels of regular, engraved double-lattice, with a ring and dot ornament in the centre of each diamond.
There are two close parallels for the scheme of decoration on this scabbard: one was found in Lawrence Lane, in the City of London (*Antiq. Journ.* XII, 1932, p.177, fig.1) and the other comes from Hexham, in Yorkshire, (British Museum Anglo-Saxon Guide, 1923, p.106, fig. 129). Both of these are roughly dated to the 10th or 11th century.
(19/79, Berkeley Street; under Street 3; S.F.7).

Wood by Carole Morris

37. Ropewood. Oak, with fragment of shaft c. 95mm long, through hole D.28mm. The shaft consisted of a length of branch from which the bark had not been removed. See the similar object in Heighway, Garrod and Vince 1979, p.199, no.12.
(33/76, VIII, Worcester St., Under Street 11, 11th century ??, SF 3).

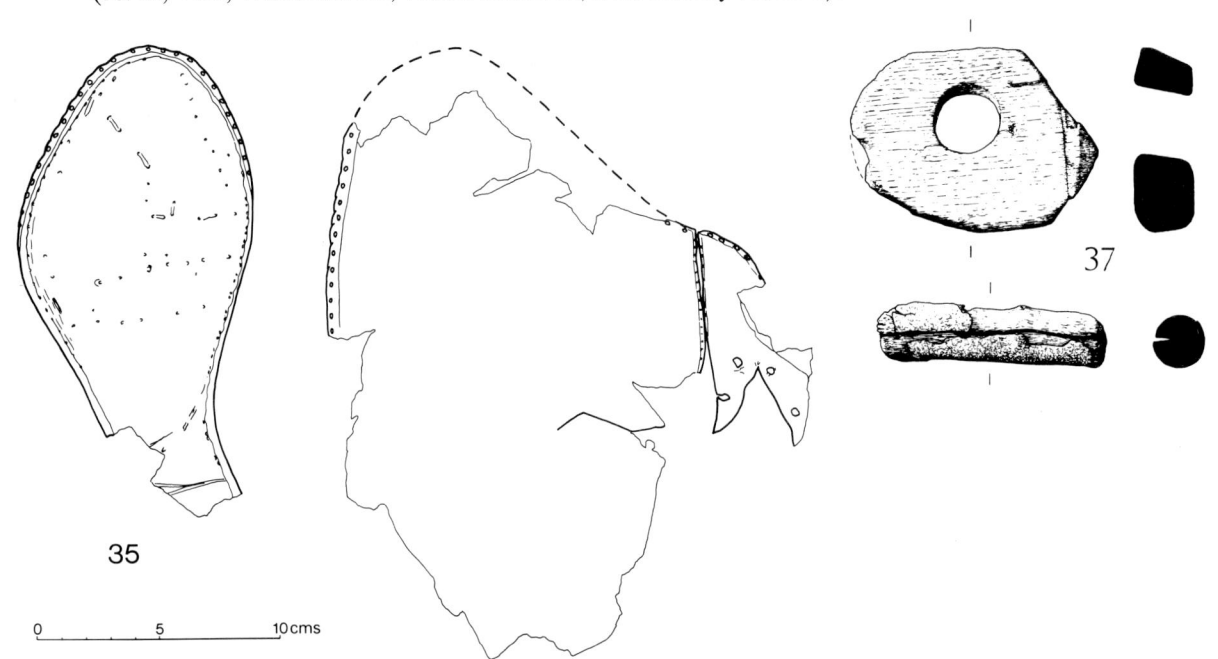

Figure 67. Leather and wood from Minor sites. No. 35, shoe or boot from site 33/76, 13th century. Drawn by L. Marley. No 37, ropewood, 11th century? Drawn by G. Morris.

PART 8 SMALL FINDS FROM 10 LOWER QUAY STREET.

See Microfiche VII for full list.

Bone

1. Antler tool (red deer). Alan Saville notes: The tool has been sawn and artificially perforated, and the tine is highly polished. This polish is more likely to have developed through handling; e.g. in use as a handle, because of its extensiveness and the lack of abrasion, than through the tine itself being a working part of the tool. The damage to the end of the tine may be post-use and associated with the evidence of burning which I also take to be post-use. I assume that this is not a prehistoric item, on the grounds that a prehistoric antler object is unlikely to occur in such a good condition in a superficial urban context. (U/S, SF 1).
2. Knife handle (9A, early 13th cent, SF 126).
3. Part of knife handle (9A, early 13th cent, SF 127).

Copper Alloy

4. Spoon, Roman (4, 3rd cent, SF 70).

Hooked tag; by James Graham Campbell.

5. The tag has corroded edges giving its plate a circular appearance, although this must originally have been in the form of an eight-lobed rosette. The front is incised with a double-contoured cross with expanded arms, within a plain border; the arms of the cross are bisected by transverse lines and it has a central panel of indeterminate shape. Both of the upper quadrants, between the arms of the cross, are perforated. The reverse is plain. Length: 205mm.

   Small hooked tags came into use in the seventh century and were employed throughout the rest of the Anglo-Saxon period (Graham-Campbell 1982). Many of them, like this Gloucester example, are so slight that they could only have been used on light fabrics in the manner of a modern 'hook and eye'. No exact parallels for the outline or the ornament of the Gloucester tag have been traced amongst the published examples of these fasteners, but that from a probable tenth/eleventh-century context at Beckery Chapel, Glastonbury (Rahtz and Hirst 1974, fig. 23.14), is incised with a double diagonal cross, whereas an unpublished hooked tag from Mr. Keith Wade's excavation of a mid to late Anglo-Saxon site at Barham, near Ipswich, Suffolk, is incised with a contoured straight-armed cross.[1] Both these examples have a pair of perforations pierced directly through their circular plates, in the manner of the Gloucester tag. Thus, although it is not possible to offer a precise date for the Gloucester hooked tag, there is no reason to suppose that it is other than contemporary with the eleventh-century context in which it was found. (6B, late 11th cent, SF33)

6. Ring brooch or breech buckle (11F, 13th–16th cent, SF 3).
7. Buckle plate. (11F, 13th–16th cent, SF 150).
8. Hairpin. (11F, 13th–16th cent, SF 117).

Iron

9. Point of military weapon, probably a Roman catapult. (S 1 and 2, early 2nd cent, SF 85).
10. Knife, possibly Saxon (8B, early 13th cent, SF 34).
11. Pointed object possibly an ox-goad (9A, early 13th cent, SF 39).
12. Key (9B, early 13th cent, SF 123).
13. Strip, curved and splaying at either end, with 2 nails at each end. Coffer handle? (11F, 13th to 16th cent, SF 146).

Leather Footwear by C. E. Goudge.

14. Most of one-piece upper, in fragmentary condition, from turnshoe. Sections of lower edge with lasting margin survive with regular grain/flesh stitching, S.L. (stitch length) 4mm. The upper has a side seam, with finer, edge/flesh stitching, S.L. 2.3mm., and finishing at a V-shaped notch in the top edge. Another V-shaped piece has been cut from the top edge, on the vamp side of the seam. The edges of these notches have been sewn, with very fine, edge/flesh stitching, S.L. 2mm., and originally, triangular pieces may have been inserted. The top edge itself has regular, edge/flesh oversewing, S.L. 3–4mm.

1. I am most grateful to Mrs. Leslie Webster for drawing this parallel to my attention, as also for her general advice and assistance.

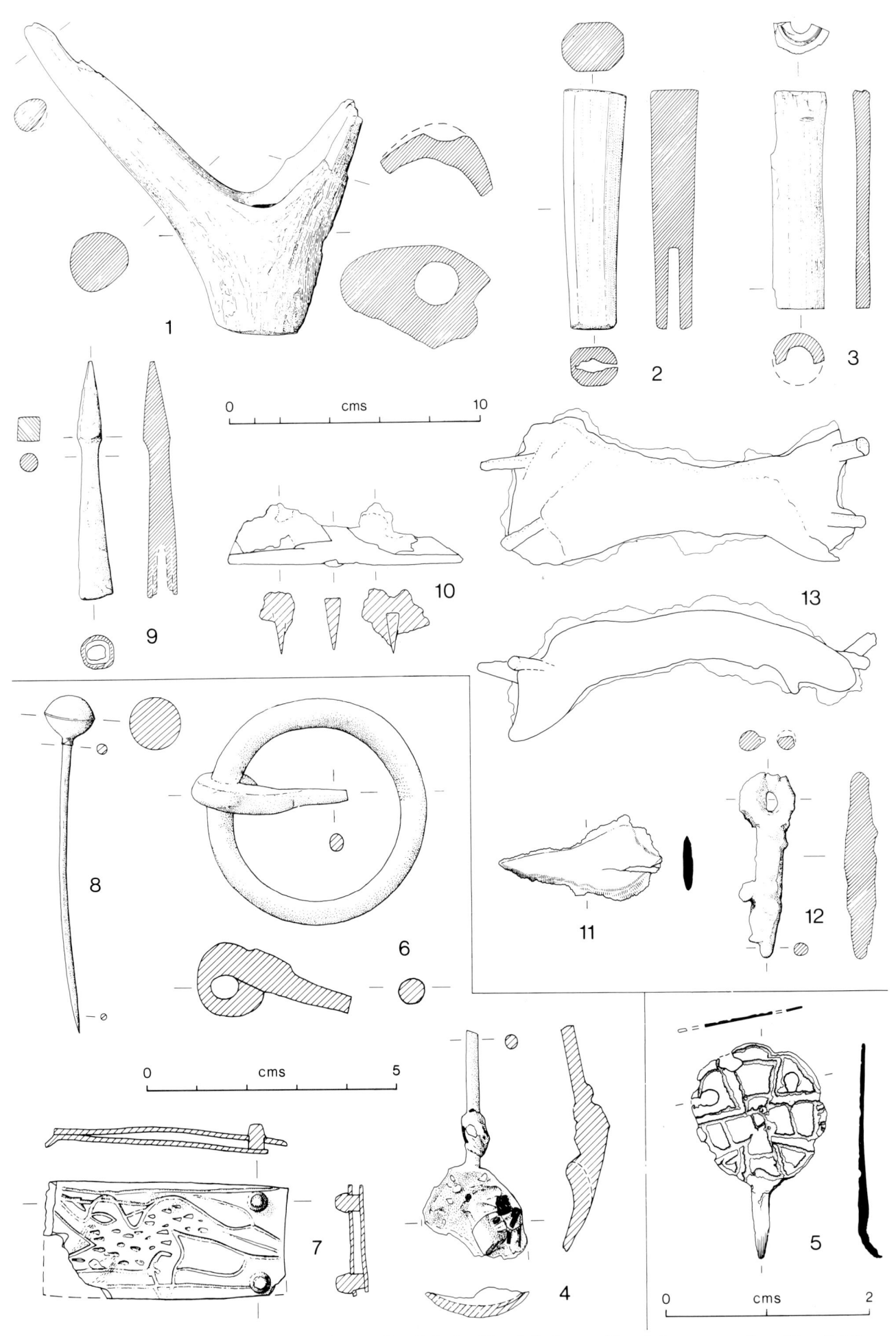

Figure 68. Site 28/79, Lower Quay Street. Small finds. Nos 1–3, bone. Nos 4–8, copper alloy. Nos 9–13, iron. Drawn by Western Archaeological Trust.

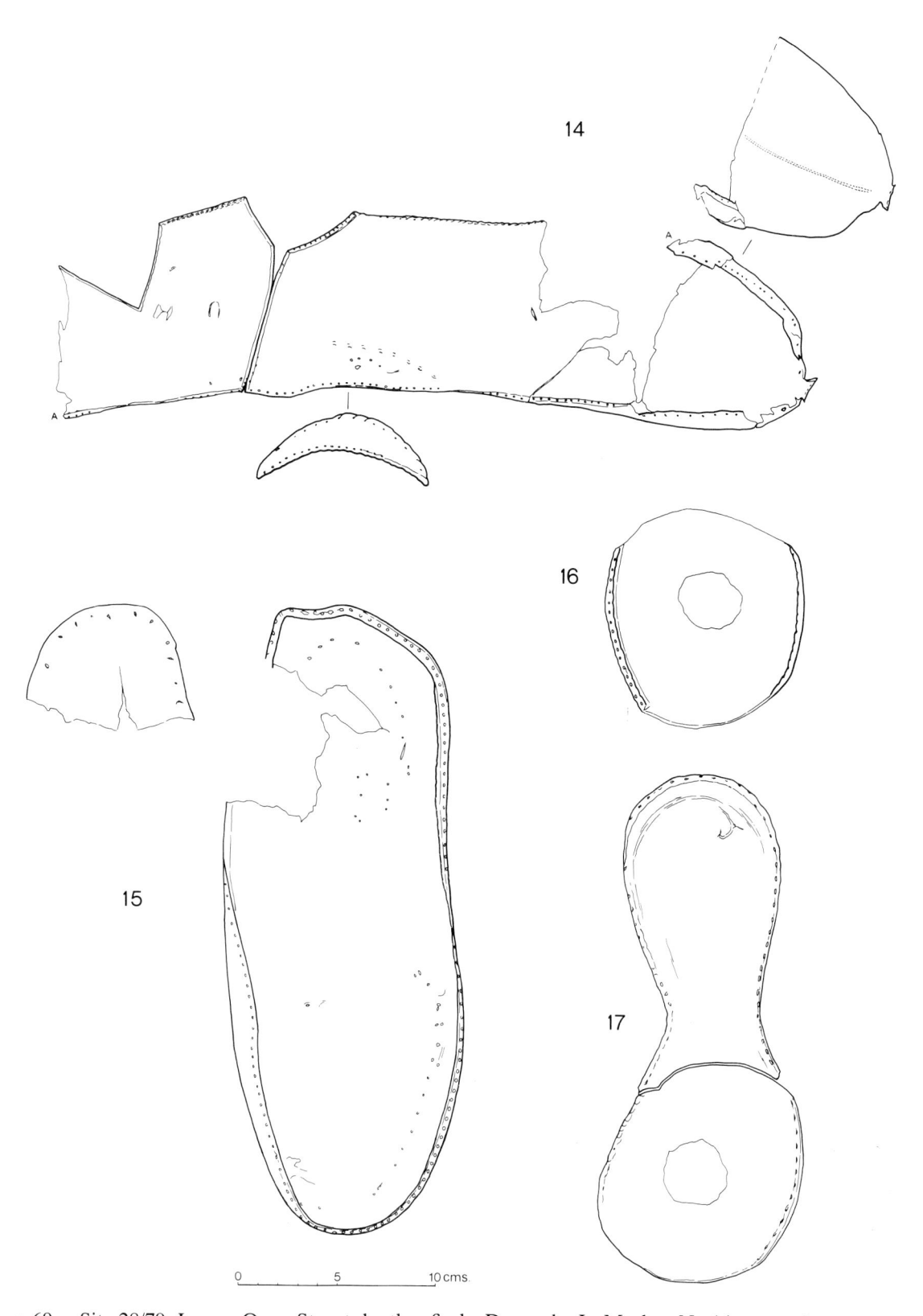

Figure 69. Site 28/79, Lower Quay Street, leather finds. Drawn by L. Marley. No 14, upper from turnshoe, early 12th cent. The upper joins at the positions marked 'A'. No 15, turnshoe sole, early 13th cent. No 16, forepart of turnshoe sole, early 13th cent. No 17, turnshoe sole, early 13th cent.

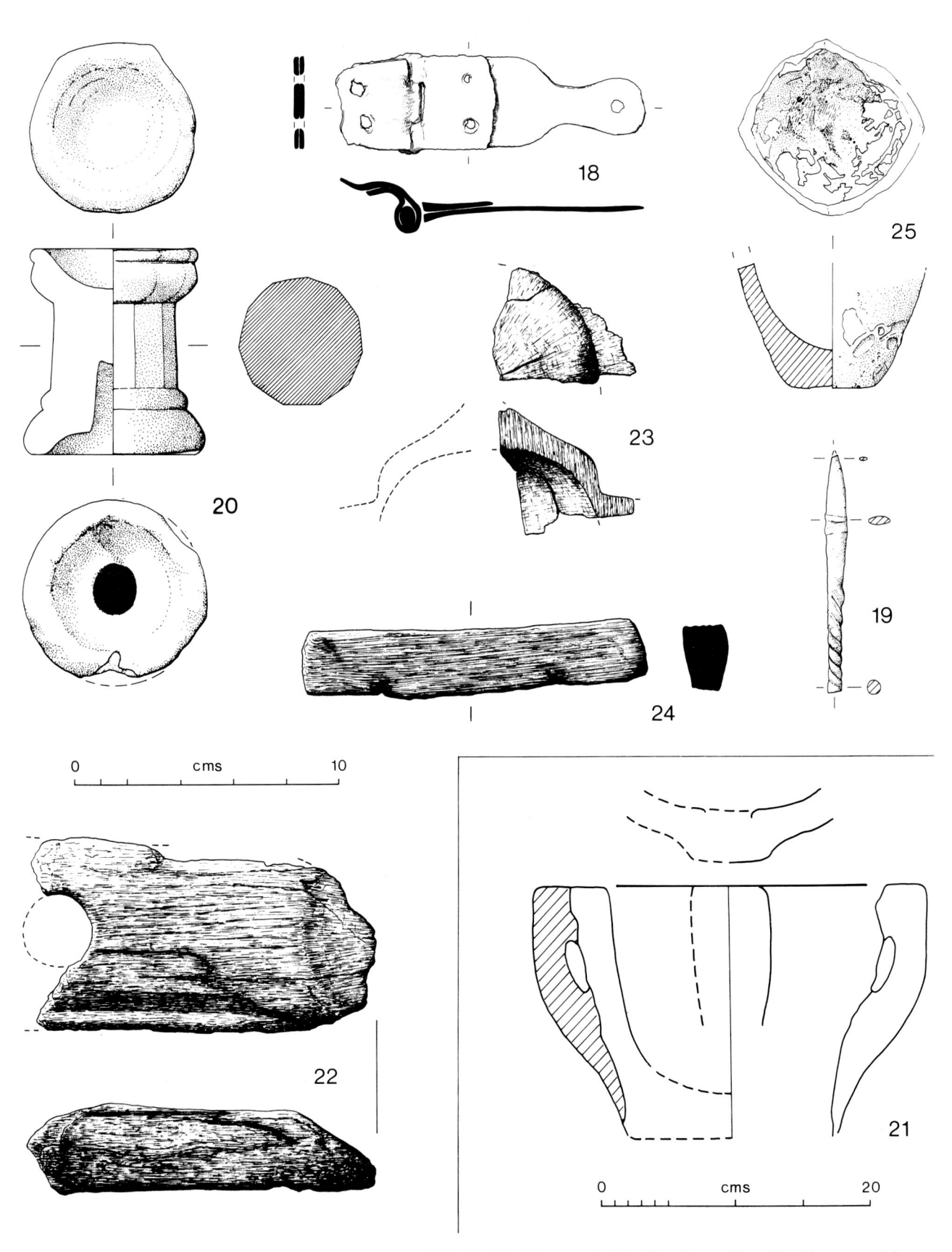

Figure 70. Site 28/79, Lower Quay Street, small finds. No 18, metal. No 19, silver. Nos 20–21, stone. Nos 22–24, wood. No. 25, pottery crucible.

The edges of the vamp fragments have additional rows of stitching, which are more irregular than the original stitching along the lasting margin, probably indicating that the seam around the toe came apart, and a crude repair was made. Down the centre of the vamp there is a double line of very tiny stitches making a decorative ridge; this is a fairly common feature of Saxon and medieval turnshoes. On either side of the ankle, there are two pairs of near vertical slits, through which thong–ties would have been threaded, although how they were arranged is not known.

A separate, crescent-shaped piece of leather, with stitching along both edges, is an original heel stiffener; the stitching along one edge matches that on the lasting margin, and there is a curved line of stitch-holes on the inside surface of the upper, at the heel position, matching that on the other edge of the stiffener (drawn separately). This shoe is probably late eleventh or twelfth century.

The published illustration is based upon original drawings made of each separate fragment, shortly after excavation. (7A, early 12th cent., SF28, 97).

15. Very large sole, in fragmentary and delaminated condition, from turnshoe. It measures 310mm. long, and c.130mm. across tread, and has the characteristic 'dished' appearance of early medieval turnshoe soles. The toe is round in shape and there is little narrowing at the waist. The lasting margin carries grain/flesh stitching, S.L. 5–6mm. Rows of tunnel-stitching on the forepart and seat show where repair patches have been sewn onto the sole; part of the seat repair patch remains (drawn separately) (8A, F19, early 13th cent., SF 78, 99).

16. Forepart of sole from turnshoe, probably right foot. It measures c.100mm. across tread, and has a circular hole, c.30mm across, worn in the centre. It has been cut away at the toe and waist to form a roughly circular shape. The sections of lasting margin which remain have edge/flesh stitching, S.L. c.5mm. (8B, F21, early 13th cent., SF 30).

17. Almost complete sole, in two pieces, from turnshoe, probably left foot, and making a pair with No.16. The total length is c.250mm., and it measures c.100mm. across the tread. The forepart has been cut away, and shaped the same way as No.16, and has a similar circular hole worn in the middle. The remaining piece of sole has a fairly narrow waist, c.50mm. across, and a rounded seat. The lasting margin carries edge/flesh stitching, S.L. 5–6mm. It is not known for what purpose the foreparts were subsequently used. (8B, F21, SF 31).

Metal

18. Hinge in very light metal alloy. (8B, early 13th cent., SF 29).

Silver

19. Silver or bronze alloy rod, twisted and flattened at one end. (U/S, SF 141).

Stone

A number of grey lias and white tesserae, the earliest in Period 4, 3rd century, hint at the presence nearby of a Roman pavement.

20. Candlestick of oolitic limestone. 1:1 (U/S, SF 6).

21. Mortar of Purbeck stone. One surviving handle, tooling marks around one side. (8B, early 13th century, SF 151).

Wooden objects

22. Broken Mattock-head.
    Surviving L = 132mm; W = 70mm; Th = 30mm.

    Part of the head of a mattock or digging tool used to break up earth for cultivation. It is solid and well-made and has very slightly curving sides. The head has broken in half across an augered, circular shaft-hole probably once c. 26mm D, and only half of the head remains, now very broken and battered. The surviving end is wide and blunt, but a chamfer has been cut towards the end of the mattock, giving it a chisel-like appearance in cross-section, and very useful for digging. This tool is very similar to the complete mattock head found on Eastgate St., which still retained a fragment of its shaft, and was of very similar dimensions. It could also have been of a similar date (Morris 1983, no.6) (Period 7A early 12th cent., SF 52).

23. Fragments of a lathe-turned vessel.
    D & H = not reconstructable; Th varies from 6–14mm.

    Two battered fragments of a small lathe-turned vessel lid. It is not really possible to establish the exact form of this vessel, although it was probably spindle-turned, i.e., with the wood grain parallel to the main axis of the lathe on which it was manufactured. It has a deeply curved outline, and is either a small bowl with an everted rim, or more probably a hollow lid with an everted lid seating. Tool marks are faintly visible on both the exterior and interior surfaces, but there is no sign of decoration (Period 8A1, early 13th cent., SF 13).

24. Small rectangular object.
    L = 129mm; W = 24mm; Th 14mm.

    Small rectangular piece of wood, now splitting along the grain. On one of the long sides, there are traces of two nail holes, through the thickness of the wood, still containing fragments of iron corrosion. The object appears to be complete, but its use is uncertain (Period 11D, 15th to 16th cent., SF 143).

Miscellaneous

25. Base of small Roman pot, used as gold crucible (Period 5B; late 3rd to early 4th cent., SF 67)

APPENDIX: CATALOGUE OF ARCHAEOLOGICAL SITES IN GLOUCESTER DISTRICT BEFORE 1974

Site numbers are Museum Accession numbers. Some archaeological sites were not given accession numbers and have been inserted here against the year in which the work was done.

For alphabetical index see p.110ff.
Collections of finds are not included here, only sites which produced a stratigraphic record.

If unpublished the records are at Museum or Excavation Unit unless otherwise stated.

Sites outside the District are only included if recorded by the Unit 1973–79.

Site number or year	Address or OS ref	Records or publication
1883	St. Michaels Square (*RB burials*)	NP
1893	4–5 Eastgate St. (*RB or med bldg*)	*Glos N. & Q.* 6 (1894), 167–70
1894	2 Southgate St (Tolsey) (*Med. Church, RB bldg*)	*TBGAS* 10, 6–8.
1920	Barnwood, (*Roman cemetery*)	*TBGAS* 52, 221–42.
1930	2–8 Barton St.	*TBGAS* 86, 199.
1931	Brunswick Rd; R. wall	*TBGAS* 53
1933	18 Commercial Rd; sections	N.P.
1933	Deans Way (*inhumations*)	*PNFC* 25 (1933)
13/34	30–44 Northgate St.	*TBGAS* 56 (1934) 72–9
1934	Barbican Lane/Commercial Rd.	*TBGAS* 56 (1934), 65–71
1934	Kings Square	*Antiq. Journ.* 29 (1949), 197–200
1935	16–18 Westgate St.	*Antiq. Journ.* 29 (1949), 202–4
41/36, 42/36	(*Quay Wall*)	*Journ. Roman Stud.* 32 (1942), 47
1937	Saintbridge House SO 849 163	N.P.
1938	Kingsholm: Recreation ground	*Journ. Roman Stud.* 32 (1942)
118/1938	Estcourt Road, power station	*Antiq. Journ.* 55 (1975) 279, 282
157/1939	CoOp Creamery, Upper Quay St.	*TBGAS* 60 (1938), 165–8
45/47	Estcourt Rd. RB well	*TBGAS* 67 (1948), 347–58
46/47	36–8 St Aldate Street, now Kings Square	N.P. Mus. Cat. A1515–A1556
1948	Newark Camp. SO 816 173	J.R.S. 39 (1949), 107
1952	21 Southgate St. Roman remains	N.P.
95/52	Podsmead Moat SO 821 160	N.P.
184/1953	Matson moat SO 850 158	N.P.
3/55	Oxbode/Kings Square; Bon Marché site	*TBGAS* 80 (1961), 50–8
1955	Blackfriars. (*cellars*)	N.P.
17/56	Commercial Rd. (*City wall*)	N.P.
67/56	Westgate Street, (*Booth Hall*)	N.P.
1956	St Mary Lane (*RB floors*)	N.P.
116/57	Bull Lane (*RB column*)	N.P.
56/58	St. Michael's Church (*Excavation*)	*TBGAS* 80 (1961), 59–74
-/1958	St. Aldate St., Bon Marché store. (*Excavation*)	*TBGAS* 82 (1963), 25–43
-/1958	31–3 Northgate Street (*RB floors*)	N.P.
20/60	1–5 Kings Square (*Roman and medieval defences*)	*TBGAS* 86 (1967), 88–94
28/60	2–4 Northgate Street (*Roman building*)	*TBGAS* 99 (1981), 79–107
62/60	3 Westgate St. (*Roman bldg*)	*TBGAS* 87 (1968), 56–64
71/61	5–7 Kingsholm Rd. (*Roman street*)	N.P.
1961	30–34 Northgate Street, Bon Marché	N.P.
98/61 (& 75/65)	Parliament Street. Friars Orchard. (*Roman city wall*)	*TBGAS* 81 (1962), 10–40
1961	Kingsholm recreation ground. Excavation by I. Richmond	*TBGAS* 81 (1962), 14–16
90/62	Hucclecote, (*R.B. villa*)	*TBGAS* 80 (1961), 42–9
102/63	Shire Hall, Westgate St. (*Roman(?) foundations*)	N.P.
50/64	11 St. John's Lane (*Roman street*) also sites 28/64, 77/65	Heighway et al 1983 p.15
1964	64–6 Kingsholm Rd. (*RB burials*)	*TBGAS* 86, 197–8
1964	Kings School Gardens (*Roman city wall*)	*TBGAS* 84, 15–27
116/64	30–44 Northgate St., "Bon Marché Store"	N.P.
15/65	33–9 Eastgate St.	N.P.
52/65	Shire Hall	*TBGAS* 86, 95–101
18/66	33 Southgate Street (*Roman floors*)	N.P.
51/66	New Market Hall, Greyfriars Lane	*TBGAS* 93, 15–100
52/66	6–16 Longsmith Street	N.P.
54/66 (= 55/66, 56/66, 87/66, 83/68)	College of Art, Brunswick Rd. (*Roman kilns*)	*TBGAS* 91, 18ff.

Site number or year	Address or OS ref	Records or publication
57/66	College or Art, Brunswick Rd. (*RB cemetery*)	*TBGAS* 98, 66–71
–/1967	30–44 Northgate Street, Bon Marché	N.P.
–/1967	Technical College, Brunswick Rd. (*RB mosaic*)	N.P.
85/67 (= 84/67, 86/67)	St Oswalds Priory	N.P.
74/68	63–71 Northgate Street	*Antiq. Journ.* 52, 63–6
85/68	11–17 Southgate Street	*Antiq. Journ.* 52, 52–62
25/69	Kingsholm Court	*Antiq. Journ.* 55, p.278, no.10 (note)
26/69	66 Kingsholm Road	*TBGAS* 86, p.197–8 *Antiq. Journ.* 55, p.278, no.17; p.282, p.13, p.284
49/69	41–51 Eastgate Street	*Antiq. Journ.* 52, p.52
53/69	10 Eastgate Street	*Antiq. Journ.* 52, 50–52
77/69	13–17 Berkeley Street	*Antiq. Journ.* 52, 35, 37–50 *Antiq. Journ.* 54, 13, 23–7
94/69	Upton St Leonards (corn drier) SO 86631588	*TBGAS* 90, 44–9
106/69	Bijou Court, 5–7 Kingsholm Rd.	N.P.
1969	medieval pipeline to Robinswood Hill.	Notes by F.W. Rowbotham Unit records, MSO
1/70	St Mary's Street and Square (*Roman and medieval pottery*)	N.P.
2/70	Market Parade sewer	N.P.
14/71	4 Westgate Street, Roman columns	*Antiq. Journ.* 52, 62
25/71	Cathedral Boiler House	*Antiq. Journ.* 54, 13
29/71	Kings Square Subway	*Antiq. Journ.* 54, 9–10
30/71	Kings Square Subway	N.P.
37/71	96 Northgate Street	*Antiq. Journ.* 54, 31–33
52/71	Cathedral south Aisle heating duct	N.P.
10/72	St Mark St, Kingsholm	N.P.
21/72	Technical College extension (near Priory Place)	*Antiq. Journ.* 54, 11–12
23/72	Commercial Rd/Ladybellgate Street	*Antiq. Journ.* 54, 12
24/72	12–13 Eastgate Street	*Antiq. Journ.* 54, 27
44/72	Kingsholm Close	*Antiq. Journ.* 55, 267–94
60/72	Priory Gardens, Priory Rd.	*Antiq. Journ.* 54, 41
66/72	Commercial Rd/Southgate Street see 23/72	
68/72	St Barts Water Trench, Westgate St.	*Antiq. Journ.* 54, 42–6
69/72	58–66, Southgate Street	*Antiq. Journ.* 54, 28
79/72	Kingsholm/Longford roundabout	noted in *Antiq. Journ.* 55, 278, no 21
1973	Queen Street, observations	*Antiq. Journ.* 54, 11
3/73	St Barts road widening	*Antiq. Journ.* 54, 41–6
4/73	Co Op extension, Brunswick Rd; Site of Old Baptist Church	*Antiq. Journ.* 54, 28
14/73	Westgate Bridge	*Antiq. Journ.* 54, 49–51
15/73	Westgate Flats: 116–148 Westgate Street (*Roman Quay, 10th cent. timber buildings*)	*Antiq. Journ.* 54, 46–9
26/73	78–88 Northgate Street ('Triangle')	*Antiq. Journ.* 54, 30–33
27/73	Northgate Methodist Hall, St Johns Lane	Heighway et al. 1983, pp.15–18; *Antiq. Journ.* 54,14
30/73	68 Westgate Street	*Antiq. Journ.* 54, 15
31/73	16–18 Clarence Street	*Antiq. Journ.* 54, 28, 14
38/73	38–44 St Catherine Street	*Antiq. Journ.* 54, 39–41
45/73	Churchdown Hill	*TBGAS* 95, 5–10
50/73	106 Northgate Street	*Antiq. Journ.* 54, 33–4
51/73	Lower North Gate	*Antiq. Journ.* 54, 17
54/73	4–8 Deans Walk	*Antiq. Journ.* 54, 41
60/73	69 London Road (corner of Heathville Rd)	N.P.
64/73	Denmark Rd/Kingsholm Rd.	N.P.
65/73	73–77 Northgate Street (Halifax Bldg Soc)	N.P.
67/73	Lower Westgate Street road improvements	*Antiq. Journ.* 54, 48
78/73	31–5 Worcester Street Early Roman levels, Excavated 1971	*Antiq. Journ.* 54, 39
79/73	Technical College extension, Brunswick Rd.	N.P.
81/73	72 Deans Way.	note in *Antiq. Journ.* 55, 275
82/73	same as 79/72	
83/73	Longsmith St Bull Lane sewer trench.	N.P.
84/73	Bull Lane, junction box for GPO	N.P.
1/74	45–9 Northgate Street (*Roman and medieval North Gate*)	Heighway *et al* 1983, pp.20–37
2/74	Robinswood Hill Well House	Above, p.11

Site number or year	Address or OS ref	Records or publication
		Above, p.72
5/74	Bell Lane/Queen St. service trench	Above, p.11
9/74	Brunswick Road: (*stone coffins, Roman*)	*TBGAS* 98, p.66; Heighway et al 1983, p.39. Above, p.12.
26/74	Stenders Hill, Mitcheldean. (*Lime kiln.*)	Above, p.69.
27/74	Silver St., Mitcheldean. (*Roman road.*)	Above, p.69.
28/74	Greyfriars	N.P.
34/74	26 Priory Road	Above, p.12.
35/74	Squires Gate, Longlevens. SO 8504 2020	Above, p.13.
37/74	Market Parade (*Whitefriars church*)	Above, p.13.
38/74	Kings Walk, viewing chamber for medieval bastion.	Above, p.16.
42/74	40 Southgate Street	Above, p.16.
44/74	68 Westgate Street	Above, p.16.
45/74	Saintbridge (*prehistoric and Roman settlement*)	See 98/75.
46/74	38–44 Eastgate Street (*Roman and medieval Gates*)	Heighway 1983, 41–76.
57/74	9–11 St Oswalds Rd.	Above, p.61.
58/74	Longsmith St.	Above, p.16.
59/74	Clare Street	Above, p.17.
65/74	Robinswood Barracks (*Roman settlement*)	Above, p.18.
77/74	Norris' Garage, Market Parade	Above, p.19.
84/74	Newent, Glasshouse	Vince, 1977.
93/74	Ladybellgate Street	Hurst, forthcoming
5/75	Horsebere Bridge, Cheltenham Rd. known as the Elmbridge.	Above, p.19.
6/75	Hempstead School	Above, p.20.
9/75	Ladybellgate Street	Above, p.20.
10/75	Longford School.	Above, p.20.
12/75	17 Ladybellgate Street (*Blackfriars W. Range*)	Above, p.20.
13/75	Greyfriars	N.P.
16/75	Estcourt Road, bus laybyes	Above, p. 63
25/75	Worcester St., Railway viaduct	Above, p.20.
41/75	St Oswalds Priory	Heighway 1978, 1980a, 1982.
42/75	Longford Lane (*ridge and furrow*) SO 843 208	Above, p.20.
49/75	1 Westgate Street. (*late Roman, sub-Roman, Anglo-Saxon*)	Heighway, Garrod and Vince 1979; Heighway and Garrod 1980.
55/75	1–3 Longsmith Street	Above, p.20.
56/75	Lamprey Estate, Painswick Rd.	Above, p.20.
57/75	Greyfriars Lane	Above, p.21.
58/75	45–9 Northgate Street (*Medieval North Gate*)	Heighway 1983, p.13–37
59/75	Painswick Rd.	Above, p.21.
62/75	Field Court, Quedgeley	Above, p.70.
63/75	Upton St Leonards, the Wheatridge	Above, p.21.
66/75	Ladybellgate House, Longsmith St.	Above, p.22.
67/75	5 Northgate Street (*street surface*)	Heighway et al 1983, p.18.
74/75	66 Westgate Street	Above, p.22.
77/75	71–3 Southgate Street	Above, p.22.
78/75	55 St. Catherine Street.	Above, p.22.
93/75	Glasshouse, Newent	Vince, 1977.
98/75	East Gloucester Development: Saintbridge	Above, p.23.
5/76	23 Kingsholm Rd.	Above, p.63.
6/76	Severn Street	Above, p.28.
7/76	Wellington St. Car Park (*Roman ditches and burial*)	Heighway et al. 1983, p.39. Heighway 1980b, p.66–7.
9/76	13–23 Northgate Street	Heighway et al 1983, p.18.
11/76	Tanners Hall, Hare Lane	Heighway forthcoming (b).
14/76	19 St Johns Lane (*Abbey wall, RB buildings, NS Roman street*)	Heighway et al 1983, p.19.
25/76	Berkeley Street.	Above, p.28.
26/76	148 Barnwood Rd.	Above, p.30.
27/76	St Margarets Almshouses, Wotton Pitch, Gloucester. (*Roman cemetery*)	Heighway 1980b, p.64–6.
28/76	Gloucester to Hardwick link road (Roman burial; Roman settlement)	Above, p.30.
29/76	148 Westgate Street. (S end Swan Lane)	Above, p.32.
30/76	Estcourt Rd.	Above, p.63.
30A/76	Barclays Bank Accounting Centre, Barnwood.	Above, p.33.
32/76	Painswick Rd.	Above, p.33.
33/76	Trunk sewer extension: Longsmith Street to Eastern Avenue.	Above, p.33.

Site number or year	Address or OS ref	Records or publication
50/76	Churcham, Queens Farm. (*Roman Road*)	Above, p.37.
51/76	Upton St Leonards. (*Portway*)	Above, p.37.
52/76	Kingsholm Rugby Ground	Above, p.63.
63/76	Cathedral: new Treasury.	Above, p.37.
69/76	17A St Johns Lane (*Roman NS street; Roman buildings; early metallings of St. Johns Lane; Abbey wall*)	Heighway et. al. 1983, p.19.
70/76	23 Brunswick Road.	Above, p.39.
75/76	Dymock Church.	Above, p.70.
80/76	Castle Meads, water trench.	Above, p.39.
82/76	Wotton Pitch	Above, p.39.
91/76	St Nicholas Church.	Above, p.39.
10/77	13, 17, 21, 23 Llanthony Rd.	Above, p.39.
11/77	1–5 Park Street.	Above, p.39.
12/77	King Edwards Gate, College Street.	Above, p.39.
23/77	Poulton Priory, nr. Cirencester.	Above, p.70.
24/77	Stow on the Wold, church.	Above, p.70.
27/77	31 London Rd.	Above, p.43.
29/77	Heron Estate, Saintbridge. See 98/75.	Above, p.43.
30/77	Barton Street.	Above, p.43.
31/77	Pitt Street (*Medieval streets*)	Above, p.43.
32/77	46 Barton Street. (*Medieval streets*)	Above, p.43.
33/77	Kings School Garden, Cathedral.	Above, p.43.
35/77	Castle Tump. Dymock.	Above, p.70.
36/77	Heron Estate, Saintbridge. See 98/75	Above, p.22.
44/77	4–8 Deans Walk.	Above, p.43.
50/77	Prinknash Park.	Above, p.71.
51/77	St Marys Lane.	Above, p.44.
54/77	27 Court Gardens, Hempstead.	Above, p.44.
55/77	76 Kingsholm Rd.	Above, p.63.
56/77	Bristol Road. (*undated street surfaces.*)	Above, p.44.
57/77	30 Westgate Street. (*Roman column and buildings*)	Heighway and Garrod 1980.
1/78	Hempstead Lane (*Medieval lane*)	Above, p.44.
4/78	76 Kingsholm Rd.	Above, p.65.
5/78	St Mary de Lode Church. (*Roman, sub-Roman, Anglo Saxon, and medieval*)	Bryant 1980.
12/78	74 Kingsholm Rd.	Above, p.65.
13/78	Little Cloister House, Millers Green.	Above, p.44.
20/78	Sandhurst Lane.	Above, p.65.
21/78	Matson Lane.	Above, p.44.
22/78	Whaddon Church.	Above, p.71.
32/78	Ladybellgate House, Longsmith Street.	Above, p.44.
35/78	30, Westgate Street.	Above, p.44.
36/78	Northern Bypass.	Above, p.44.
38/78	Station Rd. Prince Albert flats.	Above, p.45.
5/79	Cathedral Crypt.	Above, p.46.
12/79	St Catherine Street, Mechanaids.	Above, p.46.
13/79	49 Victoria Street.	Above, p.46.
14/79	28 Pitt Street.	Above, p.47.
15/79	28 Pitt Street.	Above, p.47.
19/79	Berkeley Street	Above, p.48.
22/79	Whaddon, Pound Farm.	Above, p.71.
25/79	34 Kingsholm Rd.	Above, p.65.
27/79	Barbican Way.	Above, p.48.
28/79	10 Lower Quay Street.	Above, p.48–51.
30/79	St Catherine Street.	Above, p.51.
31/79	St Catherine Street/Skinner St.	Above, p.52.
33/79	Edwy Parade	Above, p.65.
34/79	Hare Lane	Above, p.52.
40/79	46–8 Denmark Rd.	Above, p.69.
41/79	Waterpipe, Haresfield to Berkeley	*Glevensis* 14, 29 (note)
43/79	Brunswick Rd, College of Art.	Above, p.52.
46/79	Pitt St., Dulverton House. (*Fullbrook Culvert*)	Above, p.52.
3/80	28 Deans Way	Above, p.65.
7/80	Gloucester Club, Mercers Lane	Above, p.52.
11/80	Church House, Gloucester Cathedral	Above, p.53.
12/80	St Mark St., Kingsholm	Above, p.65.
13/80	Boots Store, Queen Street.	Above, p.55.

Site number or year	Address or OS ref	Records or publication
14/80	St Catherine Street, Deans Way, Serlo Rd.	Above, p.55.
15/80	Barnwood Court	Above, p.55.
18/80	Edwy Parade, gas main	Above, p.66.
19/80	3 Hare Lane, Kings Arms	Above, p.55.
21/80	Gloucester Hospital, Gt. Western Rd.	Above, p.55.
25/80	Southgate Street, Royal hospital	Above, p.56.
26/80	Shire Hall car park, new printing works	Above, p.55.
27/80	78 Worcester St.	Above, p.55.
30/80	99 Deans way	Above, p.66.
34/80	Church House Garden, Gloucester Cathedral	Above, p.55.
37/80	St Mary de Lode Church	Above, p.55.
39/80	3 Hare Lane, Kings Arms	Above, p.55.
40/80	College Green, gas main	Above, p.55.
1/81	Robinswood Hill; finds by Metal Detectors Club.	N.P.
2/81	46 Kingsholm Rd.	Above, p.66.
3/81	13 St Oswalds Rd.	Above, p.66.
4/81	South Gate, medieval and 17th cent.	Above, p.55.
5/81	17 Sandhurst Rd.	Above, p.66.
10/81	49 London Rd. Gas main	Above, p.55.
11/81	2 College Green	Above, p.55.
13/81	St Luke Street	Above, p.55.
14/81	Westgate St., outside St Nicholas Church.	Above, p.56.
15/81	91 Westgate Street	Above, p.58.
16/81	162 Barnwood Rd.	Above, p.58.
17/81	Bus depot, London Rd.	Above, p.58.
19/81	Horsebere Brook, Longford.	Above, p.58.
20/81	35 Kingsholm Rd.	Above, p.66.
22/81	Kingsholm Rugby Ground, Kingsholm Rd.	Above, p.66.
25/81	15 Sandhurst Rd.	Above, p.66.
26/81	Saintbridge, balancing pond	Above, p.58.
27/81	72 Deans Way	Above, p.66.
29/81	Kingsholm Rd., toll house	Above, p.66.
30/81	St Oswald Rd., Kingsholm Rd. roundabout	Above, p.66.
32/81	11 Barbican Rd.	Above, p.58.
33/81	50–52 London Rd.	Above, p.58
34/81	1 Berkeley Stret.	Above, p.58.
35/81	Derby Rd.	Above, p.58.
36/81	5 Denmark Rd.	Above, p.68.

INDEX by Street or Parish

Barbican Lane corner Commercial Rd.	-/1934	Eastgate St., nos. 41–51	49/69
Barbican Rd, area	-/1923	Eastgate St., St. Michael's Church	56/58
Barbican Rd, No. 11, Castle Ditch	32/81	Edwy Parade	33/79, 18/80
Barbican Way, Service trench	27/79	Estcourt Rd	-/1933, 118/38, 45/47, 16/75
Barnwood, Roman cemetery	-/1920	Estcourt Rd., no. 15	30/76
Barnwood, Barclays Bank Accounting Centre	30A/76	Great Western Rd.	21/80
Barnwood Court	15/80	Greyfriars	21/72, 28/74, 13/75, 57/75
Barnwood Road, no. 148	26/76	Greyfriars Lane, New Market Hall	51/66
Barnwood Road, no. 162 (Barnwood Manor)	16/81	Grosvenor Rd., no. 2A	38/80
Barnwood Rd.	33/76, X	Hare Lane, Tanners Hall	11/76
Barnwood Rd. at Railway Bridge	33/76, VI	Hare Lane, BR Bridge	34/79
Barnwood Rd., at Wotton Brook	33/76, IV	Hare Lane, Kings Arms	19/80, 39/80
Barton St. Nos. 2–8	-/1930	Hare Lane, see also Park St.,	
Barton St. water main trench	30/77	Haresfield, parish of. Waterpipeline	41/79
Barton St. No. 46	32/77	Hempstead, parish of. New School	6/75
Bearland – see Quay St.		Hempstead, parish of. 27 Court Gdns.	54/77
Bell Lane, New Market Hall	51/66	Hempstead, parish of. Hempstead Lane	1/78
Bell Lane, corner of Queen Street	5/74	Hucclecote, parish of. Trevor Rd., RB bath block	43/57
Bell Lane, see also Southgate Street.		Hucclecote, parish of. Villa	90/62
Berkeley St. Nos. 13–17	77/69	King Edward's Gate – see also College St.	
Berkeley St. sewer trenches	25/76 19/79	Kings School; Roman wall	-/1964
Berkeley St. No.1	34/81	Kings School, – see Park Street.	
Berkeley parish. Waterpipeline	41/79	Kings Square	-/1934
Blackfriars	-/1955 9/75	Kings Square, nos. 1–5	20/80
Bourton on the Water, church	-/1977	Kings Square, see St. Aldate St.	
Bristol Road	56/77	Kings Square, subway.	29/71, 30/71
Brunswick Rd. Technical College (Mosaic)	-/1967	Kings Walk, Bastion chamber	38/74
Brunswick Rd. Technical College	79/73	Kingsholm Recreation Ground, Sebert St.,	-/1938; -/1961
Brunswick Rd. Technical College (Friar's Orchard(	-/1961	Kingsholm Rugby Ground, Kingsholm Road.	43/75,
Brunswick Rd. G.P.O. trench	4/82		52/76, 22/81
Brunswick Rd. College of Art	87/66, 54/66, 55/66,	Kingsholm Close	44/72
	56/66, 83/68, 43/79.	Kingsholm Rd., nos. 5–7	71/61, 106/69
Brunswick Rd. Old Baptist Church	4/73	Kingsholm Rd., no. 34	25/79
Brunswick Rd. opposite Old Baptist Church	9/74	Kingsholm Rd., no. 35	20/81
Brunswick Rd., No. 23 (St Michaels Square)	70/76	Kingsholm Rd., no. 23	5/76
Brunswick Rd./Parliament Street.	-/1931	Kingsholm Rd., no. 46	2/81
Bull Lane	-/1956, 116/57, 83/73, 84/73	Kingsholm Rd., nos. 64–66	-/1964
Castle Mead	80/76	Kingsholm Rd., no. 66	26/69
Castle Tump, see Dymock		Kingsholm Rd., no. 74	12/78
Cathedral	52/71, 25/71, 63/76, 33/77,	Kingsholm Rd., no. 76	55/77; 4/78
	13/78, 5/79, 11/80, 34/80	Kingsholm Rd., junction Denmark Rd.,	64/73
Cathedral, see also College Green		Kingsholm Rd., junction St. Oswald's Rd.,	82/73 79/72
Cheltenham Rd., Horsebere Bridge	5/75	Kingsholm Rd., clay bank	43/75
Cheltenham Rd., Fleece Hotel, Wotton Pitch	82/76	Kingsholm Rd., Toll House	29/81
Chosen Hill, see Churchdown Hill.		Ladybellgate House; see Longsmith St.	
Churcham, parish of. Roman road.	50/76	Ladybellgate St.	23/72, 93/74, 12/75, 9/75
Clare Street	59/74	Llanthony Road, Nos. 13, 17, 21, 23.	10/77
Clarence Street, nos. 16–18	31/73	London Road, no. 31	27/77
Cole Avenue, to Hardwick link road	28/76	London Road, no. 50–52	33/81
College Green	40/80	London Road, no. 69	60/73
College Green, no. 2,	11/81	London Road, St. Margarets Almshouses	27/76
College of Art; see Brunswick Rd.		London Road, Gas main	10/81
College St., King Edward's Gate	12/77	London Road, bus depot	17/81
Commercial Rd., no. 18	-/1933	London Road, junction Oxford St.	33/76 VII
Commercial Rd.,	-/1934, 17/56, 66/72, 23/72	London Road, junction Horton Rd.	33/76, III
Cromwell St., Car park	7/76	London Road, junction Heathville Rd.	33/76, II
Crypt Lane	-/1956	London Road, at Hillfield Gdns.	33/76, I.
Dean's Way, no. 28,	3/80	Longford Lane, School,	10/75
Dean's Way, no. 72,	81/73, 27/81	Longford Lane, ridge and furrow	42/75
Dean's Way, no. 99,	30/80	Longford Lane, Queens Dyke	36/78
Dean's Way, gas trench	14/80	Longford Lane, Horsebere Brook	19/81
Dean's Walk, nos. 4–8	54/73, 44/77	Longlevens, Squires Gate	35/74
Denmark Rd., nos 46–8	40/79	Longsmith St. nos 6–16	52/66
Denmark Rd., junction, Kingsholm Rd.	64/73	Longsmith St., nos. 1–3	55/75
Denmark Rd., GPO trench	79/72 98/76	Longsmith St., to Quay Street	58/74
Denmark Rd., sewer trench	36/81	Longsmith St., junction Bull Lane	83/73
Derby Rd.,	35/81	Longsmith St., Ladybellgate House	32/78; 66/75
Dymock, parish of. Dymock church	75/76	Lower Quay Street, no. 10	28/79
Dymock, parish of. Castle Tump	35/77	Lower Westgate Street	67/73
Eastern Station – see Station Rd.,	1/82	Market Parade, Norris' Garage	77/74
Eastgate St., nos. 0–10	53/69	Market Parade, sewer	2/70
Eastgate St., nos. 4–5	-/1883	Market Parade, gas pipe (Whitefriars)	37/74
Eastgate St., nos. 12–36	24/72	Matson, parish of. near church	21/78
Eastgate St., no. 53	1/1934	Matson, parish of. Moat.	184/53
Eastgate St., nos. 33–9	15/65	Mercers' Lane, the Gloucester Club	7/80
Eastgate St., nos. 38–44 (East Gate)	-/1882, 46/75	Mitcheldean, parish of. Stenders Hill, Lime kiln	26/74

Mitcheldean, parish of. Roman Road	27/74	St. Johns Lane, no. 17A	69/76
Newark, parish of. 'Camp'	-/1948	St. Lucy's Garden, Via Sacra walk	33/77
Newent, parish of. Glasshouse & pottery	84/74; 93/75	St. Luke Street	13/81
New Market Hall; see Greyfriars Lane.		St. Mark Street	10/72, 12/80
Northern Bypass, Gloucester	36/78	St. Mary de Lode Church	5/78, 37/80
Northgate Street, nos. 2–4	28/60, 30/60, 31/60	St. Mary's Square	1/70
Northgate Street, nos. 13–23	9/76	St. Mary's Lane see also Crypt Lane	51/77
Northgate Street, no. 5	67/75	St. Mary's Street, nos. 14/24, Priory Rd. Gardens	60/72
Northgate Street, nos. 31–3	-/1958	St. Michael's Church, Eastgate St.	56/58
Northgate Street, nos. 30–44 "Bon Marché"	13/34, 3/55, 19/55, 36/55, -/1958, -/1961, 116/64, -1967	St. Michaels Square, no. 23	70/76
		St. Michael's Square, west side.	-/1883
		St. Nicholas' Church	91/76
Northgate Street, nos. 45–9 (North Gate)	1/74, 58/75	St. Oswald's Priory	84/67, 85/67, 86/67, 41/75
Northgate Street, nos. 63–71	74/68	St. Oswald's Road, nos. 9–11	57/74
Northgate Street, no 73	65/73	St. Oswald's Road, no. 13	3/81
Northgate Street, nos. 78–88	26/73	St. Oswald's Road, nr. Kingsholm Rd.	30/81
Northgate Street, no. 96	37/71	St. Oswald's Road, junction with Kingsholm Rd.	82/73
Northgate Street, no. 106	50/73		= 79/72
Northgate Street, Lower North Gate	51/73	Saintbridge, Saintbridge House	-/1937
Northgate Street, junction, Oxbode	33/76 V	Saintbridge, Roman burials	45/74
Northgate Street, Junction Worcester St.	33/76 VIII, XI, XII, XIII.	Saintbridge, Section across the 'Portway'	51/76
		Saintbridge, Heron Estate	29/77, 36/77
Over, Castle Meads, Water Board trench	80/76	Saintbridge, Heron Estate, Balancing Pond	26/81
Oxbode, see 30/44 Northgate St., Painswick Rd.,	56/75, 59/75 32/76	Sandhurst Lane	20/78
		Sandhurst Road, Kingsholm Court	25/69
Park Street, nos. 1–3 Kings School building	11/77	Sandhurst Road, No. 17	5/81
Parliament Street, Roman wall	-/1931, 98/61	Sandhurst Road, No. 15	25/81
Pitt Street	31/77	Sebert Street, no. 43	33/82
Pitt Street, no. 28	14/79, 15/79	Sebert Street, Recreation ground	-/138, -/1961
Pitt Street, Dulverton House (Abbey Infirmary)	46/79	Skinner Street: see St. Catherine Street.	
Podsmead, Moat	95/52	Southgate Street, no. 2	-/1894
Poulton Priory, near Cirencester	23/77	Southgate Street, no.11–17	85/68
Prinknash, Park	50/77	Southgate Street, no. 21	-/1952
Priory Place (near); Technical College	21/72	Southgate Street, no. 33	18/66
Priory Road, no. 26	34/74	Southgate Street, no. 40	42/74
Quay, excavation	41/36, 42/36	Southgate Street, no. 58–66	69/72
Quay Street, Shire Hall. See Westgate St.		Southgate Street, no. 71–3	77/75
Quay Street, New printing works, County Library, Shire Hall Car Park.	26/80	Southgate Street, junction with Commercial Rd.	66/72
		Southgate Street, Royal Hospital, pavement	25/80
Quay Street, Bearland, Longsmith Street: Water main.	58/74	Southgate Street, South Gate	4/81
		Station Road: See Russell Street	
Quay Street, Lower: see Lower Quay Street.		Stow on the Wold Church	24/77
Quedgeley, Field Court	62/75	Tanners Hall, see Hare Lane	
Quedgeley, M5 Link Road	28/76	Technical College, see Brunswick Road; see Priory Place	
Queen Street, corner with Bell Lane, service trench	5/74		
Queen Street, observation 1973	-/73	Upper Quay Street, Co-op Creamery	157/1939
Queen Street, new sewer shaft	13/80	Upton St. Leonards, 'Portway'	51/76
Robinswood Hill, Well House	2/74	Upton St. Leonards, RB corn drier	94/69
Robinswood Hill, medieval pipe line	-/1969	Upton St. Leonards, merestones	63/75
Robinswood Hill, barracks	65/74	Victoria Street no. 49	13/79
Robinswood Hill, Country Park	1/81	Wellington Street, car park	7/76
Russell Street, area between Whitfield Rd., Station Rd., and Bedford St.,	50/74, 38/78	Westgate Street, no.1	49/75
		Westgate Street, no.3	62/80
St. Aldate Street, nos. 36–8	46/47	Westgate Street, no.4	14/71
St. Aldate Street, Bon Marché site. See Northgate Street.		Westgate Street, no. 16–18	-/1935
		Westgate Street, no. 30	57/77, 35/78
St. Bartholomews, Westgate Street. Water main trench	68/72	Westgate Street, no. 66	51/75, 74/75
		Westgate Street, no. 68	30/73, 44/74
St. Bartholomews, Westgate Street, Road widening	3/73	Westgate Street, no. 91	15/81
St. Bartholomews, Westgate Street, redevelopment	7/82	Westgate Street, no. 116–148	15/73
St. Catherine's Church, London Road. *(Cinerary urn.)*	-/1912	Westgate Street, no. 148	29/76
		Westgate Street, Shire Hall	102/63, 67/56, 52/65
St. Catherine Street, nos. 26–8	9/82	Westgate Street: see also St. Bartholamews, St. Nicholas' Church, Lower Quay Street.	
St. Catherine Street, nos. 38–44	38/73		
St. Catherine Street, no. 55	78/75	Westgate Bridge	14/73
St. Catherine Street, Mecanaids	12/79, 12/82	Westgate Street, Lower, road improvements	67/73
St. Catherine Street, Railway Bridge	30/79	Whaddon, church	22/78
St. Catherine Street, Service trench, junction Skinner St.	31/79	Whaddon, Pound Farm	22/79
		Whitefriars: see Market Parade	
St. Catherine Street, Gas trench, junction Deans Way	14/80	Worcester Street, nos. 31–35	78/73
		Worcester Street, no. 78	27/80
St. Johns Lane	28/64, 50/64, 77/65	Worcester Street, railway viaduct	25/75
St. Johns Lane Methodist Hall, old Graveyard	27/73	Wotton Pitch	26/76, 82/76, -/1968
St. Johns Lane, no. 19	14/76		

BIBLIOGRAPHY

BIDDLE, M. 1970. — 'Excavations at Winchester, 1969. Eighth Interim Report,' *Antiq. Journ.* 50, 277–326.

BIDDLE, M. 1967. — 'Two Flavian burials from Winchester', *Antiq. Journ.* 47, 238–40.

BIDWELL, P. T. 1977. — 'Early Black-Burnished Ware at Exeter', in Dore and Greene 1977.

BIDWELL, P. T. 1979. — *The Legionary Bath-house and Basilica and Forum at Exeter.* (*Exeter Archaeological Reports* i, Exeter)

Board of Health 1852. — *Ten feet and two feet plans of Gloucester surveyed by the Ordnance Survey Department under the provisions of the Public Health Act*

Cam. — *Camolodunum*; see Hawkes and Hull 1947

CASE, H. 1977. — 'The Beaker Culture of Britain and Ireland' in Mercer (ed), *Beakers in Britain and Europe* (*Brit. Archaeol. Rep.* Oxford), pp. 71–89.

CLARKE, D. L. 1970. — *Beaker Pottery in Great Britain and Ireland* (Cambridge)

CRUMMY, N., 1979. — 'A Chronology of Romano-British Bone Pins', *Britannia* 10, 157–63.

DANNELL, G. B. 1971. — 'The Samian Pottery' in B. Cunliffe, *Excavations at Fishbourne 1961–69 ii: The Finds* (*Soc. Antiqs. Res. Rep.* xxvii)

DARLING, M. J., 1977. — 'Pottery from early Military Sites in Western Britain', in Dore & Greene 1977, 57–100.

DARVILL, T. C. 1978. — 'Problems and perspectives in the study of Gloucestershire in the third and fourth millenia BC', *Glevensis* 12, 13–22.

DUNNING, G., 1976. — 'Salmonsbury Camp, Bourton on-the-Water, Gloucestershire', in G. Harding (ed.) *Hillforts* (London).

FOWLER, P. J. 1977. — 'Archaeology and the M5 Motorway', *TBGAS* 95, 40–46.

FRERE, S. 1972. — *Verulamium excavations* i, (*Soc. Antiquaries Research Report* xxviii).

FULLBROOK-LEGGATT, L.E.W.O., 1952 — *Anglo Saxon and Medieval Gloucester* (Gloucester).

FULLBROOK-LEGGATT, L.E.W.O., 1964 — 'The River Twyver and the Fullbrook', *TBGAS* 83, 78–84.

GILLAM, J. P. 1976. — 'Coarse fumed ware in North Britain and Beyond' *Glasgow Archaeol. J.* 4, 57–80.

GOUDGE, C., 1982. — 'The Roman Pottery', in Heighway and Parker 1982, 38–57.

GRAHAM-CAMPBELL, J. 1982. — 'Some new and neglected finds of 9th-century Anglo-Saxon ornamental metalwork', *Medieval Archaeol.* 26, 144–51.

GREEN, C., 1942. — 'Glevum and the Second Legion' *J. Roman Stud.* 32. 39–52.

GREEN, C. 1948. — 'A First Century Well in Estcourt Rd. Gloucester'. *TBGAS* 67, 347–58.

GREENE, K., 1973. — 'The Pottery from Usk' in *Current Research in Romano British Coarse Pottery* (ed. A. Detsicas), *CBA Res. Rep. 10*, London), 25–37.

GREENE, K., 1979. — *Report on the Excavations at Usk, 1965–6. The Pre-Flavian Fine Wares* (Cardiff).

HALL, R. and PINNELL, T. 1780. — *A Plan of the City of Gloucester.*

HART, W. H., 1863. — *Historia et Cartularium Monasterii Scti Petri Gloucestriae vol. i* (London).

HASSALL, M. and RHODES, J. 1974. — 'Excavations at the New Market Hall, Gloucester, 1966–7') *TBGAS* 93, 15–100.

HAWKES, S. C. and DUNNING, G. C., 1961 — 'Soldiers and Settlers in Britain, fourth to fifth century', *Med. Archaeol.* 5, 1–70.

HAWKES C. and HULL, M. R., 1947. — *Camolodunum* (*Soc. Antiqs. London Res. Rep.* xiv).

HEIGHWAY, C. M. 1978. — 'Excavations at Gloucester: Fourth Interim Report: St. Oswalds Priory 1974–5' *Antiq. Journ.* 58, 103–132.

HEIGHWAY, C. M. 1980a. — 'Excavations at Gloucester: fifth interim report. St. Oswalds Priory 1977–8. *Antiq. Journ.* 60, 207–226.

HEIGHWAY, C. M. 1980b. — 'The cemeteries of Roman Gloucester', *TBGAS* 98, 57–72.

HEIGHWAY, C. M. et al 1983. — *The East and North Gates of Gloucester* (Bristol).

HEIGHWAY, C. M. 1984. — 'Anglo-Saxon Gloucester to AD 1000' in M. Faull and T. Rowley (eds.), *Proceedings of the 1981 conference on Anglo-Saxon Landscape Studies* (Oxford).

HEIGHWAY, C. M. forthcoming a. — 'Anglo Saxon Gloucester' in J. Haslem (ed.) *Anglo-Saxon Towns in Southern England* (London and Chichester).

HEIGHWAY, C. M. forthcoming b. — 'Tanners Hall, Gloucester', *TBGAS* 101.

HEIGHWAY, C. M. and GARROD, A. P. 1980. — 'Excavations at Nos. 1 and 30 Westgate Street, Gloucester', *Britannia* 11, 73–114.

HEIGHWAY C. M. and GARROD A. P. 1981. — 'Gloucester' in *'Waterfront Archaeology in Britain and N. Europe'* (*CBA Res. Rep.* 41), 123–4.

HEIGHWAY, C. M., GARROD, A. P. and VINCE, A. G. 1979. — 'Excavations at 1 Westgate Street, Gloucester, 1975', *Medieval Archaeol.* 23, 159–213.

HEIGHWAY C. M. and PARKER A. 1982. — 'The Roman Tilery at St. Oswalds Gloucester' *Britannia* 13, 97–149.

HULL, M. R. 1958. — *Roman Colchester* (*Soc. Antiqs. Res. Rep.* 20).

HUNTER, ALAN, 1981. — 'Building excavations at the Cross, Gloucester, 1960. Nos 2–4 Northgate Street and 1–3 Eastgate Street.', *TBGAS* 99, 79–107.

HURST, H. 1972. — 'Excavations at Gloucester 1968–71, First Interim Report', *Antiq. Journ.* 52, 24–69.

HURST, H. 1974. 'Excavations at Gloucester 1971–73, Second Interim Report', *Antiq. Journ.* 54, 8–52.
HURST, H. 1975. 'Excavations at Gloucester, Third Interim Report, Kingsholm 1966–75', *Antiq. Journ.* 55, 267–94.
HURST, H. 1976. 'Gloucester (Glevum): a Colonia in the West Country' in K. Branigan and P. J. Fowler, eds., *The Roman West Country: Classical Culture and Celtic Society* (Newton Abbot), 63–80.
HURST, H. forthcoming. 'Gloucester Castle', *TBGAS*.
IRELAND, C. 1983. 'The Roman Pottery' in Heighway et al 1983.
JONES, M. U. 1976. *'Neolithic pottery from Lechlade, Glos.' Oxoniensia* 41, 1–5.
KIP, J. 1712. *Prospect of Gloucester.*
KIRBY, I. M. 1967. *A Catalogue of the Records of the Dean and Chapter including the former St. Peter's Abbey* (Gloucester).
KNORR, R. 1919. *Töpfer und Fabriken verzierter Terra Sigillata des ersten Jahrhunderts.*
KNORR, R. 1952. *Terra-Sigillata-Gefässe des ersten Jahrhunderts mit Töpfernamen.*
LOBEL, M. (ed.) 1969. 'Gloucester' in *Historic Towns Atlas*, i (London and Oxford).
MARGARY, I. D. 1957. *Roman Roads in Britain* ii (London).
MELLOR, M. 1980. 'Late Saxon Pottery from Oxfordshire; Evidence and Speculation', *Medieval Ceramics* 4, 17–28.
MILNER, J. 1980. 'A medieval road to London' *Glevensis* 14, 17–20.
MORRIS, C. 1983. 'Objects of wood' in Heighway, C. et al 1983.
O. F. Oswald, *Index of Figure Types on Terra Sigillata* (1936–7).
O'Neil, H. E. 1965. 'Excavations in the King's School Gardens, Gloucester, 1964', *TBGAS* 84, 15–27.
OSWALD, A., 1969. 'Excavations at Barford, Warwickshire' *Trans Birmingham Archaeol. Soc* 83 (published 1969).
PAGE W. (ed.) 1907. *A History of the County of Gloucester* ii (Victoria History of the Counties of England, London).
PEACEY, A. A. 1979. *Clay Tobacco Pipes in Gloucestershire* (Bristol).
PEACOCK, D. P. S. 1967. 'Romano-British pottery production in the Malvern District of Worcestershire', *Trans. Worcestershire Archaeol. Soc.* 3 ser, 1, 15–28.
PUGH, R. B. 1972 (ed). *A History of the County of Gloucester* x (London).
RADFORD, R. 1978. 'The Pre-Conquest Boroughs of England' *Proceedings of the British Academy* 64, 131–53.
RAHTZ, P. and HIRST, S. 1974. *Beckery Chapel, Glastonbury 1967–8* (Glastonbury).
RAWES, B. 1972. 'Roman pottery kilns at Gloucester' *TBGAS* 91, 18–59.
RAWES, B. 1977a. 'Wells Bridge Barnwood: Appendix: Roman sites near Gloucester, East of the Severn,' *TBGAS* 95, 32–39.
RAWES, B. 1977b. A Romano British site on the Portway' *Glevensis* 11, 31–2.
RAWES, B. 1979. 'The possibility of Roman land boundaries near Gloucester', *Glevensis* 13, 5–9.
REECE, R. 1983. 'The Roman Coins' in Heighway et al 1983.
RICHMOND, I. 1962. 'The earliest Roman occupation of Gloucester', *TBGAS* 81, 14–16.
RIGBY, V. 1973. 'Potters Stamps on Terra Nigra and Terra Rubra found in Britain' in A Detsicas (ed.), *Current Research in Romano-British Coarse Pottery* (CBA Res. Rep. 10, London), 7–24.
RIGBY, V. 1982. 'The Coarse Pottery' in J. Wacher and A. McWhirr, *Early Roman Occupation at Cirencester* (Cirencester), 153–98.
ROGERS, G. B. 1974. *Poteries Sigillées de la Gaule Centrale* I (*Gallia* supplement 28).
ROGERS, M. 1975. *Ladybellgate House, Gloucester, and Robert Raikes* (Gloucestershire Record Office).
ROWBOTHAM, F. W. 1978. 'The River Severn at Gloucester with particular reference to its Roman and medieval channels' *Glevensis* 12, 4–9.
SAUNDERS, A. D. 1963. 'The Blackfriars, Gloucester' *TBGAS* 82, 168–176.
SCOBELL, E. C. 1899. 'The Common Fields at Upton St. Leonards and the recent enclosure 1897', *PCNFC* 13, 215–30.
SMITH, A. H. (ed) 1964. *The Place Names of Gloucestershire*. 39.2 (English Place Name Society, Cambridge).
SMITH, I. F. 1974. 'The Neolithic' in Renfrew C. ed. *British Prehistory* (London).
STANFIELD, J. A. and SIMPSON, G., 1958. *Central Gaulish Potters.*
STEVENSON, W. H. 1890 (ed.), *Rental of all the houses in Gloucester AD 1455 from a roll . . . compiled by Robert Cole, Canon of Llanthony* (Gloucester).
STEVENSON, W. H. 1893. *Calendar of the Records of the Corporation of Gloucester* (Gloucester)
THOMPSON, A. HAMILTON, 1921. 'The jurisdiction of the Archbishops of York in Gloucestershire' *TBGAS* 43, 85–180.
TROTTER, A. W. 1936. *The Dean Road* (Gloucester)
VINCE, A. G. 1977. 'Newent Glasshouse: a late 16th and 17th century Glasshouse, and late 17th and 18th century pottery' (*CRAAGS Occasional Paper* 2, n.d., Bristol).
VINCE, A. G. 1979. 'The Medieval pottery' in Heighway Garrod and Vince 1979, 170–181.

VINCE, A. G. 1981.	'The medieval pottery industry in southern England: 10th to 13th centuries' in *Production and Distribution: a Ceramic Viewpoint* ed. H. Howard and E. Harris (Oxford), 309–22.
VINCE, A. G. 1983.	'The Medieval and Post-Medieval pottery' in Heighway et al. 1983.
WAINWRIGHT, G. J. and LONGWORTH, I. 1971.	*Durrington Walls Excavations 1966–8 (Soc. Antiqs. London Res. Rep*, London).
WASHBOURNE, J. 1825.	*Bibliotheca Gloucestrensis* (Gloucester).
WEBSTER, P. V. 1976.	'Severn Valley Ware', *TBGAS* 94, 18–46.
WHEELER, R. E. M. 1930.	*London in Roman Times* (London).
YOUNG, C. J. 1977.	*Oxfordshire Roman Pottery* (*Brit. Archaeol. Rep.* 43, Oxford).